Roar: Primed for Peace

Sophia M. Elan

Published by Mediterranean Me, 2022.

While every precaution has been taken in the preparation of this book, the publisher assumes no responsibility for errors or omissions, or for damages resulting from the use of the information contained herein.

ROAR: PRIMED FOR PEACE

First edition. June 17, 2022.

ISBN: 979-8201658793

Written by Sophia M. Elan.

Table of Contents

Dedication

In Recognition of:

www.savethechildren.org for providing humanitarian aid to the children of the world

www.cetaglobal.org for your inspirational, innovative approach for addressing multiple mental and behavioral health challenges in an accessible, evidence-based manner

www.panzifoundation.org for compassionately providing holistic healing care to transform victims into survivors

Dedicated to:

Carol - there could never be enough words; I am forever indebted for your integral role in my healing. Thank you for the blessing of your unconditional, endlessly supportive, empowering friendship. I sprouted thanks to you. Forever grateful and looking forward to a lifetime of aperitivos together...

"When everything is uncertain, everything that is important becomes clear." Rumi

In Gratitude - to my "importants"

Kurt - thank you for your love and support, your belief in me and for deeply caring about my "story"

Kathy - thank you, my longest friend, for always loving me as family and being my forever "home"

Mike - thank you for being my archangel and always "saving" me. You said I would be climbing a mountain to heal. I've "summitted" thanks to your unwavering support.

Mandy - Thank you, my dear friend, for your generous support and staunch belief in me; it truly buoys me. Cheers to a lifetime of celebrations and adventures together!

Barış - thank you my "prince" for enveloping me in a loving space to heal, helping my spirit shine authentically, dancing with my soul and embracing me in the peace and beauty of true love. Looking forward to sharing happily ever now with you. You make my heart smile endlessly...

My "earth angels" - to all those who have blessed me along the way, including Silvia and Sean, your love for each other and kind spirit are heartwarming and inspiring. #bethekindnessyouwanttosee

In Tribute to my Precious Little Self...

I lovingly dedicate the song,

"Have a Little Faith in Me" (© Universal Music, written by John Hiatt), as performed by Olivia Penalva

In Memory of My Nephew, Zack Miczalek, #nomore

FOREWORD: MASTERING HAPPINESS

"I am not what happened to me. I am what I choose to become."
Carl Jung

I *chose happy*... I am fundamentally a happy person - always have been, always will be. No one will ever take that from me. Perhaps that seems like a strange introduction for a book that recounts a number of abuses running the gamut from childhood sexual abuse to attempted spousal murder.

You don't *"find"* happiness though - you **make** it. That's how I have maintained my happiness, my smile, my laughter, my open spirit, my **unbreakable** zest for life and my ability to **love profoundly**, despite traversing through those events. ***Happiness is within you, not without***. It's not dependent on someone, some thing, some place. That to me, my friends, is one of the most beautiful thoughts I can think of. If you harness the power of happiness within you, **no one, no trauma, no event** can take it from you. If that's not empowering I don't know what is....

This is not a book about abuse. Although I endured various traumas throughout interludes of my life, they do not reflect the "story of my life". They represent brief chapters at most. I am not one-dimensional. I live multi-dimensionally, spherically. This is a book about **blessings**. Yes, I have experienced dark moments of trauma - as have we all. That's all they are though - dark moments interspersed in an otherwise bright life. My abuses never defined me or my life and those dark moments cannot extinguish my light. Indeed, you need the darkness to see the luminous twinkling light of stars...

This is my journal of love. **Self** love. The most loving thing I have ever done for myself. Indeed, I have never worked harder on anything in my life. I'm writing this as a cathartic expression of a lifetime that encountered traumatic experiences along the way. I finally realized that this cathartic release is sufficient motivation in and of itself.

I also realized that although my periodic moments of darkness could not extinguish my essence - my light of happiness - my light could not shine as brightly as I wanted it to until I truly healed from my unresolved traumas. I needed to release the *grip* the *past* had on my *present* to live life *authentically*, to the *fullest*.

This is also a story of the incredible power of *self healing* and the transformative power of *gratitude*. This story chronicles my healing journey including the priceless contribution of my "earth angels", my truest friends and random beautiful souls, who helped me get through and past the darkest moments of my life.

My journey of self-healing is an *empowering* one. I was finally able to appreciate that it was fully within my control to stop the cycle of abuse I had endured throughout my life. I remember seeing a quote along the lines of "Don't blame the clowns for being clowns. Ask yourself why you are going to the circus?" I don't know the author's identity but the quote profoundly resonated with me. I needed to *stop going to the circus*. This book is the story of how I was able to gain *control* and *stop the abuse*, something that had eluded me for decades despite my desire and determination that things be different.

This is a very raw, vulnerable account chronicling my very personal journey of healing. I share the details to give context and insight into the trauma psyche, not because I want anyone to feel sorry for me or for shock value. Quite the opposite, as my "ending" is a happy one. Indeed, I view it as the "beginning", free of the figurative psychological and physiological shackles of my traumas.

I've lived an incredible life and I truly believe the best is yet to come. Both of those distinctly in and of themselves are extraordinary blessings which I do not take for granted. I am writing this book to truly put the dark moments in my life behind me. For decades, I had thought I was moving "forward" by repressing past traumas and running from one distraction to another. In reality, my unresolved past haunted me, continuing to condemn me to a pattern of abusive, disrespectful relationships and numbing behaviors. I finally realized *why* I needed to heal and, equally importantly, *how*. These realizations catapulted me on my healing journey. Despite my long and varied history of abuse, I was able to start *profoundly healing* from my traumas relatively *simply and quickly* once I *appreciated I needed to, believed I could and discovered the guidance as to how I could.*

I humbly and fervently hope that this is an empowering book of inspiration to help others in some small way navigate overcoming their own unique traumas. Everyone's healing will uniquely be their own but I humbly share my pathway in hope of providing some useful insights to others. *Healing does not happen in silence.* It's time to *"Roar".* It's time to *embrace yourself* and *your limitless life* with *savage self respect and love.*

I never gave up. I hope you never give up on you, your dreams and your desires. *You owe you* to live your fullest, most authentic life. My healing enabled me to stop running aimlessly and *truly move forward* with the passionate open hearted intensity that has always defined me. I am *primed for peace.* I am now firmly on a path where I confidently believe the rest of my life is the best of my life. Life is good; it's going to get great. *Happily ever now.* Watch out world. Here I (we) come. Let's *roar.*

PART ONE: CHILDHOOD: LOSS OF INNOCENCE

"See the world with the innocence of children.
Approach the world with the daring of children.
Love the world with the readiness of children.
Heal the world with the purity of children.
Change the world with the wisdom of children."
Neale Donald Walsch

Chapter 1
The Flashbacks

I didn't start having flashbacks of my childhood sexual abuse until after several therapy sessions that I had gone to following my first husband's attempted murder. I could sense a number of times that my therapist was trying to tactfully and gently get me to delve into my childhood, particularly my relationship with my father. I offhandedly brushed her efforts aside, a little irritated she seemed to be trying to guide the sessions to tangential, irrelevant topics. I assumed she was just fixated on traditional psychotherapy, a la Freud's Oedipus complex, never imagining she suspected I had been a victim of childhood abuse based on our sessions. Sure I had lifelong issues with my father, I kind of silently scoffed. "What on earth relevance did that have insofar as my relationship with "BS" (my shorthand reference for the first husband) was concerned?" I ignorantly and tacitly chastised her.

I hadn't even wanted to go to therapy at all, having resisted my best friend Mike's pleas to go after the attempted murder. I had had an unsettling therapy session decades earlier following an attempted suicide and I was not exactly a fan of conventional psychotherapy. Nonetheless, I finally acquiesced to appease Mike. He apparently thought therapy was a good idea after having survived attempted murder at the hands of my husband of fifteen years. Probably and sadly in large part due to my low sense of self worth, I didn't appreciate the gravity of the incident nor the need for therapy. I am very introverted and independent (an undesired necessity from not feeling I could trust or rely on anyone). I generally recoil at being the focus of attention or letting anyone help me. Therapy seemed to be in stark opposition to my fundamental persona and I was vehemently opposed to it. To me, it felt like attending therapy based on BS' attempt to kill me would be wallowing in it, something I had no interest in doing. What happened,

happened, I thought, with my trademark "c'est la vie" approach. I just wanted to "move on".

I think largely it was that fact that I didn't appreciate the gravity of what had happened that made Mike lovingly but assertively persist. As my resistance to therapy increased, his insistence did too. He was more aware of the likelihood that I would continue to subject myself to abuse if I didn't appreciate the significance of the situation more than I was. I finally agreed to pacify him, knowing he had nothing but the best intentions for me and feeling like it was the path of least resistance, something I had been gravitating towards after the incident.

To be honest with myself, I'm sure somewhere deep down, I knew I could use some sort of "therapy". I hadn't resembled my usual passionate, energetic, happy self since BS had tried to kill me. Nothing interested me and I was in serious jeopardy of slipping into an abyss of depression I was likely not going to emerge from without some intervention. My doctor had put me on Lexapro but it only made things worse. I hated how it numbed me and made me feel like my brain was literally sloshing around physically, as well as figuratively in a sea of apathy. I was feeling increasingly distanced from my normal persona, fearful we would never reunite. It also shocked me how I was told that Lexapro could cause delayed orgasms. This somewhat amused me, making me ponder whether I was likely to spontaneously "erupt" at some inappropriate time like during a work conference. Intuitively, I also knew that I absolutely didn't want to take something that had such potent potential to change my physiology in such a manner. Again, I agreed to take it in my "path of least resistance mode" at the time.

It was after several therapy sessions that I spontaneously and seemingly out of nowhere started having extremely disturbing and vivid flashbacks of my childhood sexual abuse by my father. He and I often had a volatile relationship during my childhood. Since childhood to this day, I am not comfortable being alone with him. I always felt like I could never do "right", walking on eggshells, waiting to be accused of having done something wrong. He was emotionally immature and melodramatic. He seemed incapable of accepting accountability for anything and I always felt like I was his scapegoat for anything that went wrong. He actually called me after the attempted murder (BS had called him and told him he had tried to kill his daughter) and *yelled* at me as if I were somehow responsible. I also remember physically fighting with him periodically - a lot of the details are a blur but I remember him describing me as "scrappy" and I would get in trouble from leaving marks from my long fingernails on his skin during our sporadic altercations. Despite this uncomfortable dynamic, I loved him though, as children do, and I knew he loved me as much as anyone. I was never consciously cognizant of any sexual abuse before my flashbacks.

To my surprise, however, the flashbacks did not shock me though they deeply disturbed me. I distinctly remember the weekend after they started, screaming at the top of my lungs alone in my house in some sort of intuitive primal release. I felt completely unsettled/ungrounded, like life would never be the same, mourning the loss of my prior superficially blissful ignorance. My swirling thoughts instantly fixated on my mom, not my father. I remember the flashbacks making me feel profound confusion and a sense of abandonment by her, right, wrong or otherwise. Interestingly I seemed to "accept" my father's role relatively easily. Feelings often defy logic.

Although I was troubled by a host of unanswered questions that plagued me, I absolutely did not want to reveal my flashbacks to any family member - again, right, wrong or otherwise. I always protect others - even the less than innocent ones - over myself. I had a profound need to raise the issue with my mom though - somehow, indirectly. My most potent feelings from the flashbacks were ones of abandonment and fear and *I felt them in the present sense*. I didn't feel angry at my father at the time, surprisingly. I was more concerned with something terrible having happened to me in my mom's absence. I really wanted to figure out where she had been. I needed to figure it out. It was all I could fixate on.

Even in my adult body, fully capable of taking care of myself and geographically distanced from my father, I felt a deep indescribable foreboding based on my flashbacks - not based in reality, of course. I didn't appreciate it at the time but it was as if I were my vulnerable five year old self again. I needed to figure out the pressing enigma of where my mom had been to enable the abuses to have happened to me *in order to stave off any more trauma*. Of course, my mom is not responsible for my father's abuse and I wasn't attributing accountability to her at all. I just needed to understand the logistics to arm myself for some potentially pending hypothetical trauma I illogically was terribly fearful of.

Presumably most of us all view our mothers as our primary caregiver and protector. I've always had a particularly deep attachment to my mom though and I don't mean that in a typical mother-daughter sense. I had never before appreciated the source of my somewhat unhealthy extreme attachment to her.

I have never loved anyone more than my mom but we view our mothers as our source of comfort, our fiercest defenders, etc. and I felt like I had been let down. I apparently didn't have much in terms of expectations of my father but my mom was an entirely different story. She was my confidante, my protector, my hug-all-the-hurts away go to. My mom always joked how I talked into her armpit as a young child. I was very shy and introverted and either burrowed my way in under her arm or was forever on her lap. She was always joking about how my "bony butt" tore into her thighs. My mom has often recounted how terrible she felt taking me to kindergarten. I would literally wrap myself around her leg, clinging to her for dear life and begging her not to leave me. I distinctly remember feeling petrified about her departure like something terrible was inevitably going to happen. I remember hating the game show "Password", a game I had previously enjoyed watching with my mom. When kindergarten started, the beginning of Password signified it was time to go to school. I have always had a death phobia - not about me dying - but about loved ones dying. The ultimate "abandonment" if you will. I made my mom promise me when I was about 5 or 6 that she would not die before me. That is how deep my fear of abandonment from my mom is. I just realized that I wrote that in present tense. At 56, I know I still have to come to grips with my mom inevitably "being gone" one day lest I truly unravel when it happens. I can't even use the cold, clinical term for being gone associated with my mom. I have in recent years told her she was off the hook for her promise, provided she doesn't leave before my father.

In my 30's, my mom confided in me that she should have left my father years before when my sister and I were in grade school but then she got pregnant with my brother and decided not to. I remember silently trying to come to grips with my mom ever having thought of leaving me and my sister with my father. Of course that last part was a panicked assumption on my part. I remembered her always chastising a female family friend who had left her husband and three daughters. I was deeply pained trying to reconcile the two. It haunted me so much for years that I finally raised the subject with my mom. To my great relief, she dismissed my concerns by quickly clarifying that she would have taken my sister and me. But for that deep-rooted fear of abandonment - which I associate with something awful happening to me - I would have never assumed she meant she would leave me and my sister. It makes me sad that I did and highlights to me the far-reaching impact that abuse can have not only on the psyche of the abused and the abused's relationship with the abuser but with others as well - in my case, my beloved mom. I was filtering my mom through my panicked childhood eyes. In my head, terrible things happened when my mom was gone. That's why I always clung to her in general and went into crisis mode when I had to go to kindergarten.

The flashbacks sent my emotions askew and I had to get to the bottom of this mystery in order for my world to ever be aligned again - to the extent it ever was. At the time, I felt a bit something akin to anger towards my mom - not my father, which is also telltale to me. I didn't expect better of him. Despite my feelings, I didn't want to divulge my actual flashbacks to my mom, desperately wanting to shield her from that pain despite my feelings that she had "abandoned" me in some way, enabling the abuse. Again feelings defy logic but I was fixated on my mom, not my father, the actual perpetrator of the abuse.

My maternal grandparents had divorced when my mom was an adolescent and one of my grandmother's boyfriends tried to sexually assault her as a teenager. Thankfully, he was unsuccessful but the attempt obviously continued haunting her in adulthood. She had confided in my grandmother who apparently didn't believe her. To this day, my mom resents my grandmother (long deceased) for dismissing her divulgence. My parents left my sister and I with my grandmother and this man innumerable weekends during childhood so my parents could have free time to socialize, aka, go out drinking. As an adult, this situation had always troubled me but I had never questioned my parents. This history however came to the forefront of my mind as I was initially trying to "process" my flashbacks.

I channeled my "anger" and confusion vis-a-vis my mom indirectly, inquiring of her via her "secret" email my father did not access, why she used to leave my sister and I in the care of the man who had tried to sexually assault her. She responded that she knew we were in better hands with him there than just my grandmother, who smoked and drank a lot, saying my grandmother would accidentally burn us with her cigarettes. She also said she didn't think he would ever try anything because we were so young and she had been a teenager when he accosted her. A wholly unsatisfactory response to me in many ways for leaving us - not because they had to for an emergency or work or anything - just so they could go out and enjoy themselves.

I didn't get the response I expected when my mom chose to share a "confession" instead of responding to my question. I don't know what prompted her response; it was seemingly off topic but seemed to spot on answer the question where she could have been while I was being abused. My mom told me that she had finally started cheating on my father after the second pair of parents came to our home to chastise my father for having impregnated their daughter. In a way I felt I got more than I bargained for in terms of too much information. It did, however, give me a possible answer as to where my mom was during the abuse and an insight into the anger my parents had to have felt towards each other at the time. To this day, it seems odd to me that my mom chose this time to divulge this information when I was inquiring as to why we were left in the care of the man who tried to assault her.

That was the extent to which I indirectly delved into the subject of the abuse at the time with my mom. I felt I had some sense as to where she was and that was that for the moment. I "moved on" to try to come to grips with what had happened. My mom seemed clearly ignorant of the abuse itself. I had even asked my therapist if my father had repressed the memory of the abuse as I had done so "successfully" for so many decades. Even as I write that, I realize I wrote that as if I asked that as a factual question, not a hypothetical one - not whether he could have possibly repressed it. As if she could possibly know. It truly took me until this moment as I'm writing this to appreciate that I was hoping for some objective absolution of some bizarre sorts. Of course even had he repressed it, that most definitely would not excuse it.

I think, sensing my need at the time, she kindly confirmed the possibility that he could have repressed the abuse - albeit not very convincingly - but sufficiently enough to help my adult mind segregate from my childhood past and enable me to coexist with him.

Practically in an instant, the flashbacks explained so many previously inexplicable anomalies to me. Some may seem objectively trivial but each and every one is burned into my memory from even the tender age of five years old. I had a stuffed animal that went with me everywhere. It was a pink little monkey with green feet and hands - always been one for the ugly duckling/ the misfit. I creatively named "him" "Monkey" and put one of my baby doll's dresses on him because he was my babydoll in my little eyes. As a constant trustworthy companion, Monkey got pretty filthy and even the wires that supported his arms and legs started popping out. He may even have lost one of his button eyes at one point. I didn't care one bit. To me, he was perfect and my constant comforting companion.

I remember coming home one afternoon from kindergarten to the devastating news that Monkey was gone. I can't remember exactly what my poor beloved Monkey's demise was. I was too traumatized and distraught that my best friend, my confidante, was gone. No one had even thought to let me say goodbye. It was probably a failed attempt to wash him or a decision that the wires were dangerous. In any event, Monkey was gone forever and I thought my heart would never heal. I was not only devastated with grief. I was *petrified*.

Good family friends were visiting that afternoon. I fondly remember the couple who were always so kind and generous to my sister and me. Monkey's importance to me was not lost on this loving couple. Having heard of Monkey's demise, they had thoughtfully come that afternoon to bring me a new gift. I still remember the range of my emotions from my happy smile about unexpectedly seeing them, to my gut-wrenching realization that I would never hold Monkey again, to the facade of trying to be pleased with the new little tiny normal looking stupid brown monkey they gave me. I'm a very polite person and was a very polite child. I tried to express real gratitude and pretend like I was happy with the cold, nondescript new monkey. I was utterly shocked, however, how no one could see that Monkey was irreplaceable.

I believe I initially took my emotions out via anger expressed to the innocent new stuffed animal that I knew I would never hold tenderly or even name, despite my fixation with naming things. Eventually, I let him tag along with me, letting him dangle by my side with a nonchalant, lackluster grip. I think I could have become attached to him. I have that sort of personality, but it was too soon for my tender traumatized heart. Alas, I didn't have sufficient time to develop a bond with the scrawny little monkey because something happened to him as well. I didn't get the opportunity to say goodbye to him either because my parents thought I was so detached from him that I didn't care. I remember, however, that his unexpected departure saddened and frightened me again; it had become a sort of replacement for Monkey albeit not a perfect one as Monkey was irreplaceable.

I always slept holding a stuffed animal. Even as an adult, stuffed animals used to take center stage in bed to the dismay of my sleeping partners. In more recent years as travels necessitated leaving my inanimate "buffers" behind, the stuffed animals were replaced by a pillow I clutch protectively over me. I absolutely cannot sleep without such a "buffering" comfort. I didn't realize this was unusual until I had a boyfriend who appreciated that something underlay that constant need. He intuitively always suspected I had been abused even before I did and said he would know I was "healed" when I no longer required the comforting "protection" of the pillow.

Before my flashbacks, I didn't appreciate the reason Monkey had had such an esteemed role in my childhood life. I just assumed he was my first real inanimate attachment/source of comfort so many young children have - like Linus' obsession with his blanket in the Peanuts cartoon.

Monkey and I were reunited again - via memory in the form of my flashbacks. I vividly saw myself clutching Monkey protectively against my chest as my father opened my bedroom door, the light from the hallway illuminating his face briefly before he shut the door, flooding the room in foreboding darkness. I tried to back away while gripping Monkey tightly, apparently expecting something terrible was about to happen based on the familiarity. I was trying in vain to use Monkey as a sort of protective shield - psychologically helpful if not physically. I also remember subsequently frantically grabbing for Monkey as my father was leaving the room, closing the door behind him, leaving me again enveloped in darkness with the soft embracing consolation of Monkey.

I vividly remember him saying as he left - and many other times - "You know I love you more than your sister." I have always become attached quickly. Others would definitely say "too quickly." Admittedly, they are likely correct. I have this desperate need for "connections" and to feel loved. I knew I always had a distorted association between sex and love. It is literally just today as I'm writing this that I fully realize the origin of that association - my father's attestation that he loved me more - juxtapositionsed with something sexual. Lightning bolt moment.

The abuse - and that critical repulsive statement that he loved me more than my sister - created extraordinarily difficult emotions for my little five year old self to comprehend. It was like the "act" was our little secret and it was my duty to protect him by not divulging it. The statement was programmed to make me feel special, uniquely bonded, uniquely loved. Even as a child, the abuse as well as the clandestine nature of it intuitively made me feel extremely uneasy but of course I wanted to "obey" my father and desperately wanted to feel worthy and to be loved.

My worth was being defined and love was being conditioned. Comply, obediently subjugate or be worthless, unloved. Even at such a tender age I was able to understand the existence of the quid pro nature of the relationship. My unique unhealthy relationship with sex was cemented in my impressionable brain. It was all too much for my little brain to fully process or comprehend though and presumably that is why I protectively repressed the abuse for so many decades. As an adult, it repulses me that he would say that he loved me more, especially in juxtaposition to the abuse. In an utterly revolting way, love had been inextricably intertwined with the abuse that had been inflicted on me. For the first time as I'm writing, I see it as a twisted, manipulative way of acquiring my compliance and my silence. Even at a tender age, I was sensitive enough to know the mere statement wasn't "right" and would have never divulged it for fear of hurting my sister.

As I noted, it was like a floodgate of explanations of sorts was opened when I started having flashbacks. It was like my childhood flashed before me. My flashbacks included abuses in our bathroom and instantly shed light on some particularly embarrassing childhood recollections. I had "bed wetting" problems until I was about 9 or so. It seemed to oscillate between being an annoyance and a joke in my family, at least that's how I remember it. I never consciously understood it until I had the flashbacks. It clearly wasn't a matter of having too much liquid and sleeping through it accidentally. I say "bed wetting" in quotes because I wet my pants in numerous unbelievably embarrassing contexts while fully awake, petrified to go to bathrooms. I distinctly remember two school episodes. One when I was in kindergarten, I wet my pants in a cushioned rocking chair in the classroom library area. To this day, I remember being in line as the teacher was making us each pass by to determine who the "culprit" was after she discovered the wet cushion. I thought for sure the sound of my fiercely beating little heart or the crimson color of my blushing cheeks would have "ratted" me out as I nervously stood in line. Intervention came in the form of the school bell indicating the end of the school day before I got to the front of the line. The second time was in 1st grade and I wasn't so fortunate to be cloaked in anonymity. I literally just peed my pants sitting in my chair, the puddle under my chair leaving no doubt that time as to the responsible party. I still remember being frozen in my seat, so terrified to go to the bathroom that I chose such an embarrassing option instead.

I also remember in around fourth grade, frequently engaging in an elaborate "ruse" to make it look like I had taken a shower at home, running the shower water, wetting the towel as if I had dried off and splashing my hair with water. I never undressed though. Instead, I calmed myself, "escaping" in the transformative pages of books. I remember my scheme eventually being discovered by accident. I had a huge library fine for the book "Escape to Treasure Island" being woefully overdue when I couldn't locate it. I had hid it in the back of the bathroom linen closet under towels during one of my "fake" showers. This also was another source of embarrassment for me but amusement to my family. To this day, I remember its jacket cover and the source of comfort the distraction of reading had given me.

As an adult, the first thing I always did when I returned to whatever home I was living in was to go to each bathroom and check behind the shower curtain to make sure no one was there. Interestingly, I only did this in my own home. Home was where I had been harmed. I eventually just started buying see through shower curtains. I also have a lifelong habit of locking the bathroom door regardless of whether I was alone or with whom I was living. I also remember recoiling in high school when I had to "draw" my father's bath. I have no recollection why I was told to do it but distinctly remember the unease with which I did it.

I have also always been obsessed with brushing my teeth, dentists chastising me for the force with which I do it. Although my flashbacks immediately explained certain behaviors to me, like my fear of bathrooms, I didn't instantly appreciate my oral health obsession. A lightbulb went off when my best friend from high school, Kathy, reminded me that we would use our high school lunch breaks to pick up lunch for her then walk a mile or so to my house simply for me to brush my teeth. It was a daily ritual with which I was obsessed, notwithstanding that I wasn't eating.

I distinctly remember being so "traumatized" by a little boy, Ellery, at nap time in kindergarten. He would harmlessly tickle me. I was so distraught though that I got to sit at a table doing puzzles while the other kids napped. I actually fondly remember this past time. I always loved puzzles at a young age and was apparently very adept at them. My mom has told me she would even mix two puzzles together for me to do. I think I enjoyed the sense of order and control it gave to me. I also got to drink orange juice while I was doing puzzles, allowing me to skip milk time which made me happy because I hated milk. Despite the "Ellery" incidents, I also remember liking boys quickly thereafter at the early age of six; I remember my first crush vividly in first grade. Promiscuity started at a relatively early age as well. I hadn't appreciated at the time my habit of equating sex with love that would disserve me so many times throughout my life.

Like I said, the flashbacks explained some of my historical behavior to me. I had yet to have any real appreciation, however, about how deeply impactful my childhood abuse had been - and was - on adult me, my sense of self worth and my relationships. That would still take time. Unfortunately, a lot of time, an attempted suicide and a lot more abusive relationships....

Chapter 2
An Intoxicating Life: Overdose #1

It's fascinating to me how vividly I can recall certain details from the lowest parts of my life, despite said points generally being accompanied by some form of intoxication. Some remembrances are so intense, so vivid, so painful I feel like I'm reliving the event. I think maybe in a way I am trying to come to grips with them by "reliving" them. Some details remain irrepressibly noteworthy somehow through the prevalent thick haze of memories I would just as soon forget.

In high school, I overdosed on the sleeping pills prescribed to me for relentless struggles with insomnia, aided and abetted by a cocktail of my parents' antidepressant and anti anxiety pills. Immediately before typing the preceding sentence, I was going through some of my notes from my dreams when I was trying to lucidly dream - more on this later. The sleeping pills had been prescribed because I was having horrific scary dreams as a teenager. One of the details from one of my recent dreams while trying to lucidly dream included my sister getting married (in the dream, not the reality). That detail helped trigger my memory to remember that the scary dreams had begun when my sister was no longer sleeping in the same room - in the same double bed - with me. I remember this was a time when she and I were not getting along. It took me until now to realize that I was afraid of sleeping alone and her absence is what triggered the seemingly inexplicable violent dreams. To this day, I absolutely struggle sleeping alone. I distinctly remember that the sleeping pills were counterproductive. They exacerbated the problem, resulting in even more 'bizarre" and terrifying dreams. Certain essential oils and teas have the same effect on me now; they have the power to put me in a state of subconsciousness where I don't want to consciously go.

I have no recollection of what the teenage dreams were, just that they terrified me and set me on a lifelong path of insomnia. I struggle to go to sleep because I don't want to experience my subconscious. My subconscious potently protects my day time with repression. The inner workings of my brain are only available while sleeping. I've never been able to nap alone. Even when I try when I'm exhausted from not sleeping, I wake up in a panic. I know it's because I'm not inebriated and, hence, I'm cognizant of my dreams and their revelations. It's human nature to avoid pain, physical and mental. I distinctly remember always falling asleep in classes in college given by my absolute favorite professor. It was as if I were drugged. I struggled so hard to stay awake knowing full well how disrespectful it was to fall asleep and obviously counterproductive to my education. I now realize my body gave into exhaustion in an environment - objectively highly inappropriate for sleep - but subjectively a safe haven. That's why I sleep much better when I am with someone. Anyway, I digress, but an important digression to me and an excellent reminder/motivation for me to write down my dreams.

I was in my bedroom alone with the door shut, beginning to drift into the drug-induced abyss of never never land I had chosen. My parents barged into the room, startling me from the warm embrace of blackness that was beginning to engulf me - the segregation from reality, from life, that I had chosen. My father yelled at me. ***Yes, yelled at me.*** May startle you but apropos. It was something to the effect of "Sophie, what the hell are you doing?", an oft-repeated question hurled at me so many times, my best friends from high school bring it up to this day. Don't get me wrong. I know my father loves me as much as anyone but he has always been ill-equipped to deal with stress and compassion has never been his strong suit in these types of circumstances. This query - one of the isolated recollections of my first overdose - is also noteworthy because, as I said, it is the exact same thing he said to me after my husband tried to kill me. People always wonder why I apologize for things that are not my responsibility or fault whatsoever, why I always feel responsible for others and why I avoid asking for help like the plague. Being responsible and made to feel like everything was my fault was programmed into me from a young age.

Fortunately, two of my "earth angels" made fateful appearances that prevented me from being successful at the ultimate escape. Shout out to my high school boyfriends who were instrumental in saving my life. My boyfriend at that time, Tim, had spoken to me on the phone shortly after

I had taken the pills. It was obvious to him that I was in grave danger. Not knowing what to do he called Mike, my subsequent boyfriend who has literally and figuratively been saving my life ever since, remaining my blessed friend to this day. Mike told Tim to immediately call my parents, which he did. I don't know what would have happened but for their intervention.

Next vivid recollection was the emergency room doctor asking me why I had tried to kill myself while I was retching up the pitcher of black charcoal he forced me to drink to rid my stomach of the drugs. I can still remember the thick chalky taste and desperately wanting everyone to go away and just leave me alone. Despite my drug-induced haze, I remember being struck by the fact that he asked me this insightful question in front of my parents. I have no idea how I answered or whether my answer would have been different absent my parents but I do remember I thought it was something that should be asked privately.

I have a fierce constitution, of which I am mighty proud and grateful. I've always been relatively small but I have great inner strength and a survivor instinct. When I hadn't succeeded as planned at drifting off into never never land in solitude, I physically recovered from the overdose quickly.

I'm not sure what happened next but I remember being in some sort of mental institution, where all the possessions I had with me were being thoroughly inventoried. The staff took a tiny change purse I had away from me. I still remember it. It had a diminutive mirror and apparently they thought I might possibly use the glass to cut myself. I don't really know what the nature of the institution was nor the politically correct term for "guests" thereof, particularly sensitive to the denomination since I apparently was one of them. I vividly remember some "patient/client/customer/other institutionalized person" screaming and wailing uncontrollably as I was being shown around my new "residence"? Temporary, I hoped. I remember a room with a circle of chairs for group meetings presumably where everyone divulged their deepest, darkest feelings. I felt extremely uncomfortable with the novel surroundings - particularly with the ongoing wailing and the fact that I was painfully shy under the best of circumstances. However, I also remember feeling vaguely optimistic that I wouldn't be alone - my kryptonite if you will - and that maybe somebody felt the way I did and maybe someone could help me process it and move on with my life.

I kind of remember feeling abandoned but like I deserved to be left there for upsetting and embarrassing my parents. Writing this just jogged my memory - that's the fascinating thing about memories - even the ones we think we lost. They are generally there somewhere - the retrieval process may take awhile and something may need to jog the retrieval - like reflection or desire to remember. I now believe that I went from the ER of the hospital to the hospital's psychiatric ward.

The next thing I remember is my father loudly insisting at "reception" that no daughter of his would be staying in such a place. Classic father - laser focused on how things would reflect on him - and with an insensitivity - a vocally loud one - for the "institution" and the "institutionalized." My father is the quintessential parent who lives to brag about his children's accomplishments, almost ad naseum. It wasn't until years later that I appreciated the depths and full ramifications of that pride vis-a-vis me when his pride faltered. More to come. I remember a discussion between a doctor and my father, the doctor indicating that my parents would need to sign me out with an acknowledgement that my departure was against his recommendation. I remember my father hastily, angrily signing. *I do not recall anyone asking me what I wanted or even looking at me. I was in the background, metaphorically and in reality*, being neither seen nor heard.

I remember ending the day at Red Lobster - normally a big treat back then - with my parents and best friend, Kathy, and her boyfriend. I also remember thinking that was odd given the circumstances. I didn't view it as a celebratory occasion but I was comforted to be with my friend. My parents always seem to be uncomfortable around me when something disturbing has happened. *I do not recall a single conversation with either of my parents about why I had overdosed. Ever.*

I was forced to go to psychiatric therapy. I think maybe my parents had agreed to that as a condition when they whisked me away from the ward. I only remember two things about therapy. First, my mom insisted on being in the room with me. To this day, I don't know why - it's inconsistent with her personality. I was very uncomfortable about being honest or open about anything given her presence. This was especially true given my persona of shielding everyone from anything contentious or unpleasant to them, often to my own detriment. Side note, my father insisted on being in the room with my mom when she went to therapy years later to her unexpressed (to him) dismay. Full circle.....Second, the therapist asked if I had been trying to get attention. To this day, this infuriates me, I shall assume for evident reasons without expounding. I left feeling dejected and despondent, like I was responsible for pain, chaos and shame I inflicted on my parents because of childish antics. In high school, I had wanted to be a psychologist - something drew me to helping others and I was fascinated by the mind. Perhaps that desire was an unconscious reflection of my troubled psyche and realization that I needed help. I think this dissatisfactory interaction with the therapist briefly intensified that desire. In any event, I became a lawyer, so neither here nor there.

I'm gratefully one of the lucky ones, having survived not only one but two intentional overdoses (the second detailed later). Difficult to get insight into the tragedy of suicide when the victims aren't around to reveal their feelings or motivations. That was my first and only session. I still bristle recalling the therapist's misguided, insensitive query. From the depths of my soul, getting attention was not a motivation one iota. It actually was the exact opposite. I just wanted to quietly slip into peaceful black solitude...

PART TWO: ADULTHOOD: TRAUMA DRAMA:

WHY DO THE WORK

"Don't blame a clown for acting like a clown. Ask yourself why you keep going to the circus."
Unknown

Chapter 1
Attempted Murder

The Lead Up

I remember the night my husband tried to kill me as if it were yesterday. In reality, it was over 15 years ago, the same span of time we had been married before he tried to choke me to death. How could I stay with someone capable of murder for so long you may be asking yourself? Some additional background into my already troubled psyche may be of benefit...

As I noted, my father is the quintessential parent who thrives on bragging about his children's accomplishments ad nauseum. In my case, this meant my siblings. It wasn't until later in life that I really saw that side of him vis-a-vis me. To the contrary, he always predicted that I would be barefoot and pregnant with a half dozen kids at an early age. It was obvious that this was something that would be less than praiseworthy in his view.

I was a normal, sociable child and teenager who dated and frequented social events. My father focused on the less social, more academically-driven personas of my siblings, lauding the fact that they graduated high school as valedictorian and salutatorian. For the longest time - even into adulthood - I would be reminded that I finished only sixth in my class. Despite my more sociable life, I was actively involved in speech and debate and would spend a lot of the Summer break avidly researching and preparing for the start of the season in the Fall. I still couldn't get my father's approval. He never seemed too impressed with all my hard work nor even the numerous accolades I received. He loved bragging and apparently it was easier to explain perfect grade point averages and graduating 1st or 2nd in your class.

I was a good kid and conscientious student but life wasn't all about academics to me in contrast to my siblings. I always seemed to be grounded for innocuous things while they could do no wrong. Except for when I was getting in trouble, I rarely garnered much attention. This actually is somewhat shocking as I started drinking at a young age in high school but my parents never suspected nor found out.

I spent a lot of time at my maternal grandmother's house where there were frequent parties and always a well-stocked bar. My grandmother was extremely hospitable and generous and I felt more at home there, more comfortable, more "seen" and "heard". She always made me feel special and loved. She was quite the sociable host and had many relationships. I was always enamored with the classic beauty Elizabeth Taylor and her unwavering passion and zest for life. I loved how she moved on from one failed relationship to the next, never closing her heart or missing an opportunity to love. One of my uncles nicknamed me Elizabeth Taylor at a young age for some reason. The nickname flattered me and it was with great pride that I perceived a kindred spirit amongst Ms. Taylor, my grandmother and myself.

During high school, I drank often at my grandmother's house - in her absence. To this day, I cannot even stand to smell scotch or any other type of whiskey - but that was her drink of choice so that's what I drank. It felt like I spent most of my Summers there and I would also go to drink there before high school football games. I often told my parents I was going to a game when I would go to my boyfriend's house instead, conveniently located behind the high school. I always made sure to check the scoreboard before heading home so I knew who had won in case I was asked. Normally no one asked, however. Often, my parents weren't home either, they frequently were out drinking. My sister and I took turns watching my little brother, nine years my junior. Other than this responsibility, I was largely left to my own. I don't remember what little things kept getting me grounded but they were unrelated to my secret drinking and my parents were unaware that I was having sex in high school.

I silently and determinedly moved past my high school "failures", as perceived by my father. It wasn't until years later after I graduated from college (a year early with two majors, first in my class and an unblemished record of A's), passed the law school entrance exam (in the top 5%), and attended a prestigious law school (graduating with honors) that I seemed to garner my father's attention for my academic achievements.

I distinctly remember him opening the positive results of my bar exam, responding almost as enthusiastically as if he had just won the lottery. Finally, I shone brightly in his eyes and could be included in his praise. I was the first in our family to graduate from college. I seemed to have reclaimed "favorite status" in my father's eyes based on my educational success and potential lucrative stream of income. Turns out my sister was the one at home with children early on, having dropped out of college in the midst of her first semester.

After law school, I moved on to an objectively successful legal career where I worked insane hours, made great money and garnered excellent reviews and accolades.

My father never ceased bragging to anyone who would listen, beaming with pride about his daughter, the lawyer, and my lucrative job at a top law firm. As I said, he always viewed his children's achievements as positive reflections on himself.

It just dawned on me that I may have been driven to do so well in school because I was subconsciously jealous of my sister. My father's oft-repeated statements that he loved me more than he loved her not did not sync with the attention she was getting for excelling in high school while I seemed to be in the background. I was obsessed in college that I not even get a "B", awaiting grades at the end of each trimester with near petrifaction. I even took a couple of required math and science classes pass/fail because I was fearful of losing my straight "A" status. One of them to which I was particularly drawn was psychology - the subject had continued to fascinate me. Notwithstanding the pass/fail status I was driven and got an "A" in the classes, to the chagrin of my fellow classmates because grading was on a curve. I could have squeaked by as far as the college was concerned with a mere "pass" grade and I was self-conscious "ruining the curve" for my classmates, a lot of whom were my friends. Yet, it was more important to me that I not disappoint my father with an average grade, finally having garnered his attention for my academic achievements. I had put myself on a stressful pedestal and I couldn't let myself fall. I was undoubtedly an enigma to a lot of classmates. I was the promiscuous partier who excelled. No one, including myself at the time, had any insight into my troubled psyche.

It's crazy to me how profoundly impactful our upbringing can be. Some small part of me may have known my own self worth but I could not internalize it, embrace it or act accordingly. I wasn't accustomed to being lauded about my school efforts, unlike my siblings, and I needed external validation, "proof", if you will. Even when I would do well, I had a bizarre habit of expressing my gratitude to my parents for my achievements as if my genes were exclusively responsible and I deserved no credit. I would actually express this sentiment in thank you cards. I just realized that perhaps I had internalized my father's belief that the achievements of his children were an extension of himself. My mom, however, always lovingly chastised me for this habit and tried to assure me that I was solely responsible for my achievements.

My sister, whom I love dearly and with whom I have a phenomenal relationship, confided in me in just the past several years how jealous she always was of me, apparently holding the perception that everything came easily to me. She confided that she always thought I had the perfect life. My life has been such that most would not perceive my internal conflicts, my extremely low self-esteem and confidence, or my tortured soul based on the objective trappings of achievements and success and the seemingly outwardly happy relationships I had.

Breaking the **shackles** of pervasive negative or limiting beliefs instilled since childhood is no easy task and takes consistent and extraordinary determination. It was not until recently that I finally realized how deeply I had internalized the **idea** that my self worth is merely sexual or financial in nature. Even as I write this, I'm chilled by the fact that I spontaneously chose the word, "idea", instead of "feeling" or "impression" or something less concrete or objective. It's as if I've come to accept it as a fact. Indeed, I've certainly lived my life as if it were - forever allowing myself to be treated as a means to an end. More like inviting than allowing to be painfully honest. If my worth is to be a means, I am worthless by definition if I am not fulfilling that purpose...

After my flashbacks of sexual abuse, I understood that my distorted views on sex stemmed from my childhood. Aside from my father's articulated assessment that ***no man will want you for anything but sex or money*** (more on this to come), I hadn't appreciated where my need to give financially to a fault had come from. I knew my parents' relationship was one in which my mom was the financial provider for the most part and assumed, without much thought, that was where my habit of being used financially or taken advantage of had originated.

It is not until I just wrote the prior paragraphs that it dawned on me that my academic achievements, which translated into great earnings potential, are what finally got my father's attention after so many years of not being seen or heard. My earnings potential is what got me my "preferred" status back in my father's eyes. It would be unbelievable to me how insidious and pervasive our upbringing and childhood abuse or neglect can be if I weren't living proof of it. My profound belief that my worth was merely sexual or financial had been instilled in me as a child, my father literally confirming that belief with his articulation many years subsequent.

Shortly after graduating law school, my college boyfriend, Bob Smith, and I got engaged, just prior to me starting my lucrative job as a lawyer. He moved in with me in the downtown apartment I had rented. Its proximity to work was convenient given the insane work hours that characterized my several years at the law firm. I distinctly remember him not helping me with the move, stating he needed time to "bond" with his father. This was neither the first nor last time I was not his priority. As noted, I had been promiscuous in college and dated several men who excelled at school and would go on to have stellar careers. "BS", as I now prefer to refer to him, his name being as non-descript as he was, did not do well in school nor did he exhibit much ambition. I was drawn to the uninitiated and needy from the start. Bizarrely, even though he would benefit significantly from my career, he was always jealous of my accomplishments. The focus always had to be on him. My achievements would be twisted into pity for him. I will never forget my embarrassment as he sat reading a book during my swearing in ceremony for the bar association that he had attended with my parents.

Soon after I began my legal career, BS started working as a broker for a trading company but quickly decided he wanted to try to trade for himself. He wasn't making money - a good day was when he wasn't losing any money. He didn't have expenses because I was paying for everything. He still wasn't making any money to speak of a year later when we got married. His family was relatively well off and he had grown up with a certain sense of entitlement. My in-laws didn't think I was good enough to join their family because I did not come from money. They did not hide their feelings from me or my parents. I remember countless times being profoundly embarrassed in their presence, made to feel shameful for my upbringing. Another "validation" tying worth to finances. BS was fixated on money - he could spend it - however, wasn't making it.

The "honeymoon phase" of our marriage wore off quickly but, like my mom who basically supported my father, I tried to make the most of it. I continued working exhausting, stressful hours, always needing to excel for validation. Despite my outwardly successful career, I knew life was missing "something", that I could be happier under different circumstances. I lived for my vacations but it became a fight every time I wanted to take a much needed and deserved one. BS thought we should save "our" money instead, planning for retirement. Our differences went deeper though. I wanted children and to work for a charity. I wanted my hard work and long hours to go towards something I found personally more "rewarding". He was adamantly against either; they were inconsistent with his monomaniacal obsession with amassing a big bank account and material reflections of "his" success. He thought he was being supportive when he suggested that he stay home to raise children - children that he clearly articulated he did not want - while I continued working extraordinary hours at something that was not fulfilling me. I say "differences" rather than "disagreements" because I more or less caved to his desires, not even entertaining the thought that my own desires should be my priority.

Today, with my self awareness, this embarrasses and pains me that I obsequiously followed his desired courses of action, particularly with respect to such fundamental things as my career and motherhood. I was modeling - indeed, mirroring - my relationship after my parents' co-dependent relationship, however, where my mother's "martyrdom" appeared strong, independent, even heroic to me. My skewed psyche internalized that the more you "suffered in silence" and took care of others' needs, goals, desires and whims to the dismissal of your own, the "stronger" you were. Self sacrifice was modeled as "love" to me and I was copying it to an extreme - working so hard and being so exhausted and stressed that I was seriously compromising my health. It's interesting to me that there are many other women in my life, including my niece and my friend, Kathy, who similarly have perceived my mom the same way. Kathy always aspired to emulate my mom yet has always been confounded by my relationships. It was not until the past few years, when I started realizing the impetus for my relationships was my mom and articulated that to her, that Kathy also began to appreciate the fact that I was emulating my mom. She knew my father had always been at home while my mom worked. What she had viewed as my mom's enviable strength, she viewed as my weakness.

After several years of working insane hours I took another job - trading big law firm life for an in-house corporate job. At first, I was more fulfilled and much happier. My job involved frequent foreign travel and my wanderlust soul, which was repressed by BS, was given "flight". I enjoyed my work for the first time, being exposed to different cultures and being treated with respect and kindness. Jealous BS preferred when I was miserable working, however. He was upset with my traveling and quite frankly that I was having good experiences. He required frequent reassurances when he would falsely accuse me basically of "partying" when I was traveling for work. As I said, he had a bizarre sense of jealousy. Even though he benefitted from my salary and top bonuses, he would mourn how pathetic he was when I received accolades and financial rewards instead of expressing pride or congratulations for my efforts. The focus always centered around him and I would downplay my achievements to make him feel better about himself.

His jealousy didn't phase me, however, as I was used to my fathers off the chart jealousy. My mom couldn't have any communication or time with me without his inclusion. My father would call me and talk to me for hours - generally complaining about finances, my mom or just in general. She, however, had to have him pre-approve emails to me (the ones he was aware of that is). He'd walk into a room and immediately accuse us of talking about him behind his back. I fondly remember that my mom used to sing to me "You are my sunshine, my only sunshine," the fond memory transitioning to a bad one when she abruptly stopped because it made my father jealous.

BS hated my travel but loved my paycheck. I was in the awkward position of loving my job but feeling pressured to find a different one because he resented the travel - the travel I loved. My a—hole boss settled the situation when he started sexually harassing me. I didn't even tell BS, knowing if I did that his greed would insist on pursuing what he would envision as a lucrative lawsuit. Instead I silently quit and dejectedly moved back to the long, "unrewarding" hours of lawfirm life.

The utter absurdity of my life lived for someone else increasingly made me feel unfulfilled, restless and resentful but I felt unable to rectify it. I was *trapped in my belief from childhood* that my purpose was to satisfy my husband, even at the cost of my authentic greatest happiness. My life was also taking a toll on my physical well-being; my sleep deprivation, stress and underlying resentment and unresolved issues having frequently and significantly manifested themselves physiologically, including a misdiagnosis of multiple sclerosis.

At this point, BS and I got involved in his family's restaurant business. Between my career and a business I was trying to support on the side, this kept me fully distracted. I wanted to leave him but just didn't have the psyche or courage to do so. At this point, I began to realize that my mom staying in a life that made her miserable was the opposite of strength but I was no better equipped to effectuate change. *I was quagmired by my deeply-instilled, limiting belief that I did not deserve any better.*

I kept plodding along over the next year or so, making the most of circumstances as I always seemed to manage to do. The restaurant was a happy distraction for me. I had been increasingly articulating my desire to work for a charity. I wasn't as happy as I could be with my marriage or my job so I would settle for a change in the latter. I thought the restaurant may finally support a career switch for me. BS assumed a

charity would pay less and was unsupportive, which, of course, settled that at the time. I desperately needed a change though. I was working insane hours again at a job that paid well but was making me miserable; it wasn't fulfilling me and was negatively impacting my health, psychologically and physically. Fortuitously, we got a potential offer to sell the restaurant more or less at the same time I had been approached for another in-house corporate job. The company was of great interest to me but the job was in another state. I finally got the courage to say I was taking that job or looking for a job with a charity. BS decided we would accept the offer to sell the business and I would accept the new job, recognizing we would be living apart until the business sale was consummated.

I got an apartment in the new city, hours from where we were living in Chicago, and dove into my new job, energized and enthused by the change. I was working long hours because we were in the midst of a huge acquisition, my professional forte, while commuting back and forth on weekends to help at the restaurant and work on the sale of the business. I was exhausted but feeling better; engaged in things of interest and experiencing a new city. The business would be sold soon, BS would be moving to the city I was working in, he would get a job and we would get a new house, or so I thought. I could deal with a less than ideal marriage and personal life as long as I was relatively happy professionally.

As I drove the hours to Chicago on the day of the closing to consummate the restaurant sale, I happily - though briefly - even envisioned finally pursuing my desire to do charitable work in the not too distant future. I had a rude awakening instead that pierced my newly forming bubble of happiness. BS told me he didn't want to work. He had no intention to get a job and that he was going to stay in our house in Chicago to unsolicitedly, arrogantly "help" the new owners indefinitely at my literal and figurative expense. Mind you, the new owners didn't even want him there.

Something finally snapped in me given the stark contrast between my expectations and his intentions - between the life I longed for and the one I had been living. I finally had enough and got up the courage to separate from him. It was the proverbial last straw. We had already been physically separated for months by then. I had wanted to leave him for some time. He was pathetic in many ways - it's what made me want to leave but thus far had kept me bound to him. I felt "compelled" to take care of him, modeling my behavior after my mother. As I alluded, there is no one I love more than my mom. I am now deeply and painfully aware, however, that my mother's behavior in my parents' co-dependent relationship that I had perceived as strong was actually weak and subservient. She acquiesced to every whim of her husband/my father, subjugating herself and unwittingly modeling a pattern of behavior I was following. Of course, I do not desire to be weak or subservient, just as undoubtedly she did not. I couldn't stop it though when I didn't realize I was doing it.

When I first announced the separation, BS, who had always been emotionally abusive and somewhat violent at times, dislocated my shoulder.

I will never forget him questioning who would be there to take care of me if we got divorced as he drove me to the hospital for treatment of the injury he inflicted on me. During the first few months of our separation, BS flexed his emotional manipulation I had previously not recognized. Although they had never been close, he called my father daily instigating him to try to guilt me into staying with him, saying he would commit suicide if we divorced. My father chastised me about the separation because of the impact it supposedly had on BS.

It had taken me years and every ounce of courage and strength I had to separate. I would have never done it but for BS' articulated intention of not working. I longed for familial support or at least to not be questioned. My family knew how unbelievably hard I worked and how much BS took me for granted. Way to support your daughter I thought, albeit silently, not having sufficient courage or sense of self worth to stand up for myself to my father.

The Attempt

As I intimated, I had wanted to leave BS for years. I had strategized a departure in my mind over that time and hypothetically effectuated it. I remember telling a male colleague with whom I was good friends that I would leave BS but would give him all the savings from my years of working. I knew I was capable of starting over again but didn't have faith in his abilities; it had basically been a parasitic relationship at least financially. Since my worth was financial, I viewed giving up all my earnings as the cost of my freedom. My friend was understandably shocked at my mindset. For years, my departure remained a kind of fantasy of freedom; I had an all-consuming desire to be done but didn't have the courage to actually leave. BS always threatened he would kill me if I left even though I never articulated my desire to. Turns out, he was serious.

BS continued his manipulative ways and sadly I continued to allow myself to be manipulated. I had scored great baseball tickets through my employer and had invited my brother and his family, all of whom were avid baseball fans. BS begged to come, jealous of my family. I'm embarrassed to say that I acquiesced and uninvited my sister-in-law. My father told me that he had warned BS to not to drink or do anything stupid since he was trying to reconcile with me. That was my father's way of supporting me apparently even though I had no interest in reconciliation. We went to the game and even went dancing afterwards, unwisely drinking all along to help deal with the awkwardness of our separation.

I had started seeing someone after my separation. Initially I hadn't told BS. I had separated because I didn't want to be with him, not because of anyone else. I didn't need any additional reason and I didn't want to cloud that fact with anything extraneous. My father persisted that he thought it would be easier on BS if he knew there was someone else until I foolishly acquiesced against my better judgment and own wishes. His assessment turned out to be false and apparently set the stage for the events that were about to unfold. I was at work when BS got to my apartment on the day of the game. He had gone through all of my things and found (and broke) a necklace I had received through work that BS erroneously assumed my new romantic interest had given me. I wasn't aware of this until later. As I was getting ready for the game, I could hear BS trying to persuade my brother (a la the manipulative efforts with my father) to convince me to stay with him. I knew it would be an awkward night at best but I did not foresee what was to transpire.

That night after we got back to my apartment, he was in a fit of rage I didn't see coming. To this day, it makes my skin crawl that he was so upset before we even went out but kept his anger hidden as we went out, drinking and dancing, etc. I feel he was fully aware of trying to fulfill his oft-stated intention of killing me if I left. I knew him well enough to know it wasn't the jealousy of another man per se but the realization of losing my lucrative stream of income that pushed him over the edge.

He began beating me relentlessly. I was in shock, in utter disbelief, my dulling of faculties further exacerbated by my inebriation. I didn't have my wits about me nor could I muster my inner strength, my survivor instinct dissipating in the face of this surrealness. He threatened to throw me over the balcony. As if his intent weren't sufficiently clear from that threat, he literally articulated his intent with rage in his voice and eyes. He said something to the effect of "If I can't have you, I'll kill you." Surrealism up a notch. I felt disconnected as if I were in a nightmare I desperately wanted to end but was powerless to stop. His articulation spurred me into action sufficiently, as I tried to get to the door to escape. He grabbed me, dragging me by the ankles along the carpet, leaving a trail of rug burns along my scantily-clad body.

I managed to get up, reeling from the pain of the burns. He was quite a bit bigger than I am and he pushed me backwards over the couch so my lower back was awkwardly pressed back against the couch while my upper body was hanging upside down over the front of the couch; the angle giving him greater leverage. I felt my body almost give in, flailing ever so slightly but futilely. He began choking me, making good on his threat. My life flashed before me and I felt myself slipping into unconsciousness. My mind and body felt disassociated. Unfortunately though they seemed to be surrendering in unison. I was so utterly shocked by his threats and what was happening. His words didn't comport with any reality I could sync with. I just wanted it to end.

I was feebly trying to gasp for breath, the survivor instinct briefly battling with my desire to give up the surreal fight. With my already beaten body badly contorted, however, and my neck bent back so far and awkwardly, there was barely any room for air even without his hands firmly strangling me. I briefly flailed about trying to get upright, to get leverage, to get grounded on the floor, just barely out of reach of my upside down body. I felt my body go limp as it gave up any futile resistance, following the lead of my mind that apparently had capitulated. I heard persistent banging and an insistent voice over his enraged threats. I thought I was hallucinating. Finally, he released his chokehold, my head whipped forward as I crumbled into a pile like a beaten, breathless, emotionless rag doll. He barely opened the door and I heard a male voice tersely warning him to knock it off or he would call the cops.

The brief intervention spurred me into action again. I frantically searched for my phone as I gratefully gulped for air. I scrambled into the bathroom, hoping the warning would put an end to the nightmare. Before I could lock it, he was there. He didn't heed the warning. The self-righteousness of an enraged, drunken self-absorbed man knew no bounds that night as he continued to beat me senselessly. He ripped apart my phone, the pieces scattering, and continued to beat me, punching holes in walls and slamming my head against the wall. I recoiled, shrinking in pain against the bathtub and he slammed the back of my head against its cold, hard, unwielding porcelain. I felt like I was beginning to black out again.....

Fortuitously, intervention came again just in the nick of time. This time in a more official form of the police. BS remained indignant, still self-righteous, continuing to berate me and demanding I give him my car keys despite his obvious inebriation. From my recollection, the police appeared to be there just as a warning. I now know I should have had him arrested but I just saw their presence as my means to escape. In my hazed, painful, shocked condition I simply left my apartment in the middle of the night, barely dressed and obviously beaten. Perhaps attributable to my hasty departure, but they didn't ask if I needed medical assistance or if I wanted to press charges. All I knew was that I had to get out. I was petrified that they were about to leave and BS would make good on his threats to kill me. It was only with hindsight that I appreciated that the policemen's seemingly nonchalant attitudes were likely a sad reflection of the frequency with which they respond to domestic violence calls.

I returned to the apartment building a few hours later with great trepidation. I didn't know what else to do. I had gone to my work office and absolutely did not want anyone at work to see me disheveled, practically naked and obviously battered and bruised. I stayed outside the apartment complex until I was confident the day property manager would be on site and enough neighbors would be awake to answer my pleas for help if necessary. I didn't know if BS were still there or what to expect. I was trying to take comfort in the assumption the alcohol had worn off and he would be in full, slow, hangover mood, likely embarrassed and remorseful.

I was greeted with hangover mood but he was remorseless, fortunately. I say fortunately because shockingly somehow I was still struggling leaving him. He was more indignant if anything, seeming to think somehow I had justified his actions. His indignation emboldened me to insist he leave. I was scared that he could be so nonchalant having tried to kill his wife of almost 15 years. As I watched him sitting on the curb outside the apartment from the safety of my balcony - the one he had threatened to throw me over - I felt sorry for him. He was slumped over, hungover and pathetic looking. I was badly hurt, exhausted, in shock and still scared but felt pity for him, not anger. The same pity that had instructed my behavior in our relationship and had previously prevented me from leaving. I wondered if he were even aware that he had tried to kill me, possibly the alcohol had blacked his memory out. Even at that low point, it took all my strength and determination not to go console him of all things, *rescue* him and take him back. That's the thing - ***trauma brains do not work logically, rationally; they cannot be guided by conscious rational analysis and steely determination alone.***

I waited until I saw him get on the shuttle to go to the airport, fearful he would return, fearful I would change my mind. I was still in shock and shaking. I was trying to assess and ice my injuries as I surveyed the obvious physical evidence of the event, both all over my body as well as the apartment. I found my phone and pieced it back together. I would soon be getting confirmation that BS was fully aware of what had happened when my father called me. I would have never told anyone in my family what had happened. I didn't want to disturb or worry them. ***I thought that little of myself.***

I answered the phone with slight trepidation, always a bit nervous whenever my father called; something was always wrong and I was usually the reason. He responded to my barely audible "hello" with my voice still shaking from shock and pain. To my incredible surprise, he responded with "Sophie, what the hell are you doing?" I don't know if I appreciated it in the moment but you may recall that is exactly what he said to me when I had overdosed in high school. It was an oft-repeated chastisement of me throughout my life. I was clueless as to what he was talking about but didn't have the strength to address it at the time. I told him something like I couldn't talk then, that I had had a "bad night". I don't know if the night's events or his response shocked me more but I know which one pained me more. He said, "I know. Bob called me and told me he tried to kill you."

His initial query somehow attributing blame to me, fully aware that someone had tried to ***kill*** me, ***his daughter***, would be unbelievable to me were his words not forever painfully emblazoned in my memory. As I said, this man was incapable of coping with stress and was forever blaming me for everything. Apparently, he and BS had commiserated on their call and chastised me for seeing another man, notwithstanding we were separated. Notwithstanding also that my father had persuaded me, against my inclination, to tell BS about the other man. The fact that he didn't even bother to ask about my well being is unbelievably painfully inexcusable and unforgettable. I think my father saw some of BS in him and on some level realized there were parallels between my relationship and my parents' relationship. Neither BS nor my father could cope with the prospect of losing their wife's support.

I remember going to the doctor. I didn't want to. I just felt like shrinking into a little hole or at least crawling into a tiny ball of self embrace. I could barely swallow or put my head even gingerly on a pillow because of the trauma to my trachea and my head, respectively. Despite my injuries and pain, I didn't want to seek medical attention. I was too embarrassed. My mom, unlike my father, had called me with nothing but absolute concern for my psychological and physical well being and insisted they were coming to see me. As much as I just wanted to be left alone and not go to the doctor, it was preferable to seeing my father and letting my parents see the extent of my injuries. I was still trying to protect them. We compromised and my mom agreed they wouldn't come if I promised to get checked. I capitulated to honor her wishes.

My mom was as horrified as I - and incensed - about how my father handled that initial call and always told me she wished I had let him see the extent of my physical injuries. My brother was still in town when my father alerted him as to what happened. He called to ask if I wanted him to take me to the doctor. I said no. ***That's how little I felt about myself.*** My husband of 15 years had just tried to kill me. Yet, in my psyche that didn't warrant having my brother, that I had helped raise since a baby, accompany me. I didn't want to "impose".

My usual doctor wasn't there that day. At first, I wasn't sure if that made me feel more or less hesitant, ultimately deciding on the latter. It felt like greater anonymity. At the time - for a long time unfortunately - I felt ashamed, like what kind of a worthless human must I be for my husband to try to kill me? What transgression must I have committed to motivate homicidal rage? That's the thing about "programmed" low self-esteem/worth. It's that insidious, haunting, omnipresent, destructive, distorting. No one for one second would objectively make that assumption upon hearing about his heinous acts. Except, that is, maybe my father. I twinge every time I recall his initial words to me, the searing pain to my heart and psyche, trumping the relatively superficial bodily injuries that had greater potential to heal.

My doctor's colleague was an affable man of Eastern European descent I believe. He had a thick accent and kind eyes. After delicately and thoroughly examining me, he looked me solicitously in the eyes and gently asked if BS had been trying to kill me. I paused, for the first moment, fully appreciating the import of what had happened. I was strangely grateful for BS' articulated intention to kill me so the gravity would not be questioned or forgotten. Without that stated desire, I would have never defined it as such despite the extent of the beating, the choking and the threat to toss me over the balcony. Knowing me and that I would have kept it secret, the gravity likely would have soon been lost on me. As I meekly nodded yes, tears welling in my eyes for the very first time, he patted me kindly, comfortingly on the shoulder, with compassion in his eyes and told me I needed to go to the hospital to get diagnostic tests to determine the extent of my injuries.

So much for crawling into a hole of anonymity, I thought to myself. As I drove my shocked, exhausted, beaten and bruised body and ego to the hospital, I shuddered as I recalled BS inquiring who would take me to the hospital if I left him as he drove me the last time after he had dislocated my shoulder. "Me, asshole," I quietly said to myself. Always me, always taking care of myself and everybody else.

I remember sitting, embarrassed, in the waiting room for what seemed like an excruciatingly long time, hyper self conscious about the visibility of my various bruises and abrasions, amply afforded by the hospital gown. The staff were very kind and solicitous as I tried to quell that nagging oh-so-terribly wrong feeling that being beaten up surely was a glaring reflection of my worthlessness somehow. My trachea was damaged by the choking and my head was unbelievably swollen and tender, particularly from having it banged against the porcelain tub. I couldn't even lay the back of my head against a pillow for weeks without the soreness vividly bringing the incident back to the forefront. To this day, I have troubles turning my head and swallowing and I strongly suspect I have permanent damage to my brain from the cumulative effect of this beating and other head traumas.

I returned "home", surrounded by visible evidence of the horrific, still surreal events of the previous night. Evidence of the beating was obvious throughout the apartment, reflecting the ongoing nature of it. The couch was overturned and things were askew everywhere. He had obviously continued rifling through my things when I had briefly left. There were gaping holes in walls throughout the rooms from BS punching them and banging my head.

I went to work the next day wearing a turtleneck sweater, despite the Summer heat, to try to hide my visible injuries. He had choked me so hard that I had extensive black and blue bruises that I couldn't otherwise conceal. I remember feeling like I was choking and was going to suffocate. To this day, I have never been able to wear a turtleneck again or have any restriction on my throat. When I got home that evening, anxious to rip off and throw away the turtle neck, I was touched by the kindness of "earth angels" again. The apartment manager had had the holes in the walls repaired (never mentioning it nor charging me) and the weekly cleaning lady had left various indications of TLC. It's amazing how far a little compassion, especially unexpected, can go to soothe one's soul and I am forever grateful for random acts of kindness and compassion.

As you see, I vividly recall the incident. I recount it for cathartic value as well as to provide a glimpse into the pervasive effect of childhood traumatic abuse. At the time, I did not have any recollection of childhood abuses, having "protectively" repressed them. I most definitely had no inkling that my unresolved childhood traumas had anything whatsoever to do with this incident nor other incidences of abuse. This - attempted murder by my husband of almost 15 years - was a significant, unsettling traumatic event to say the least. One would objectively think that such an extreme incident would have clued me into something being seriously wrong with my psyche and needing my attention. Yet, somehow the need to address and "process" it managed to escape me. Unfortunately this was not the end of the abuses I would endure, physically, emotionally or financially. Many more were destined to come before I recognized that my unresolved childhood traumas had set me down a path of abusive relationships.

I deeply appreciate how lucky I am to be alive, thanks to the intervention of one of my "earth angels", the property manager who had interrupted the choking, and subsequently called the police when the beating continued. Many people think I have bad luck based on various experiences I have had. The eternal optimist in me disagrees. First, BS didn't succeed - that makes me lucky. Second, him trying to kill me is what catapulted me to truly "living". Living as I decided. Or so I naively thought...

The Aftermath: Glimpses into the Trauma Dynamic

After the attempted murder, I returned only twice to our joint home. First time to attend an Alcoholics Anonymous meeting (he blamed all of his abusive behavior on having a newly-identified addiction) and to attend marriage counseling at his insistence. I spent a sleepless night in a separate bedroom with the door locked followed by my one and only AA meeting and then an ineffectual, personally frustrating marriage counseling. I intuitively felt manipulated and, with hindsight, am confident I was. I don't want to sound trite or insensitive, but his conveniently-timed, newly-discovered alcohol addiction was making it even more difficult for me to leave him. My therapist would later help me gain new perspective and realize that even if he had an addiction, I didn't need to stay in a relationship with him, ***particularly since he had tried to kill me.***

My skin crawled during the marriage counseling. For some reason the entire session ended up revolving around BS and his "need" to have money and the finer things in life because his wealthy parents apparently didn't give him the love and attention he craved as a child. The session entirely revolved around him and he manipulated the direction of it. I am not belittling whatever issues he actually may have but as I sat there, trembling, literally physically afraid of him, I was shocked that we didn't delve whatsoever into his abuse of me or my feelings. I wanted no part of it to start with and completely withdrew when the therapist focused on his side of things, seemingly validating him.

On my way out of town before returning to my "home", I stopped at our bank. Mike had previously counseled me to get our assets frozen. For some ignorant, naive reason in the surreal haze that continued to envelop me, I couldn't fathom BS doing anything underhanded, notwithstanding that he had tried to ***kill me***. Turns out, however, he had moved all our money - earned from my salary - from a joint account to an account exclusively in his name. I distinctly remember my shock - though I should not have been surprised - when I tried to get some nominal amount of money and there was none. All the bank teller would disclose to me was that the funds had been moved to an account to which I had no access.

The second visit was less than an hour when I knew he would be out of the house and I wanted to grab whatever I could of my things that mattered the most. My heart pounded the whole time, fearful that he would ambush me and try to successfully effectuate his articulated intention of killing me. He had always taken care of all financial documents and I wanted to see if I could access some of them on his computer because I didn't have any. I couldn't access those but quickly turned nauseous when I found his notes from his research into a divorce strategy. He had obviously been advised about marital property and premarital assets. He had listed a stock exchange seat and some family real estate under his exclusive assets. He had borrowed the money from his parents to buy the seat before we were married. He was a trader but a good year was when he didn't lose money. It was not a lucrative career. We paid the loan from his parents back while we were married from my earnings. The asset I paid for was now valued at over $100,000 but would be excluded in a divorce given the purchase before we were married.

While he was professing his forlorn sadness about being apart and his desire to stay together, he had been strategically consulting a lawyer and inventorying assets, including some financial perks from my job that I really wasn't even aware of. I was already afraid of him and had been diagnosed with post-traumatic stress disorder. Seeing his greedy, calculating, cold strategizing intensified my fear. I was trembling from fright, as his callous nature became more and more transparent. I lost precious time, distracted by futilely trying to obtain any worthwhile documentation. I only managed to grab a couple handfuls of photos from my childhood.

His attempts at manipulation - that I never had realized before - continued. He engaged in regular conversations with my father about reconciliation and my father willingly participated even though I had made it clear that I would not stay with him. I was literally terrified of him. My father continually chastised me to stay with BS - for what reason I truly don't know. Apparently BS was able to come up with some stellar reason to stay together that trumped, in my father's eyes, his abuse and attempted murder. As screwed up as it was, I realize that my father "bonded" with BS. My father had been laid off, then unemployed for years and my mom had been the financial provider. This commonality apparently made my father empathize with BS. Mind you, no one in my family was particularly fond of

BS before he tried to kill me. He also called my sister who is a very religious, understanding, forgiving soul. Mind you also that he had never called her before. She told him she would listen to him but her kindness could not be taken as condoning his behavior. The interaction with my sister quickly stopped; he didn't foresee a useful ally he could easily manipulate.

BS had all this time on his hands to converse with my family and strategize divorce. He wasn't working or even bothering to search for employment. He didn't need to in his eyes because he was living off "our" savings. He also joined an exclusive gym and hired a daily personal trainer even though we had a house full of fitness equipment. He advised me he was looking into an expensive celebrity-frequented rehab therapy program out-of-state in exclusive Beverly Hills, California. Consistent with our marriage, his entire focus was on himself. ***Mind you, he never, to this day, expressed remorse or apologized to me.***

As I said, I was afraid of him and suffered from post-traumatic stress disorder. I became "paranoid", often thinking I could see him across the street stalking me, even though we lived in different cities, hours apart. I finally got up the courage to consult a lawyer. I wasn't thinking clearly and I did not have good luck finding a great divorce lawyer. Remember I was a lawyer and could have gotten great recommendations. I was still too embarrassed to let people know what was going on. I knew though that I needed to be done with him at whatever cost. Unfortunately the lawyers I consulted indicated that my husband would likely be able to get alimony based on me having been the provider throughout our marriage, ***despite his attempted murder.*** Talk about "no fault" divorce. We had sufficient assets at the time and he was more than capable of working. I didn't have my wits about me and couldn't realistically assess the situation. I drafted a settlement agreement, generously, ignorantly, giving BS more than half of the joint (primarily earned by me) assets even though he also had additional significant assets that would not be considered joint property. I wanted to appeal to his selfish greed and dispense with the marriage as quickly as possible for my physical safety and emotional well-being. I was also fearful of the financial hit I was taking funding his new lifestyle.

Imagine my surprise when I finally filed for divorce, only to find out that he had already filed months earlier, shortly after he had tried to kill me. He had secretly filed but hadn't had me served because he wanted to stay married, aka, wanted to continue benefiting from my salary. His greed had prompted him to file for divorce trying to ensure a strategic upper hand if reconciliation failed. His greed was particularly evident in the divorce petition as he was seeking *permanent* alimony. I didn't even know such a thing existed. I realized that his request was a par-for-the course reflection of his avarice nature and pathetic existence.

I couldn't stand the thought of feeling *financially enslaved* and attached to this person for the rest of my life. Sadly, my confidence in myself as a lawyer had also been shook from the attempted murder. My husband of 15 years had tried to kill me; it made me feel worthless in my twisted abused psyche. My impulse was to "escape". I decided to move to Argentina and quit my job even though I was counseled that BS' request could be granted and I would still have to figure out how to pay the alimony. I still didn't have my wits about me to realistically analyze the probability of that. I appealed to his base nature and hastily offered up more assets to him in my draft settlement agreement, desperate to be done in every way. It was about a year and a half after he had tried to kill me and our divorce was still dragging on. He had engaged better, more expensive counsel who likely advised him that his chances of obtaining permanent alimony were unrealistic. After all, he was getting significant assets from our "joint" assets, had other assets valued in excess of a couple of hundred thousand dollars and was fully capable of working; hardly a sympathetic case for alimony, let alone *indefinite support*. He pathetically asked for more than I had already generously offered. I quickly agreed and finally we were "settled".

A few additional noteworthy nuances, reflective of BS, my father and myself. I had "loaned" my parents about $30,000 from one of my work bonuses to pay off their second mortgage. I was financially secure enough to just give them the money but BS insisted on a fully-documented, interest-bearing loan. The money constituted "marital assets" so I acquiesced, stipulating that the loan would be paid out of any assets of the estate of the last to be deceased parent. We had a secured $1,000,000 promissory note from the restaurant that we sold; it represented the significant bulk of the purchase price. My father continued talking with BS regularly after he tried to kill me until *he threatened to foreclose on my parents' house*. This was one of the assets he had listed on his divorce strategy document. Even though he could not successfully foreclose, I wanted to shield my parents from his threats, so I relinquished my share of that $1 million promissory note in exchange for his agreement to release any claim to my parents' note. I never told my parents that. I just assured them I took care of their note. BS' threats to foreclose got my father's attention even though the attempted murder of his daughter had not. My father never talked to BS again. When BS eventually tried to foreclose on that $1 million promissory note, he had the gall to enlist my help. I stupidly did what I could but was silently happy that he likely got screwed because the business had failed. Karma is a bitch as they say.

We also had an interest-bearing certificate of deposit for $20,000 from the restaurant sale. BS insisted on waiting to distribute it in case of any liabilities from the sale of the business. When it came time to distribute it, he took advantage of a vagueness in our divorce decree to exclusively retain that asset. I also found out I got burned from vagueness when I examined one of the accounts that I had been awarded - just by brokerage name - to find out that he had sold the most lucrative holdings and kept the proceeds. I only realized this when I subsequently got a huge tax bill for the gain recognized by him from those holdings; I didn't even have the cost basis information to lower the bill since he had all the financial records. I was embarrassed and financially disadvantaged by not having my wits about me, by being naive and by choosing my divorce counsel poorly.

I recount these details to show the type of character and mindset my first husband of 15 years had and my conditioned belief that I had to unwaveringly support him despite years of disrespect and abuse. As I have said, I wanted to leave him because he was pathetic but had been compelled to stay with him because he was pathetic. I felt it was my role in life to subjugate myself - my needs, my goals, my aspirations - to him, unconditionally. I am not proud of the types of things I put up with in the first marriage nor in subsequent relationships. I share these intimate details of my ignorance, my vulnerability, my pain to provide a glimpse into the trauma brain of an abused person.

Oh how I wish I could say I had learned from my marital experiences and that this was the last abusive relationship I would endure. Unfortunately, however, I did not resolve my traumas nor did I appreciate their ongoing impacts. Not surprisingly, therefore, it was not the last of my abusive relationships. At that point in my life, I had no clue that I even needed to heal. I had not begun to connect the dots between my childhood and adulthood.

It's funny, I just remembered three things about our wedding that probably foreshadowed things to come. One, we had a super cool priest from Hawaii. I'm not Catholic and he did not pressure me to convert. As I said I have a death phobia and I refused to say until "death do us part" and the priest was fine with that. I find it ironic now since BS had tried to kill me. Second, the best man made a toast to us but I didn't have champagne to toast because BS gulped his entire glass down then proceeded to drink all of mine, clearly caught on our wedding video. Class act from the start. Finally, we had written our wedding vows. I remember I started laughing uncontrollably, hysterically while I was trying to say mine. Perhaps, somewhere deep down my nervous system knew something before I realized it....

Chapter 2
Escapism Part 1: Exotic Men & Monks

The "Boxer": "Bodyguard" #1

He was dark, foreign, mysterious. He had soulful eyes and a soothing voice. He was strong and self-assured but simultaneously had pronounced sensitivity and thoughtfulness. He was the exact opposite of my self-absorbed, needy, plain vanilla husband. He was of South American heritage and even his last name was exotic, multisyllabic and melodic to pronounce, in sharp contrast to the non-distinct "Bob Smith" I had married.

The mere contrasts between the two were probably sufficient to catapult me, head first, into a relationship that seemed to clearly delineate the past I was trying to escape from and the future I wanted desperately to embrace. I was extremely attracted to him - his well-defined physique and passion for fitness in particular caught my attention. He was the first of many "bodyguard" types I would fall for, unwittingly. At the time, I didn't realize I was looking for a "protector". He boxed as a hobby and for exercise. Although the inherent violence of boxing as a sport didn't sit well with me, I loved it for exercise. I had a weighted stationary punching bag in my home gym - not only was it a great exercise but also a wonderful release of tension. I was clueless about proper technique, I just enjoyed punching and the sense of empowerment it gave me. Marlon showed me some moves and I was hooked - both on boxing and my visibly strong boyfriend.

It was an intense whirlwind romance on hyper speed. I had started seeing Marlon while I was separated. As I said, he had a certain sensual combination of strength and sensitivity that always appealed to me. I was in my office at work after the attempted murder, "broken", figuratively and, in some ways, almost literally. I was trembling terribly from shock and pain. I felt like the most alone I had ever been. I desperately wanted to stop the shaking and find some sort of warmth to soothe my broken self. I still remember what I was wearing. I just had on a pair of shorts and light silky sleeveless babydoll shirt. I was freezing. I remember being fixated solely on that singular sensation - not my throbbing head or the pain of swallowing or the surreal fact that my husband had just tried to kill me. The only thing I cared about at that moment was comforting warmth in any form. Something prompted Marlon to call me then - in the middle of the night. He said he sensed something was wrong. I briefly recounted the night's horrors and he replied lovingly and solicitously. I remember him suggesting getting some towels from the fitness room to wrap myself in to try to stop my figurative and actual shaking. His voice and the towels gave me the soothing "embrace" I desperately needed at the moment to get through.

Marlon's fortuitous presence and thoughtfulness at that deep, dark point in my life more or less cemented our budding relationship, no matter how mismatched we may have been objectively. It felt like he was filling a void in my heart and my life. He was a figurative bridge between the suffocating confines of the past that I desperately wanted to escape and the bright, spirited life I longed for.

As I said, our relationship was a whirlwind. Within weeks, Marlon was driving across the country with all his possessions in his car to come live with me. I had desperately needed to put distance between myself and the apartment where my husband had tried to kill me. I constantly feared he would return to finish his articulated desire. I was relieved when I found a house I could close on with lightning speed. The thought of living in it alone was overwhelming me though. Marlon solved the problem. Instant roommate. My extreme discomfort at being alone had intensified after the attempted murder. I really was unwittingly seeking a bodyguard and Marlon fit the need perfectly. I remember him telling me how he had kicked the door down of a potential suitor of his younger sister because the guy had supposedly "disrespected" her somehow. I think merely through an expression of interest. I remember Mike reacting in horror at the violent nature of the incident when I ill-advisedly told him about it. All I saw was a superhero-type boyfriend who would assertively protect his "women". You likely can fast forward and predict that this relationship didn't end well - but I could not at the time in my traumatized head.

Marlon had quit his job as a mortgage broker to move in with me. I assumed he would find a job once settled. In the meantime, his unemployment status meant he was completely free to keep me company and travel with me. I was fulfilling my twofold purpose of providing sex and financial support. Everything seemed great, until it wasn't...

We traveled together quite extensively - Argentina, Granada, Thailand, Ibiza, Mexico, London, California, New York... Marlon was an avid house music fan and I quickly fell in love with it as well. I fulfilled his desire to basically travel the world to go to club openings and see his favorite djs. It was all so new to me. He was several years my junior. I wasn't exactly into this new lifestyle of "clubbing" until dawn. Marlon would take evening naps and sleep in late in preparation. Most definitely not my thing - I couldn't nap and I hated losing the next day from being out until early morning. My exhaustion was countered by my energizing new freedom and life.

Of course, this regimen was in complete contrast to my professional life. More importantly, Marlon's "style" was in stark contrast to my lackluster, conservative, stay-at-home husband who never wanted to do anything, including travel, which my restless soul endlessly craved. That contrast appealed to me and the new lifestyle spoke to my adventurous side in general, albeit not in the particulars. After BS tried to kill me, I felt complete apathy for a few weeks. I didn't recognize my normally passionate self. I was relieved that I had emerged from that apathy with Marlon's presence. The lifestyle, the venues, the travel, the logistics were all giving me the distractions from my pain I craved like a drug. I reveled in my relative freedom and independence, free to explore all things worldly and sensory.

This relationship not only helped free me from my past but also coincided with incredible experiences I wouldn't trade for anything. In particular, our trip to Thailand spoke to my spirit and my Buddhist leanings. I cried at the Grand Palace in Bangkok, which deeply touched my soul. It wasn't all music and debauchery, although music has always soothed my soul as well, and one of my fondest memories of Marlon is of him having introduced me to a new genre.

Of course, I was paying for everything and my generosity knew no limits. I was financially fine at the time and happy to share. Not only was I paying for everything but I was providing financial support in different ways as well.

I started getting inklings of problems but always dismissed them readily, feeling like I was more or less happy and not wanting to stir anything up. I would give Marlon money and find out later he had gifted money to his siblings. Oh isn't that "generous" of him I convinced myself to justify his actions. Marlon was still married to a Brazilian woman. He had married her so she could get a visa to the US and had yet to divorce so she could get citizenship. According to him, she had won some local Brazilian beauty pageant. In my head, she might as well have been crowned Miss Universe. I hadn't traditionally been jealous - maybe didn't have much reason to be - but I increasingly found myself growing jealous and possessive of my younger, exotic boyfriend. I felt like I was dating an animated masterpiece with his dark features, olive-toned skin, statuesque face, deep penetrating dark eyes and chiseled physique. I hated Marlon having any ongoing connection with the Brazilian bombshell. I considered her an existential threat to me. She owed student debt that she contacted him about frequently and I insisted on paying it off. It took me a long time to recognize any form of manipulative behavior. It wasn't until much later that I realized no one - men, family, etc. - ever had to ask for anything. They were pros, however, at making it clear what they "needed" or wanted and I quickly, without hesitation, satisfied their needs and desires.

Marlon also exhibited jealous tendencies that, at first, honestly, I enjoyed, mistakenly viewing them as a validation of his interest in me. They also bordered on violent - which, again, I viewed, positively as my superhero bodyguard protecting me.

One of the strangest/most memorable jealousy incidents took place at an airport in South America when we had a layover en route home. I wanted to get something to eat and kill some time waiting for our flight. Marlon declined my invitation to join me, choosing to wait at the gate area. I met a monk at the bar counter at the restaurant I went to. Again, I was fascinated with Buddhism and I was thrilled to have an engaging conversation with the gentleman. I returned to the gate area just before boarding and excitedly recounted my story when Marlon inquisitively asked what took me so long, obviously annoyed. As we were about to board, the toehold part of one of my sandals broke and I was making quite a comical entrance trying to magically grip onto the sole and basically "slide" onto the plane. I was in near hysterics laughing at myself and ineffectual efforts but Marlon could only focus on my "monk encounter". He was livid as the monk passed - as everyone did since I was moving at a snail's pace - and I didn't introduce him.

Things started to unravel - intensely and quickly. We actually broke up a number of times but I always let him live with me. We had ongoing passionate heated exchanges. We were both jealous and living together was a horrible idea. I absolutely did not want to be alone though and I preferred the arguments to solitude. I went to Europe a number of times throughout this period, always meeting a new male interest. I never told him about these encounters but he would rifle through my things, find some "evidence" of an encounter, get jealous and insist we get back together.

Even when we were broken up, Marlon was treating me disrespectfully and taking advantage of my generosity. I kept trying to make him feel "manly" despite me paying for everything. I now recognize that I was following my mom's lead in this regard. For instance, my mom was the one making money but my father would kind of dole her out an allowance, for which she had to account for every penny with receipts.

I was going out of town for work. I needed a new laptop. I left him several hundred dollars asking him to research what to get and buy it for me. Instead, he spent the money on himself, including doing a "bridge climb event" I had expressed interest in doing together. I also let him host a friend at my house while I was gone, telling him they could eat and drink anything they wanted, except two special bottles of wine my boss had gifted me. Undoubtedly comes as less of a surprise to you than it did to me, that those bottles were gone when I returned. After I had quit my job, I even told him he could try to sell my house and I would pay him the standard realtor's fee. Instead he sabotaged any efforts to sell it since he was cozily content living there. I paid him to paint my house - the one he was living in rent free. He took down all my artwork and "taped" the rooms to prepare them for painting. Then for some reason even though he wasn't working, he couldn't manage to finish a single wall. I was incensed each time I returned home. I desperately craved a sanctuary of peace. Instead, I was continuously greeted with a house in disarray, unsightly blue tape everywhere and my artwork strewn around haphazardly, blank walls waiting to be painted, all a constant tangible reminder of my freeloading "partner's" disrespect.

Unfortunately there were countless examples like this - too many, too embarrassing, to recount but you get the picture. Unfortunately, it was the first of many times I would let men live with me at my exclusive cost in exchange basically for being disrespected and treated poorly. I had one deal breaker and one deal breaker only - be faithful to me. That really was my red line - the only thing I would have acted on because it would have rendered me meaningless in my head since I viewed my worth as only providing financial support or sex.

Things got to the point where Marlon announced his intention one night to return to New York. Things had been abysmal, we were constantly fighting, our interactions increasingly heated, and our happy times becoming a distant past. Nonetheless, I was crushed and couldn't bear the thought of him leaving. I vastly preferred misery to solitude. I was extremely unsettled and borderline petrified at the prospect of being alone. We got into a terrible fight that night because I was so distraught about the prospect of him leaving me. It ended with a protracted physical altercation and him physically hurting me, extensively evidenced by bruises and marks all over my body, including ankle bruises and rug burns (again) from him dragging me around for some reason.

I continued pleading with him to stay despite my injuries and pain. I could take the physical pain but not the crushing psychological weight of the thought of him leaving me. It was a very bizarre night. In large part, it was like my bruises were from his sheer strength and trying to "contain" me. I was spiraling out of control at the thought of him leaving, choosing what had become our miserable heated interactions over solitude. He added deep emotional injury to my physical injuries when he said he understood why my husband had tried to kill me. Of course, that was particularly cruel and should have been my "last straw" but I still couldn't bear to be without him, to be alone. To me, solitude was foreboding. Subconsciously I associated being alone with something terrible happening - something so awful that it trumped the current physical and emotional abuse I was experiencing.

Marlon ended the night's events by leaving - in my car of course - as he did so many times before, staying out all night and returning late the next morning making me late for work. Something prompted me to take photos of my extensive bruises. I knew I would never share them with anyone. I think intuitively I wanted to keep a stark reminder for myself so I wouldn't let anyone ever physically harm me again.

My thoughts continued spiraling out of control all day. I was desperate to get home to him and beg him - the man who had been living off of me financially for months, the man I had treated to vacations all over the world and innumerable gifts, the man who had physically and emotionally harmed me the night before - not to leave me. This is how little I thought of myself and the extent of the abuse I chose to endure to not be left alone. Alone petrified me and made me feel unbelievably worthless since my low sense of self worth required validation by another by definition. ***If I weren't being used, I was nothing.***

Overdose #2

Despite my initial pleas for him to stay that night, Marlon reiterated his intention to leave that weekend. I couldn't take any more. This time I didn't choose dramatic outbursts and futile pleading. I chose dramatic withdrawal in the form of another overdose. I had given another man my heart and soul to be cast aside in my head. The incomprehensible nature of it combined with my fear of being alone was too much for me. I didn't care to go on thusly and my skewed psyche didn't see a path forward at that low moment. My "worthlessness" had been confirmed again in my messed up head. While Marlon packed, I chose to quietly slip into dark oblivion over having to cope with the searing pain of solitude. Marlon discovered me passed out later.

I remember him shaking me hard to arouse me from my drug-induced deep haze, shoving the phone at me and ordering me to take it. He hadn't known what to do when he first discovered me practically unconscious so he had called Mike, who had intervened to save me from my first overdose so many years ago. Mike had instructed Marlon to dispose of any remaining pills and awake me from my drugged stupor. He wanted to call an ambulance and I pleaded with him not to. I just wanted to be left alone. Although I was heavily drugged, I managed to get my wits about me sufficiently to persuade Mike there wasn't any real threat of me dying. He agreed not to call an ambulance with Marlon's promise to check on me regularly and report back to him. Marlon delayed his plans to depart to make sure I was ok. I know we're not nominating him for a Nobel Peace Prize for that but it enabled me to stay home this time in relative anonymity and I was grateful for that.

The next day, I was still reeling, emotionally from my pain and physically from my bruises and cocktail overdose of muscle relaxants, pain pills, Xanax, Valium and Lexapro. I apparently have an extraordinarily strong constitution. I was shaky and exhausted. I had to use a straw to take sips of water because I couldn't even hold a glass, I was trembling so badly. Of course, Mike didn't see this. He and Marlon continued their consultations. Marlon couldn't get me to eat so called Mike for support. Mike threatened to call my mom, which I would have done anything to avoid. I agreed to eat if he didn't call her. It took me a week to get the drugs out of my system and return to some semblance of normal.

Mike had come to my rescue - again.... Even in my deep fog, I vividly remember my conversation with him. It was a wake up call. When you're suicidal, at least in my case, it's like you're in your own little world. You don't think about how you will impact others because you truly mistakenly believe no one cares. Remember Marlon had just told me he understood why BS had tried to kill me. I had never felt more worthless, more misunderstood or more alone. When Mike shared his feelings with me about my possible absence, it affected me profoundly. I promised him that he would never have to rescue me again thusly. I would love to say suicide never entered my head again but unfortunately cannot. I kept my promise to Mike however even when I had fleeting suicidal thoughts in my darkest moments, when slipping away into oblivion seemed momentarily preferable to continuing my existence. Mike, one of my "earth angels", got me through those moments again.

The Racecar Driver: "Bodyguard" #2: Argentina Bound

Marlon eventually left and so did I, finding my next distraction in another country and another exotic man. As you may recall, I had decided to leave my career and move out of the country when BS kept pursuing permanent alimony. I was relieved to be finally done with that chapter of my life and beyond ready for a complete change of scenery after my relationship with Marlon ended so dramatically. I was completely free again and planned to make the most of my independence, which for me always meant traveling.

I had fallen in love hard with Argentina and her endless charms when I traveled there extensively for work during my prior job. I also associated Argentina with a time in my life when I felt valued and respected, having had incredible work experiences and making new lifelong friends. Argentina has a European "sense" about it. I loved buzzing cosmopolitan Buenos Aires with its incessant pulsating heartbeat and the geographical diversity and natural splendor of the country in general. The people were passionate, warm and hospitable. I couldn't think of a better place to start a new chapter in my life.

I embarked on a number of new engaging distractions. I bought an idyllic piece of property with an awe inspiring backdrop of the Andes mountains and dove head first into designing the house of my dreams. This was a comical adventure in and of itself as the architect only spoke Spanish and I only spoke English. Not to mention that I knew absolutely nothing about building a house. My relatively new freedom, however, after years of obsequiously following BS' whims, gave me a glorious feeling of heady confidence.

My brief but memorable house designing experience is when my "expertise" at a kind of rudimentary charades began. I would try to "act things out" with gestures and facial expressions in my fledgling effort to bridge the language barrier. The logistics and challenges served their purpose; they were time consuming, comical, enjoyable and, importantly, distracting me from unresolved traumas and pains.

I still have the basic sketches the architect gratuitously made for me. I was designing the "sanctuary" of my dreams. It was only with hindsight that I realized I was gravitating towards "compound-like" properties where I would feel protected and safe, just as I was gravitating towards "bodyguard-like" boyfriends. I was unaware that I was seeking protection and a sanctuary although my hyper vigilance and guarded nature were obvious to me and anyone who spent any time with me. Having been diagnosed with post-traumatic stress disorder, I had just kind of accepted that I would always live with a kind of fear-based orientation.

My dream house was going to be completely gated, the wrought iron entryway gate affording a view down the lengthy driveway to the glass entrance that would afford a view of the fountain centerpiece I would have in my interior courtyard. The courtyard - hacienda-style - was the most distinguishing feature of my hypothetical house. I wanted the luxury of spending time outside while still being within the safe confines of my home, enjoying unspoilt nature with a view of the Andes mountains, immersed in the crystal clean air of the unspoiled village I had chosen for my new home. I envisioned evenings gazing up at the stars, sipping the famed Argentinian Malbec I had fallen in love with during my work travels and smelling the equally famed Argentinian steak grilling on my rustic outdoor grill. All from the tranquil peace and safety of my bricked-in "compound".

My musings kept me company and helped distract my head and heart from my growing list of traumas. Still reeling from Marlon leaving me, I planned my companionship to be in the form of an Akita, the regal strong breed of dog I envisioned as my new form of "bodyguard". Again, things often don't work out as "planned". The house never materialized. I had been told the house should cost less than $60,000 but was quoted $300,000. I had designed a small house of my dreams with all the comforts that spoke to me. The architect had designed a grandiose home with several bedrooms and a huge dining room with a table for eight. Not only did the house price not sync with me but the whole prospect seemed comical if not sad, his designs having made me painfully feel my "aloneness".

After the dream sanctuary I had envisioned and enjoyed designing didn't come to fruition, the next "distraction" came in the form of Mariano, "bodyguard-type" boyfriend #2. I truly didn't realize at the time that I was gravitating towards a pattern of boyfriends - as contrasted as possible with vanilla BS in terms of physical appearance as well as personality characteristics. Mariano was dark, exotic, even stronger than Marlon, and confident while also simultaneously sentimental and thoughtful. His smiling soulful eyes and soft spoken demeanor immediately melted me.

While Marlon had been passionate about music and boxing, Mariano's passion was extreme sports. He had been a race car driver until a devastating accident and was now actively engaged in hobbies like kayaking off of bridges and rock climbing. He presented himself in sharp contrast to BS who had no adventurous side and he synced with my restless, spirited soul. I felt exhilarated, our somewhat reckless natures juxtapositioned. He also co-owned a restaurant, "Malbec" (with his beautiful ex-girlfriend, a fact I was unaware of at the time) which excited my foodie soul.

I met Mariano the first of many nights I dined at his restaurant, having fortuitously chosen it, its name having intrigued me. The food, the wine, the ambiance and the music entranced me as well as I savored a languid meal. I was confident as I ate dinner there my first night that my body language reflected my introverted being. With hindsight though, I realize that I was projecting a certain vulnerability that certain people easily picked up on. Despite my introverted nature, the wine and the music were working their uninhibiting magic on me. I had noticed a gorgeous gentleman, with beautiful silver gray hair, classily dressed, and also dining solo. I am not a presumptuous person but his intent gaze was not lost on me and I felt my cheeks beginning to flush from the Malbec and his obvious interest. My waitress brought me another glass of Malbec, indicating it was from the gentleman and I shyly smiled my appreciation at him from across the room. I was surprised and disappointed when I returned from the ladies' room later to discover he had apparently abruptly left.

With my ego slightly bruised and the impending doom that always accompanies me with the approach of nightfall and my uncomfortable solitude, I left a short while later feeling deflated. I had just begun my walk to my hotel, when a car approached with a man I recognized from the restaurant - Mariano. He had obviously been at least the manager, overseeing the restaurant, and had been responsible for the sultry Cafe Del Mar music I had been enjoying. He asked me in Spanish if I wanted a ride. I thanked him and declined with my limited Spanish, trying to explain that I wanted to walk. He stopped the car, got out and indicated he would like to accompany me then, not awaiting my response.

We walked the short distance through the charming town to my hotel, trying to make polite conversation despite our language barrier. Fortunately I'm pretty well versed in other languages when it comes to food and wine and can make small talk about myself and the other person. I managed to discern that Mariano owned the restaurant and had told the silver-haired gentleman that I was with him. I should have been upset about Mariano presumptively "staking claim on me" and dismissing a potential suitor in whom I had been interested. Instead, I was flattered and took solace in the fact that I could avoid dreaded solitude for the night in whatever form.

I hadn't noticed when he got out of the car that Mariano had brought another lovely bottle of Malbec, my "kryptonite", and I was pleasantly surprised to not have the evening end, my unease with being alone delayed at least. We ended up having a lovely evening despite the language barrier and surprise, surprise, he spent the night. When he left the next morning, I nonchalantly said, "Adios, amigo," indicating my assessment of a one night stand. He immediately "corrected" me, referring to me in Spanish as his girlfriend and inviting me for dinner that night. I declined at the time because I wasn't sure if I wanted a relationship with him and was self conscious again with the age gap; he was several years younger. I was also moving to a new hotel that day and wasn't sure precisely where I would be located.

That evening, I enjoyed myself at the cocktail reception the hotel was hosting in their stylish lobby. A group of businessmen from Colorado was also staying at the hotel and I was enjoying the company, the attention and not feeling so foreign and alone. I had every intention of ending the night with one of the men who had been monopolizing my company until I saw Mariano outside in his car, looking in, obviously having been watching for some time. I should have taken issue with him "staking claim" on me again, in an almost stalking manner, but instead, I felt a combination of flattery and guilt, like I had cheated on him in some way.

That night, Mariano spent the night with me again and insisted the next day that I have dinner at his restaurant. I agreed this time and had a lovely evening - he personally took care of me and treated me like a princess. His attentiveness and compliments sharply contrasted with my marriage where I had largely felt "unseen" and definitely not heard. Of course, I realized the language barrier was a problem but we seemed to be communicating fine for the time. Indeed, I felt he was more interested and "listened" to me more than BS ever had. I was also so relieved that he was gainfully employed, unlike my recent relationships. This time in my life was punctuated with a lot of laughter, great adventures and memories. I was particularly pleased with my profound feelings of independence. I felt for the first time that I was living as I chose, untethered from any confining relationship or the need to conform to anyone's expectations or desires. I felt uncharacteristically free and more alive than ever.

I left before Mariano did that night because he had to close up the restaurant. Afterwards though, he came to my hotel bringing me *a puppy* as a gift. It wasn't the "bodyguard" Akita I had been adamant on getting but a melt-your-heart golden Labrador puppy. I'm a pushover for puppies and a Labrador was the breed I had actually wanted before getting fixated on a burly, protective Akita. Of course, having a puppy made no sense as I was in a hotel. What was less obvious to me was the manipulative nature of the gift, as sweet as it was in the abstract. No one had ever gotten me a puppy or anything like it and I fell for both Mariano and the puppy.

The next day, Mariano took me to look at rental houses and we found a beautiful huge property with a resident Rottweiler and golden retriever service dog. Mariano also moved in with me without question or my resistance. I had my "sanctuary" and endless distractions in the form of my bodyguard-type boyfriend and a group of dogs with wildly different personalities and needs for my loving attention.

I walked everywhere in the charming little village and kind of "stuck out". These facts had garnered attention and I had been approached to do a restaurant as an amenity for one of the boutique hotels located across from the town's main park. The hotel was beautiful, the setting was exquisite and the rent was free. The hotel owner, an eccentric wealthy man, wanted to have the best restaurant in town. He was happy to lease the space rent free in exchange for having the amenity for his guests.

It seemed like a dream come true and added a nice layer of distraction to keep me from having to deal with my past traumas. Again, major language barrier but that didn't stop me. We spent hours "negotiating" in some sort of humorous child-like exchange, another welcome time-consuming distraction. All I had to do was complete the kitchen and furnish the empty restaurant space. The "shell" was gorgeous though - the first floor had a charming dining area with floor to ceiling windows overlooking the natural beauty of the park with its towering green trees and a lower level "cellar" I envisioned using as a wine and music bar. I had enjoyed having a restaurant before and had incredible passion for all things food and wine-related. Unfortunately and ignorantly, this made me feel fully qualified to open up a restaurant and wine bar in a foreign country where I spoke baby level Spanish. I jumped in head first, as I always did, patting myself on the back having successfully negotiated a ten year lease, rent free! I apparently have a deep reservoir of some sort of bravada despite having low self-esteem. Not much phased me and the more challenging a situation was, the more determined I became. I was not a risk averse person. Whatever happened to me, happened to me.

I had felt my lifeblood draining during my marriage. BS was risk averse, conservative and incapable - all he cared about was amassing possessions and a bank account, at my literal and figurative expense. With my relatively new found freedom I was voracious for life, living in the moment, heady with my unconstrained freedom, having no one to answer to. I abhorred feeling "confined" in any way and was reveling in my independence.

Now I was fully immersed in distractions from my pain, without a second's thought that I needed to heal from my recent traumas. Mariano quit working at Malbec; he had gotten into a fight with his ex-girlfriend/"co-owner" over me. Turns out he didn't co-own on paper. It didn't really phase me at the time that another boyfriend had quit his job, was unemployed and living off of me. He could help me with my new restaurant, I thought. I named it "Girasole" (Italian for sunflower - a nod to the other country I was head over heels in love with), had hundreds of pretty business cards with sunflowers made and amused myself planning the menu, picking out furniture, decor, dining ware, appliances, etc. I was in distraction heaven with my new "home", boyfriend, business and puppies.

Long story short, the landlord had promised to finish the structural portions of the restaurant but immediately ceased once we signed the lease. I wanted to get out of the deal. I was contractually stuck, however. The hotel owner, who was very prominent in the community, threatened me with legal action. I was advised that he would win and that he would take my land - my empty land that was supposed to be the site of my sanctuary house that never transpired - in settlement. I was totally deflated and settled in resignation. I had been paying someone as a "manager" to help me with restaurant preparations. He spoke English and could be a liaison for me with the hotel owner. He basically did nothing despite me paying him and Mariano warned me that he was pretty much stabbing me in the back, conspiring with the hotel owner. He had quit his job to work with me and had the gall to liken me to a "terrorist" for no apparent reason when I decided not to pursue the restaurant given the landlord's refusal to complete the space. Now I had no dream sanctuary, no business prospects, a threatened lawsuit and a growing group of hostile locals. I just had my stack of pretty business card...

I was also now relatively distractionless. My puppy turned out to be stressful because he had devilish qualities - not being trained at all - and I was constantly in fear for his life because the Rottweiler whom I grew to love had apparently attacked small dogs before. My Argentinian breaking point was when Wintertime approached in July.

With the approach of cold and snow, which I abhor, I didn't hesitate to decide it was time for a change of scenery and climate. Summertime in Europe was calling my name and calling me forcefully. I was feeling restless and at unease without any real distractions to occupy my time. Since Mariano conveniently wasn't working and I hated being alone, it was calling his name too - at my expense, of course.

Before leaving, I cancelled my house rental and the real estate agency returned my security deposit to the guy who had called me a terrorist because his wife had helped me with the rental paperwork - for a fee. Mariano was incensed and violently demanded that the agency give me my money, breaking a table in their office. I saw inklings of sociopathic behavior - like Mariano shielding me and refusing to socialize with others - as well as this kind of Neanderthal approach but, again, I viewed it as "protecting" me. We left the mischievous Labrador puppy with one of Mariano's friends who had other labradors while we were gone. I was hoping they would help reign him in in my absence. I have no better ability to "discipline" a little puppy love than I do a boyfriend - I am the anti-Alpha/ a push over.

Reminiscent of my initial time with Marlon, my latest boyfriend and I traveled extensively together throughout Europe that Summer - Mallorca, Athens, Crete, Croatia, and Slovenia plus extensive travels throughout Italy, the geographical site of my heart's desire. I was in full on distraction from my traumas and the realities of my present unhealthy relationship as well. I continued to repress my budding fears and make the most of my new experiences, trying to soak up everything and beyond happy to not be alone. Remember, Mariano had been a race car driver too and the skill and speed with which we were zipping around Italy was exhilarating. I knew he was being fairly reckless - not everyone else on the road has the skill set of a professional and recall that his career - and almost life - had ended due to a terrible accident. I stayed silent, however, not wanting to irk him.

We got into a lot of fights, despite the glorious venues, vistas and adventures. Nonetheless, I was doing what made me the happiest - exploring - and doing what I had perfected - pacifying - so the fights didn't particularly weigh on me. I still enjoyed Mariano's company and was thoroughly appreciative of being escorted around. I don't even remember what the fights were about, but he was definitely controlling and very jealous. I would try to make light of the situation but he would brood and go silent. I responded by doing my own thing which only served to make him angrier. One night when we got into a fight in Sicily and I went for a walk to try to calm down. A local approached me. I rejected his advances but all Mariano could "see" from the hotel balcony was that another man had approached me. My walk was long, enabling me to calm down and tire myself. I returned to the hotel looking forward to sleep as we were leaving early the next day for a new destination.

Despite the language barrier, it was quite evident that Mariano was very upset with me when I returned. He berated me for having "left to be with" the guy who had briefly approached me - the one that I had immediately declined. I was exhausted from arguing and my creeping realization that we should not be a couple. My efforts at sleep were ineffectual though because he threw water on me in bed, repeatedly, stealing the blanket I was trying to shield myself with in vain, until I finally got up in resignation allegedly to move on to the next town. We ended up sleeping in the car for the night instead, my physical discomfort surpassed by my gnawing psychological discomfort that our interactions were unhealthy at best. I was exhausted but stayed awake, partly out of trepidation and partly to think about what to do. I didn't want to be alone - the ongoing underlying theme that colored my assessments and dictated my decisions. I was in a rental car - stick shift - something I couldn't drive. I was in Sicily and eventually needed to return the car to Rome. I had already paid for accommodations at the next town where we were staying. So forth and so on. I seemed to have an endless litany of excuses not to separate.

I chastised myself for having left the hotel the night before and upsetting him. I had also suspected that Mariano took steroids, given his physique and questionable personality traits, and chalked up some of his behavior to side effects of the drugs. I wasn't fully appreciating that there were some violent and sociopathic tendencies I should be wary of, regardless of the impetus. Inevitably, when I was questioning myself, Mariano would do things to further de-escalate my growing unease. He didn't believe in a God. We would go to see a church though and he would make the sign of the cross over me before entering. I asked him why he did that when he didn't believe and he immediately responded because I did. He asked me to marry him a number of times. Funny, the first time he asked me, I accidentally answered yes thinking he was asking me if I were tired. The Spanish word for marriage and tired are interestingly similar...

So I chalked up the prior night's events as a fluke, taking some responsibility for it myself, and looked forward to the next destination. We were going to Calabria, in the South of Italy, a very genuine, rustic gem with breathtaking scenery. I had chosen a townhouse that I was really looking forward to spending a week at based on its simple elegance and laid back chic style. I was not disappointed when I entered the stunning townhouse and I was very excited to live like a local and explore the beautiful seaside surroundings. We spent a lovely day at the local beach and I felt confident I had made the right decision not prematurely cutting the trip short.

We both immensely enjoyed cooking and cuisine. That night, we enjoyed cooking dinner together and had a lovely candlelit dinner with a beautiful bottle of wine. I didn't want the night to end and expressed the desire to take an evening walk to explore more of the town. Mariano didn't want to go out and expected me not to. That expectation made me feel uncomfortable, having finally escaped the controlling, confining behavior of BS after so many years. I wasn't ready to part with my new found independence so easily. I probably should have had some foreboding from the prior fiasco when I had gone out solo but I was wine-fueled and adamant I wasn't staying inside. Mariano was equally adamant that I wasn't going out. We got into a protracted physical altercation in which I got severely bruised extensively all over my body - again. My injuries were basically the result of my very strong boyfriend trying to restrain me while I refused to capitulate. I did not realize at the time (nor with Marlon) that I was in "fight or flight" mode, often, in my case, intense simultaneous fight *and* flight mode. I also didn't fully appreciate that I was somewhat stuck generally in that hyper vigilant, anxious state as a result of my prior unresolved traumas.

At one point, I went into an upstairs bathroom with the ill-advised thought of trying to escape out the window. As I was starting some sort of crazy descent, Mariano came into the bathroom and grabbed my face very hard between his strong hands in a viselike grip that I instinctively recoiled from vehemently. In my determined effort to free myself, I ended up banging my head extremely hard against the cement wall. As my head was reeling from the intense jarring, I remember looking across the street where a young man's eyes met mine. I silently pleaded with my eyes for help but was met with an emotionless response. I realized then that even if I could "escape" somehow, I had no idea what I would do in this foreign town where I didn't know anyone or speak the language. So I gave up. Once I stopped trying to leave the house, the fight stopped.

The next day, we both acted as if nothing had happened, me in an instinctual effort not to get hurt any more and he in what appeared to be a nonchalant indifference to the prior night's events that scared me. I silently and gingerly tended to my obvious bruises and he seemed to think things were ok. We explored a nearby town and went to another beach. While we were there, a male friend called me. I needed a confidante and Mariano didn't speak English. In a quiet and shaky voice, I started recounting the prior nights' events, seeking some sort of objective assessment of the situation. I was a little distance from Mariano and didn't think he could hear or understand but he apparently at least heard a male voice. My conversation was abruptly interrupted when Mariano forcefully grabbed the phone from me, scratching and bruising my cheek in the process and refusing to give me my phone back.

I decided enough was enough and we needed to return to Rome the next day. We had to meet the owner at the townhouse to return the keys. I was very self conscious about my obvious bruises but noted with mounting trepidation that Mariano did not appear to care one iota if someone noticed my injuries. His demeanor seemed frighteningly callous and he appeared blatantly remorseless.

My plan had been to send him back to Argentina when we got to Rome and for me to continue my travels solo. When I got there, my friend - the

one with whom the call got interrupted and with whom I was very close
- basically accused me of lying about how bad things were or being crazy
for putting up with it. However well intentioned he may have been, I felt
completely alone again and petrified at the thought of Mariano leaving me.
Instead of sending him home, we moved on together to the next destination.

We continued to muddle through the trip. Things went pretty smoothly
with me now on my "best behavior", not daring to try to do anything solo
and being vigilant about any interactions in person or on the phone. We were
about to go to Santorini when fortuitously I had some business colleagues
asking me to come back to the US to do some temporary consulting work. I
couldn't lie to myself any longer that things were ok with Mariano and a new
distraction/excuse to cut our holiday short had conveniently dropped in my
lap.

I remember being at the airport in Rome about to separate from
Mariano. I gave him money to buy a kayak in Argentina to use for a tour
guide business he was planning. I simultaneously had trepidations about
separating (given my unease with solitude) and some relief as I finally was
honest with myself that he scared me. Nonetheless, with my skewed psyche
I truly envisioned the separation as a temporary one, promising to return to
Argentina as soon as I finished the short-term consulting project.

I finished the project pretty quickly after I returned to the US and I
found myself really missing Mariano. Our separation diluted my gnawing
fears and concerns about my safety while heightening my unease with
solitude. I was anxious to return to my "distractions", Argentina and
Mariano, my boyfriend, for good or worse.

I think I had an angel intervene on my behalf. It feels that I have been
thusly blessed many times. Mariano called me, apologizing that he had
gotten back together with his ex-girlfriend whom he referred to as "the love
of his life", while insisting to me that he still had the biggest heart. Although
it was fortuitous and undoubtedly best for me not to return, I was utterly
crushed. I had viewed Argentina as home now. I had a big piece of land
there. I had a puppy. Most of my possessions were there. Despite how he
had treated me, I had had every intention of reuniting with Mariano. Now
I had been cast aside after taking him all over Europe and giving him some
money for a new business. I recount these facts as they reflect my traumatized

psyche. I should have left Mariano the first time he had tried to control me/ hurt me. I should have been grateful that he broke up with me even though I didn't have the wherewithal to do it. I was scared of him and physically separated, affording an easy and safe separation. Yet his breaking up with me devastated me because I opted for misery over solitude. I was irrationally deflated. Deflated again....

Time for a new distraction I immediately thought without hesitation. Italy was calling my name with the magnetic pull it always had on me. It had been the site of my first European departure after my marital demise and I gravitated there again and again. It always instilled a simultaneous sense of peace and excitement in me. Mariano and I had taken a day trip from Chianti to the Tuscan town of Cortona when we were traveling around Italy. Its charms had immediately captivated me and I ached to explore her beauty more. It was the setting for the book and movie, "Under a Tuscan Sun". I had loved both and a number of people commented they thought my life was akin to the protagonist in the movie in certain ways - heartbroken following a divorce, looking for a new life in a foreign place. The movie had a happy ending and perhaps mine would too...

Fainting: Time to Heal (Inklings)

My decision being made, it didn't take me long after my break up with Mariano to plan my return to Italy. I found a former convent turned apartment building in the center of town, an Italian sanctuary of sorts synced perfectly with my heart's desire. I immediately booked an apartment online for three months. I was determined to immerse myself in local life and signed up for Italian classes. I was euphoric about the prospect of living the day to day joys of Italian life. "*Dolce far niente*", or the sweetness of doing "nothing" seemed like the best plan I had had in awhile. I was invigorated by my new planned "distractions" from my most recent trauma and heartache. I envisioned practicing my hopefully developing Italian with the local proprietors, immersing myself in languid beautiful walks in the surrounding countryside, and savoring the exquisite but simple pleasures of the food and wine I always enjoyed immensely.

Although my heart was compassing me to Italy, my body was staging a kind of revolt. For no apparent reason, all of a sudden, a week before my planned departure, I started feeling incredibly faint, the prospect of actually passing out overcoming me virtually every time I would stand up. At the time, I didn't appreciate that my nerves were so fraught and my body was sending me emergency signals to stop and address my unresolved traumas. I went to my trusted chiropractor in hopes somehow that an adjustment would magically fix me. I drank copious amounts of water thinking maybe it was from dehydration though I was always good at drinking sufficient water. I was clutching at straws in vain. My feelings of faintness got so bad, I could no longer convince myself that I would be fine to travel. With extreme dejection and forlornness, I cancelled my trip; I had no choice.

I knew something was "off" and I was growing increasingly uncomfortable with my sense of unease, restlessness and lethargy that inevitably creeped up when I was alone. At Mike's prodding, I reluctantly agreed to go to another therapy session. It turned out to be a wise decision because my therapist referred me to a craniosacral practitioner. I had no familiarity with this therapy but the way my therapist described it, it seemed almost magical to me. I was eager to dive in head first, hoping the therapy could quickly "adjust" whatever was off with me, enabling me to "escape" my increasingly lifeless soul and resume traveling.

I didn't understand the mechanism at the time but the therapy was so positively impactful, I immediately believed in it wholeheartedly. For the first time in my life, I experienced profound physiological releases, manifested through sighs, sobs, crying and unknotting of my ever present shoulder knots. It felt like an "out of mind" experience if you will. I didn't feel any conscious thoughts per se in terms of a "release". Despite my tears and sobs, I wasn't the least bit sad. Indeed, the opposite. I instantly felt "lighter" and markedly less tense as if my childhood trauma were escaping me somehow. I didn't recognize my voice, my sobs and whimpers reminiscent of a small child. I still was wholly ignorant as to the need to resolve or "release" the trauma from the attempted murder or the physical abuse of subsequent boyfriends, etc. To the small extent I was aware I needed to deal with any trauma at the time, it exclusively related to the childhood sexual abuse.

After the first session, my near fainting spells magically disappeared and I thought I was miraculously healed. I was ready to move on. Paolo, my former Italian boyfriend (in between Marlon and Mariano), had been in contact with me recently. I always preferred the company of men to solitude so I decided to go to Rome instead of Cortona initially. I was happy to see Paolo again and most definitely thrilled to be back in Italy. He lived outside of the historical city center though and was busy with work. There were insufficient distractions for my restless head and soul. He wanted me to stay indefinitely. I wanted to go immediately. As a compromise, I suggested I go somewhere and he could meet me on weekends when work permitted. I was going to Santorini after all I decided. My Greek isles tour had been cut short previously and I was anxious to island hop. I was looking forward to a whirlwind of new sites and experiences. I had yet to appreciate my wanderlust was also my strategic avoidance of resolving my mounting list of traumas.

Chapter 3

Escapism Part 2: "Greek God"/"Bodyguard" #3

He was Greek, his name was Yanni, he was a chef/manager of a charming little Greek tavern - or so I thought at our initial encounter. What I did know without a doubt was that he was incomparably charming and gorgeous. I was instantly smitten. The first time I ever had occasion to use that word. I fell and I fell hard like never before or since. I had intended to stay on the idyllic island of Santorini for a few days and then move on to other Greek islands.

"Yanni" changed all of that. I had had dinner at his restaurant the night before. I was feeling very uncomfortable about being alone and was still upset about Mariano. I had been trying to contact him to try to arrange getting my possessions from Argentina. I was tired of parting with things that mattered to me. Additionally, Paolo had informed me he would not be joining me.

Distracted by my unease and sadness, somehow I managed not to notice "Yanni" although apparently I had garnered his attention. I had been on the phone most of the evening and his colleague was free flowing with my wine. I ended up spending the evening with that waiter after I managed to lose my key to my hotel.

The next morning, I returned to the restaurant to see if I had lost my keys there. "Yanni" was there and I was instantly enamored with him. No surprise, I couldn't find my keys but checking was worth the visit. To my pleasant surprise, he invited me for dinner at the restaurant that night. I accepted excitedly and had a lovely evening. "Yanni" took care of me and I also enjoyed watching his interactions with the other customers. He continued to exude endless charm and had the customers smiling and laughing with his gracious hospitality and witty quips. He was the consummate host and everyone - men, women, children, his colleagues - seemed as taken by him as I was.

He was the polar opposite of BS and I fell for him. Hard. I had never felt so intensely before about someone so quickly. He was tall and slender with a very muscular physique, highlighted by his stylish well-fitted clothes. He was confident and self assured. He oozed charm and had swagger, another term I had never had occasion to use before to describe a potential romantic interest. He fit the new mold of protective "bodyguard" I seemed subconsciously drawn to, something I still didn't even realize.

The mirth and merriment continued after he finished work while the undeniable chemistry intensified. I felt like he was out of my league, appearance wise, but he was very attentive and complimentary and I was flattered by his attention. I would be leaving in a few days anyway, so no harm no foul, I thought as I accepted his invitation for another drink in the main square. I was trying to make the most of my little time with this beautiful man and I enjoyed witnessing his presence and basking in his undeniable charisma. We spent the night together and he asked why on earth I would leave. Why indeed I thought, despite already having paid for my non-cancellable flight and accommodations on the Greek island of Rhodes, a destination I had been anxious to visit for some time. I couldn't escape his magnetic hold on me and I immediately acquiesced when he asked me to stay longer, promising me we could visit Rhodes together another time.

We spent every moment he had available over the next couple of weeks together. It was November, off season, and I was grateful for his relatively free schedule. It was a heady experience exploring the unique charms and romantic vistas of the gem that is Santorini with a man I couldn't believe seemed as interested in me as I was in him. I had fallen in love with Greece when I went to Crete with Mariano, even seriously contemplating buying a home there. Santorini now held my heart, in large part because of "Yanni". I couldn't bear the thought of leaving as my intended time in Europe was dwindling. "Yanni" mirrored my thoughts as he implored me to stay and I warned him to be careful what he wished for. I needed to go though. I had things to take care of in the United States and didn't have the confidence to believe he sincerely wanted me to stay.

I remember being at the diminutive airport in Santorini with "Yanni" and his friend who had taken me to see me off. I was sleep deprived from lust-filled nights with "Yanni". I hadn't wasted my precious moments with him on sleep. Plus, I was hung over from celebrating our new romance with too much wine. We hadn't wanted the night to end. I was so happy though that I practically glowed and my smile was radiant. Apparently that's what smitten will do for you. The friend took our picture and "Yanni" later gifted me a mug with that happy photo of us together. I still have it.

I missed him intensely, immediately. I seriously considered going back while I was at the Athens airport for a layover that seemed excruciatingly endless. I had never met anyone like him and I knew I had to have more. He was the exact opposite of what I was used to and I desperately wanted to segregate myself from what I was used to. That desperation and undeniable desire to be with him emboldened my usually introverted self to call him and shyly ask if I returned for Christmas if he would be able to spend some time with me. His instantaneous affirmative answer lit my soul on fire. My elation energized me for the remainder of the long trip home and the ensuing weeks until I could return.

I returned a couple weeks later, thrilled to be spending Christmas and New Year's with my new romantic interest and pleasantly surprised and flattered that "Yanni" wanted to stay with me while I was there. I eagerly accepted. His obvious intelligence and charm made him a scintillating conversationalist. I loved listening to his humorous stories and his view on everything; he spoke perfect English (as well as several other languages) and was a self-trained chef. I am a foodie and was in culinary heaven having him cook for me and introduce me to classic Greek cuisine.

We continued to explore the island and her unique beauty. We enjoyed innumerable dinners out at quintessential little tavernas that quickly became near and dear to me. Wine and engaging conversation flowed with sultry music in the background and I kept falling like never before. It was off season for "Yanni" and I was happily paying for everything without a second's thought. I excitedly shopped for several Christmas gifts for him, spending quite a lot. It was my m.o. to generously gift, an expression of my feelings and a sort of validation of my worth given my ever present low self-esteem. I still felt like I was in a dream being with him, a dream I never wanted to end. We hosted Christmas dinner for his friends and we all spent a memorable New Year's Eve out together. I was in heaven and these were some of my fondest memories to this day.

I was positively giddy during my visit but nauseous at the thought of leaving again soon. I really thought that he was probably a "player" and my insecure nature told me that I was only getting so much attention and so much of his time because it was off season. My experience in total though had enamored me with Santorini and it beckoned to me as "home". I still had a home in the United States and had already rented an apartment for months in Bariloche, Argentina. Mariano had agreed to send my possessions there via bus in exchange for me not returning to the town we had lived in together several hours away. Apparently he wanted to avert a "scene" he obviously anticipated. Carol had even already planned a visit there to see me.

I always follow my heart though and it insisted I rent an apartment in Santorini no matter how extravagant it seemed for an unemployed person to have a home and two overlapping rentals. I was in a good financial position at the time and once something captivates me, my decision is made. I was desperate to feel that somewhere was "home" and I couldn't bear the thought of leaving Santorini, nay leaving "Yanni", without a tangible plan to return. As I had learned in Argentina, finding rentals in foreign countries is a lot different from the US. The best way to do it is through locals and fortunately "Yanni" found me the perfect rental. I was nervous at first if I were "calling his bluff" by planning to live there. That feeling quickly dissipated as he expressed the need for me to be centrally located so he could easily get back and forth to work.

I could barely contain myself when I realized my "Prince Charming" planned to live together in the adorable penthouse of a townhouse directly overlooking the iconic sea view with world famous sunsets. I paid for the deposit to secure the apartment and he said he would share rent with me. This idea synced perfectly with my plan as I intended to use the little apartment as a base to explore the Mediterranean - my dream come true. I had felt suffocated and confined in my lengthy marriage to BS who shunned vacations and travel in favor of amassing possessions and as large a bank account as possible. I, on the other hand, loved exploring for the sake of exploring and was determined to experience as many new places, cultures and experiences as I could. I anticipated a blissful life and felt utterly euphoric.

I left to return to the US and subsequently Argentina not only with a key to a Santorini home and a full heart but some new information. I wasn't able to rent long term so "Yanni" had to sign the year long rental agreement. It was then that I found out that he was Albanian, of Muslim heritage (hence did not actually celebrate Christmas), that his name wasn't even ,"Yanni" and that he was a waiter at the restaurant. He explained that a lot of Greeks were discriminatory against Albanians and that it was better to let people think he was Greek. My heart hurt for him to be mistreated this way. I had no appreciation for the fact that it should have been my first glimpse into his supersized ego and pride that would eventually be the downfall of our marriage.

He had also been talking a lot about his ambitions to own his own restaurant one day and I was attracted to his self assuredness and determination. His focus on this goal and frequent discussions about it with me started making me feel uneasy, however. I began getting a creeping, unsettling feeling that he was hoping I would fund his business venture. I voiced that concern one night when we were driving around and the conversation once again centered on his endless preoccupation with being chef owner of his own restaurant. He immediately brought the car to a screeching halt, kind of implying I should get out, notwithstanding that it was my rental. He seemed to want to make his point dramatically as he dismissed my inference with indignation. I wasn't confident enough to listen to my intuition or gut feelings at the time. I chastised myself for filtering him through my lens of my marriage where BS had been monomaniacal about money (my sensitivities to being used having been exacerbated by my experiences with Marlon and Mariano). I quickly apologized, hyper worried I had offended him and that he wouldn't want to be with me anymore. I begged him to forgive me, which he quickly did to my great relief.

I went as planned to Bariloche, Argentina, checking at the bus station daily to see if my belongings had arrived from Mariano as promised. This was a stressful, daunting task as I still did not speak Spanish and had less of a desire than ever to learn it since my heart and head were already in Greece. As noted, I have perfected amusing monosyllabic "communication" and charade-like movements in foreign countries to manage somehow to get my point across. Nonetheless, the answer was always the same - nothing had arrived.

I felt alone and disappointed and quickly became restless again. I was anxious to return to Santorini, my new "home" and Yanni. Throughout this story, I will continue to refer to him as "Yanni" because I want him to remain in my memory from that time.

Yanni had professed his love one evening as we were messaging and I was ecstatic that our feelings were mutual. He had already moved into the apartment "we" had rented and he was building me various thoughtful furnishings, including a coffee table with a glass top he sent me pictures of. Under the glass top he had put romantic and sentimental photos and momentos for me, including "muah" (his trademark sign off to me for figurative kisses) in stones. I was touched by the romantic, sentimental gestures and impressed with his skills. I couldn't wait to get back to him. He seemed like the embodiment of perfection to me and I was in heaven. He wasn't making money since it was off season and I happily sent him the rent money from Argentina. My first of many trips to Western Union.

Carol was about to come visit me for a week in Argentina. My heart and my spontaneous head told me to leave Argentina prematurely and return to Santorini and to Yanni. I impulsively decided that Carol and I should meet in Turkey, a country to which I had never been but suddenly felt an undeniable exotic pull, given the added benefit of being a lot closer geographically to Yanni. Carol had used frequent flier miles for her flight and I found a better deal to Istanbul, enabling her to switch flights at no expense. When I called to get her approval of the change in plans, she agreed instantly, blindly following me for the first time in what would become an endless stream of spontaneous plans and itinerary changes to come.

Fortunately, the Bariloche landlord was one of my "earth angels". He not only let me out of my rental early, penalty free, but also continued tracking shipments from Mariano. Mariano sent some of my possessions to the South of Argentina but not until after I was already back in Santorini, an ocean away. The landlord took care of getting my things, repackaging them and sending them to me in Santorini. It was a financially unwise decision as it cost me several hundred Euros but I was tired of "losing" or being separated from "my things". After the demise of my marriage, I had been at the mercy of BS shipping me whatever few things of my lifelong possessions he decided to and he hadn't been very merciful.

I didn't realize it at the time, but as I continued to experience "losing things", I began to appreciate my deep psychological need for some sort of continuity, some source of comfort, some semblance of order, something I could count on, if you will. I am not at all materialistic but as people kept fundamentally hurting me, I found I took great comfort in certain things that made me feel at "home". I kept losing relationships, connections, my belongings and *sense of belonging.* I had lost the continuity of my decade+-long marriage and home as well as all of our mutual friendships and had left my career. I was uncomfortably untethered. I have had so many "unsettling" things happen to me and I had an obsessive need for something familiar. I was *unsettled chaos*. Unfortunately it was neither the first nor the last time that I would basically "lose" all of my belongings.

Fortuitously while I was in Bariloche, my house in the US sold and I started making plans to move the bulk of my belongings to Santorini. Also fortuitously, there was a strike at the ports in Greece, however. I was told I could pay thousands of dollars to ship my things but they would be stuck indefinitely on the ship and I would pay storage costs for them. I only mention this as it reflects how psychologically important my things had become to me. Shipping my things absolutely made no sense financially or logistically. I had plenty of money at the time to replace my things in Greece. Indeed, it would have been much cheaper to do so, relatively speaking. I was moving from a huge four bedroom, three floor house to a tiny one bedroom which didn't have space for one-tenth of my things. I had a lot of heavy fitness equipment (which accounted for a significant amount of the shipping cost) and I planned to keep it outside on the balcony in Santorini. It would have been an absolute obstacle to easy movement and a horrific eye sore against the backdrop of the exquisite famous cliff vistas and sunsets. I also had planned to ship all my electronic equipment notwithstanding the different voltage requirements in Europe. Unresolved trauma often manifests itself in objectively absurd thought processes and decisions. I remember the patient yet quizzical interactions I had had with an international relocation company before I had found Santorini and Yanni. I would ask for quotes to move all of my household goods and car to anywhere in Argentina or Italy, worlds apart geographically but both similarly near and dear to my heart.

Bottom line, it was an incredibly foolish plan to ship my belongings and the strike was fortuitous for me. I was so desperate for the comfort and continuity I felt my "things" gave to me though and was still recoiling from having parted already with most of my possessions. Mike (fully aware of the foolishness of my latest plan) graciously and generously helped me make the right decision by offering to shoulder the financial and logistical burden of leaving my things behind and shipping them to him where he would store them. Again, not the best move, but it gave me the comfort of still having "my things" somewhere - even if not physically with me.

It gave me a more fundamental comfort as well. Mike was the one man in my life who did not take advantage of me. Indeed, quite the opposite. Not only had he literally saved my life a couple of times, he also helped me financially. One of the sweetest memories of my life was when I showed up back to college after a break not sure what to do as I didn't have the money to pay for tuition. I was always left to fend for myself as far as my parents were concerned. They had simply told me nonchalantly that I would figure it out. Instead, Mike had figured it out. It was one of the most touching memories of my life when I found out he had paid for my tuition, having worked extra hours to fund it, not having money himself. He truly was my figurative "buoy", saving me many times from "drowning".

I left Argentina, closed the sale of my house and had a brief but exuberant reunion with Yanni and my new "home" in Santorini, followed by the first of many glorious trips with Carol. Carol and I both fell in love with Turkey's endless charms immediately and I likely would have never left but for my intense desire to return to Yanni and my new "base" in Greece. I was exuberant about my present and my future and felt like I had "moved on" from my past traumas. Unfortunately it would take more traumatic experiences and apparent repeat of patterns I was stuck in to appreciate that I was still immersed in my trauma brain and behaviors.

Long story short. As I mentioned, I had envisioned using the apartment in Santorini as a base, while exploring other countries. Yanni had other ideas though and suggested I wait until after the Summer season in Santorini so we could explore together. As it turned out, he not only wouldn't earn enough money to pay his way but he also didn't have the necessary visas, neither of which I realized at the time. I was head over heels in love with him though and except for a couple short trips, I happily stayed put in Santorini with him. I realized that it was very foreign to his culture for a woman to travel alone and he was having a difficult time explaining that to himself, as well as family and friends who were apparently curious. I was on a trip in Morocco one time when he "beckoned" me back and I quickly obliged. I was more than happy to wait for him to accompany me.

The time I spent in Santorini flew by. Although Yanni was very busy working, we spent all of his free time together. Even though he would come home extremely late from work - like 2am or after - I was energized by his presence and always stayed up to share a bottle of wine with him after work. We grew closer and closer and I thoroughly enjoyed every minute with him. I spent my alone time exploring the island, exercising, getting a masters degree in Natural Health and various fitness and nutrition certificates and studying Italian. Yes, I was studying Italian in Greece. This was reflective of my restless soul - my head was forever somewhere other than where I geographically was. I was financially set at the time and was basically learning for the sake of learning. It was the best time of my life. Consciously I felt a comfort and peace I hadn't ever really before.

I was, however, still "jumpy"/easily startled, a lifelong subconscious hyper vigilant trait intensified by the attempted murder and subsequent incidences of physical harm. Yanni would actually get upset with me for startling so easily and noticeably, as if it were a reflection on him. He never appreciated it wasn't something I could control consciously despite my attempts at explanations. I was sleeping better than ever before though notwithstanding the late sleep schedule and I truly felt my traumas were "resolved". I didn't actively, consciously think about my childhood or spousal abuse.

Yanni hadn't seen his family in Albania for years - except for his brother who also worked at the restaurant. I hadn't appreciated his immigration or visa status at the time. As the season was winding down in Santorini in late Fall, he suggested we cut our rental short (which meant me losing my security deposit) and that he would go to Albania to visit his family while I visited mine in the US. We would reunite "somewhere" relatively soon. I quickly agreed, feeling sorry for him that he hadn't seen his family for a long time.

Additionally I had been becoming increasingly restless and wondered whether I would become a little stir crazy living off season on a small island. I was excited to explore somewhere new with him. Again, I was faced with the prospect of parting with a lot of my things. I had amassed a decent amount of things between what I had brought, what I had had shipped and what I had purchased, including furniture and fitness equipment. I shipped to the US the subset of my belongings from Argentina that had been shipped to me and packed - for not the first nor last time - an arduous and non-sensical amount of luggage to take with me.

Yanni departed a day or two before me. I distinctly remember how empty the apartment and I felt. The "distractions" and relative stability of my new love and foreign home were coming to what felt like an abrupt end after having enjoyed several months of what felt like sheer bliss. My restlessness, insomnia and nagging gut feelings that something was "off" started creeping into the forefront of my life again...

Chapter 4
The Disclosure, From the Mouths of Babes

I kept myself busy with distractions during my separation from Yanni. I traveled around Italy before returning to the US to visit family and friends. I also, uncharacteristically wisely, decided I may benefit from a couple of more craniosacral therapy sessions, having had such a powerfully positive impact before. Probably didn't need it, I naively thought but surely this would complete my healing I foolishly concluded.

I had just returned to my parents' house from a few of these sessions. They had been pretty intense, cramming them in successive sessions over a few days. I had struggled with my initial sessions because of my post traumatic stress syndrome from BS' attempted murder and my childhood sexual abuse. Not only did I have my eyes closed, which at that time always had my hyper vigilant self on edge, but the therapy also involved my therapist placing her hands on parts of me that were highly sensitive to me based on my traumas. This included my throat, in what seemed like a chokehold position - not in terms of firmness or grip - there was no grip or pressure - but based on BS' actions. I viscerally recoiled at having my throat touched, too reminiscent of a feeling of being suffocated. It also included my pelvic area, sensitive for obvious reasons (though granted I freely gave that area in a sexual context). These sessions were challenging for me somewhat initially for these reasons. I had total trust in my therapist, however, and such positive responses, I gladly accepted her recommendations.

In my last session of my three consecutive days of seeing her, she asked if I would be comfortable if she put her fingers in my mouth. She explained that this was a technique that could help open up repressed vocalization. It's funny, I'm such a person of opposites (indeed seemingly contradictions outwardly I'm sure). I am simultaneously the most expressive person I know (many would say to a fault) and the most repressive. The sessions were extraordinarily impactful in terms of physiological releases but I didn't think I felt anything particularly from this last part focused on my mouth, at least not immediately.

My parents had invited my siblings and their families over so we could all get together while I was in town. I felt very unsettled and at unease, a kind of simmering resentment and bitterness, that I normally repressed via distance and distractions, undeniably bubbling just beneath the surface. I remember everything in minute detail, the weather, what was being served and everyone's demeanor. All my senses and awareness were heightened; I was on "high alert".

I hadn't realized how profoundly effective my craniosacral sessions had been until I entered my parents' home and was instantly resentful of the jovial, lighthearted ambiance. Completely not my usual personality. I felt like an outsider. Everyone had already eaten, not having had the courtesy to wait for my arrival, the so-called guest of honor. They were already enjoying dessert. My sister-in-law had made some bread pudding with bourbon sauce that everyone, particularly my father, was raving about. I recalled that previously he had loved my blueberry bread pudding, a recipe I had tweaked to accommodate his dietary needs; her rich, decadent recipe did not similarly accommodate. There was also some cocktail that everyone was enthralled with. I remember my beloved niece commenting about liking grasshopper cocktails - my favorite and signature - and that my brother - whom I adore - had introduced them to her. Ah, no, that was I. I sulked crabbily in the corner, refusing to take part in the festivities despite knowing how petty and unjustified my feelings were.

I was in an unusually super foul mood, resenting everything and everyone as compliments and accolades were being freely bandied about, scowling as everyone laughed, conspiratorially it seemed to me in my dark mood. Again, so *not* me. Normally. Everyone had gotten together to see me while I was in town and yet I felt invisible, irrelevant. The lighthearted atmosphere was in stark contrast to the heaviness of the weight of my past that my therapist had expertly tapped into and brought front and center to the surface. Everything seemed too superficial to me and I was clearly annoyed. My previously repressed emotions were surfacing and seemed to only be intensifying. Everyone and everything, no matter how trivial, was striking a raw chord in me and rubbing me wrong.

I felt like a mini volcano of seething repressed emotions, like a burning cauldron of resentment and anger, now just below the surface. I became increasingly resentful of the persistent lighthearted normalcy juxtapositioned with my dark traumatic past that had been tapped into and brought to the surface. I was boiling with a range of conflicting emotions. My feeling that I was about to spontaneously erupt in conflict with my omnipresent repression and pattern of shielding all others at all costs.

I still had absolutely no intention of revealing anything. Apparently, however, my markedly unusual demeanor was not lost on my mom. Everyone had left and I don't recall where he was but my father was absent as well. The ensuing conversation would have never occurred had he been present. She would have never inquired anything nor I divulge anything had he been in the vicinity. This was normal course for us - discussing things secretly so as not to upset him. Note the earlier comment about her secret email. He had to read every communication she had with her kids - the ones he was aware of at least.

She point blank asked me if I had been raped. I have no idea what prompted her to ask that - so starkly and seemingly out of nowhere. My shock at the question, combined with the apparent impact of my recent therapy caused me to respond, vaguely, "Something like that." As she probed, I said that I had been sexually abused as a child. When she inquired as to the perpetrator's identity, to my surprise, I barely hesitated though I absolutely had adamantly intended on never exposing anyone in my family to this deep dark secret.

She seemed pained more than shocked. Trying to deflect the source of that pain, to my surprise, she went through a litany of men she apparently could envision may have abused me - various uncles, family friends, etc. She obviously struggled accepting the source of my abuse, implying I must be remembering it inaccurately. She would have never accused me of lying about it as my grandmother had done to her when she told her about the attempted abuse by my grandmother's boyfriend. To this day, she has never forgiven my grandmother. Although she would never outwardly accuse me of lying, she was grasping/clutching at other potential abusers, perhaps I had confused in my mind. Her response unsettled me deeply. Of course it made me question myself - my recollections/flashbacks and the fact I divulged something painful I never meant to. Plus, how many questionable characters (including my grandmother's boyfriend) were we entrusted to and where was she that she thought something like that could have happened, I unsettlingly pondered to myself.

I felt completely deflated and guilty burdening my mom with all the emotions this disclosure must have brought forth in her. Yet, to my surprise, it was very therapeutic to me. My therapist clearly knew what she was doing. "Freeing" me, so to speak, to open my mouth if I chose. I never would have chosen to do so absent my mom's completely unexpected query. Something about confiding in my mom, combined with the craniosacral therapy, made my abuse less scary as if light had been shed on the dark I had shouldered by myself for so long. Exposing the light of disclosure on my deep dark secret made me feel lighter, freer, safer....

This experience miraculously enabled me to more or less segregate my childhood from my adult present. It was as if I were no longer a petrified, confused little girl **alone without her mom.** It was as if a clearly-defined, protective delineation between my traumatized past and my current reality had been drawn. It was as if I were safely disembodied from the suffocating darkness. Tiny, helpless five year old me was now in a place from which I, the adult, could now be capable of healing my pained, troubled "inner child".

Literally as I am editing this, it **dawned** on me - fortuitous pun. Writing for me - and communicating my thoughts to my truest friends - has the same kind of profoundly positive impact on me. It exposes the darkest experiences, the deepest troubles, to a kind of "cleansing" "light". I had never journaled historically. I had heard about it as a therapeutic outlet but quite frankly it hadn't made sense to me or otherwise appealed to me. After all, I had been a master of repressing my feelings; I had no interest in "reliving" them. I think now that I had dismissed it out of hand because I simply had not been ready.

I realize while writing this though that journaling can have the same effect I described above. It's exhausting and painful but deeply cathartic and **enlightening.** It almost feels ethereal to me to write or speak about these things. It's akin to things not seeming as scary in the day of light. Exposing my deepest shadows to the black and white of paper and having the ability to articulate my repressed emotions has been incredibly therapeutic for me.

If you feel that something is so scary, so painful, that you keep it to yourself, that actually only serves to make it scarier, more painful. Having the ability to disclose it is freeing in some sense in and of itself and having the ability to "share" it with a compassionate listener is a very calming, soothing therapy for me. "Feeling alone" with your traumas is the worst possible feeling, exacerbating the pain, the fear, the hopelessness. Having an outlet - be it a best friend, a trusted family member, conventional psychotherapy or even just pen and paper - is transformative. It enables a release of sorts and a comforting delineation between past and present.

Although I didn't understand the methodology by which it worked at the time, craniosacral therapy had triggered a compelling breakthrough for me. I am forever indebted and grateful to my craniosacral therapist and my therapist who had recommended her. At the time, I felt that I was more or less "healed". I was optimistically intent on focusing on the future. My sort of unrecited "mantra" was "go forward". I naively thought I had broken completely free from the past, my traumas no longer empowered to destine my life...

Chapter 5
Illusory Peace: The Unraveling

R*eunited*

Yanni and I each visited our respective families for a few weeks and were anxious to reunite. As you recall, he had asked me to wait to travel throughout Europe until after the tourist season in Santorini so we could travel together. I had more or less acquiesced except for a few trips on my way back or forth from the United States. He had no money to travel, however, and more importantly, did not have the right to freely travel throughout Europe as an Albanian citizen. Indeed, he couldn't even go back to Greece to work. Details, details, none of which I had been aware of when we had decided to leave Santorini. The course of my life likely would have been vastly different but for those "small details".

At the time, however, I didn't care. I just desperately wanted to be reunited with him, however, wherever. My adventurous soul perused the handful of countries Yanni was free to enter. The list of countries I was interested in visiting was quite limited but included Turkey. Yanni, however, was dismissive of Turkey. I didn't really understand why and assumed it was because he had been less than thrilled about my prior trip there with Carol.

We chose Chile from the dwindling list, a country I had briefly visited years prior for work and that was of sufficient interest, relatively speaking. Our plan was for me to visit him briefly in Albania and travel to Chile together. It was the first of many decisions that made little if any sense logistically or financially. Yanni hadn't traveled before though and had no money. I had no problem making the overseas journey to Albania to basically turn around and head back overseas to Chile. I was happy to escort him.

My visit was somewhat uncomfortable given logistics and my total language barrier with Yanni's family. I enjoyed the long but scenic drive between the airport in the capital and his small village. We traversed through verdant valleys and mountainous countryside, the scenery keeping me company, while Yanni caught up with his uncle, our paid driver, in Albanian. I remember his father's striking presence and warm demeanor and his paternal grandmother's welcoming kindness. Yanni's mom was not as happy to see me, apparently viewing me as the woman who was basically making her son travel to a mysterious foreign country far far away. I remember awkward moments based on local customs, exacerbated by complete ignorance of Albanian, save for a handful of words I learned for politeness. The men (including Yanni) were to gather in one room drinking raki, the potent local alcohol of choice, while the women were left to socialize in a separate room.

It was a big deal to have a foreign visitor and it seemed like almost everyone in the village, including endless cousins, had come to pay their respects. I had bought a bottle of wine on the way from the airport and watched in horror as it was rationed out in silence amongst the endless women in diminutive little cups as I heard the raucous laughter coming from the adjacent room of men with free flowing raki. A lot of the women didn't drink and none of the women spoke English. They seemed quite shocked that I did not have a mastery of Albanian and I felt embarrassed by my obvious ineffectualness.

The women generously - and obviously - proffered their tiny tea cups with sips of wine to me one by one which I gratefully accepted to Yanni's mom's own apparent horror. It was very uncomfortable for me passing time, feeling like I was silently being "sized up", trying to fill the awkward silence with my intermittent equivalent of "cheers" and 'thank you" in Albanian. What's more is that it was very cold and we were physically distanced from the wood stove oven, the only source of heat on the chilly Fall evening. The men were benefiting from that in addition to their warming liquor. Yanni's paternal grandmother's presence warmed and comforted me, however. She kindly, protectively sat beside me, maternally patting my hand periodically and insisting on cloaking my shoulders in her shawl while Yanni's mom and her mom continued to eye me suspiciously from across the room.

I thought relief came in the form of one of the cousin's wives who arrived later, entering the room and greeting me in broken English. She was very welcoming and friendly to me and we instantly bonded. I remember Yanni's mom standing in front of me as if I weren't there, apparently telling my new "translator" about the terrible things that were going to happen to her first born son in the far away country this strange foreign woman (me) insisted on taking him to. Of course, I wasn't insisting and would have been happier staying in Europe which had been the plan but for those pesky little "details". The woman patiently tried to explain things to Yanni's mom - who still wouldn't look at me - while sending me apologetic side glances. I will never forget departing the next morning when Yanni's mom still refused to look at me, confident I was going to end up getting her beloved first born in trouble. She insisted on giving us homemade butter to take with us on the long journey. I remember thinking how impractical but sweet it was and wondering what we were supposed to put it on.

The long journey was a struggle. Yanni had chosen the biggest suitcase to take with him; it didn't even fit in the trunk of most cars. We had to switch airline companies in Rome and the immigration official, who seemed to be having a bad day and taking it out on us, was refusing to let him come with me to collect his luggage. I remember struggling by myself in baggage claim with several cumbersome bags. It was quite the comical effort. We both had a couple of roller bags and assorted backpacks. I would move mine a few feet. Then go back to retrieve his, a process I repeated for a lengthy time to get to the check in gates. The check in attendants chastised the immigration officer for not letting Yanni come with me before refusing to let me check his bags in. I persisted for what seemed like forever until they finally acquiesced after I paid an additional exorbitant fee. I was stressed and already exhausted, thinking this didn't bode well for the start of our new journey.

I barely made it to the gate in time given the unexpected luggage challenges I had encountered. I couldn't wait to reunite with Yanni on the plane though and have a celebratory toast to kick off the rest of our trip on a more positive note. For some inexplicable reason, there was no alcohol served on the long flight between Italy and Argentina, two countries renowned for their wine. I searched in vain for something to at least put the butter on... We switched planes in Argentina for our final flight to Chile. My relief to have finally made it was short-lived as we got interrogated by customs because I had an empty pepper grinder that had a few errant peppercorns left in it and a bag of unopened organic walnuts, neither of which I had declared. As customs whisked Yanni away to another room, I wondered what his mom would think of me having gotten her son in trouble so quickly. After a long wait and a hefty fine, we were let go, sans the walnuts and the grinder.

The trip was more or less nondescript. I remember getting hives for the first time in my life, stressed by trying to find accommodations and the fact that we had to keep finding special transportation to be able to fit Yanni's ill-advised behemoth luggage. In reality, I had started feeling really nervous about paying for everything with no apparent plan for Yanni to get a job, now appreciating he couldn't return to Greece as I had assumed. His cousin was very successful selling timeshare in Cancun, Mexico so we went to the embassy in Chile several times trying to get an Albanian in Chile a visa to Mexico. We got nowhere, surprise, surprise. Yanni didn't care much for Chile so we analyzed the short list of countries again where he could go. Even though he had rejected Turkey when we were practically adjacent to it, he now decided it would be fine when we were an ocean away.

The most memorable part of the trip was getting a troubling call while I was trying to celebrate Thanksgiving, my favorite holiday, in a country that doesn't celebrate the American holiday. My 13-year old nephew was experiencing a lot of jaw pain and was undergoing tests. I was very close with my sister and my niece and nephew and my Thanksgiving wasn't as much of a cause for celebration as usual. I was anxious to get good news.

We took the long flight to Turkey just before Christmas time. Fortunately, this time our physical load was a little lighter - no comically large luggage (the suitcase had broken along the way), no butter (having melted along the way) and no pepper grinder (having been confiscated along the way). My psychological load was heavier, however, as I was still awaiting news about my nephew.

Perspective

I was looking forward to reuniting with Istanbul and celebrating Christmas, another favorite holiday, even though I would be celebrating in a Muslim country. It turned out to be a memorable Christmas for the worst reason possible - my beloved little nephew had been diagnosed with cancer and was scheduled for surgery. I immediately cancelled all my plans in Turkey, sent Yanni back to Albania and turned around to fly across the ocean again to be with my family. His surgery was announced a success but the experience had rattled me so much, I decided to stay stateside for awhile. I didn't want to be so far from family. I always said if I were to live in the US again, I wanted to live in California so I went to Napa and Sonoma to find vacation rentals. I had always found the area somewhat akin to Europe in style and loved the natural scenery of the vineyards and rolling green hills.

I worked on finishing my Masters Degree in natural health and did some consulting while I enjoyed my new locale. I was quickly feeling restless again when the novelty of my new surroundings wore off. Yanni was kind of stuck in Albania with no real prospects. I had to send money a number of times to help him. We were missing each other and decided to apply for a fiancé visa for him to join me in the US. I hadn't previously researched it and didn't really appreciate that you couldn't just stay engaged. You have to get married eventually.

Once he got the visa, he came to meet me in California. That whole time of my life is a bit of a blur. He seemed to remain fixated on having a restaurant of his own, skipping the step of getting a job and working towards that goal. We had a lot of disagreements, some heated arguments and foolish and expensive "escapades". He spoke perfect English but refused to conform to normal American employment-seeking processes. He didn't want to apply for job openings and send in a resume - or even create one. He just expected to show up at restaurants or wineries and wow them with his presence. When that didn't work in California, we foolishly moved on to other states, spending a month here or there, somehow I always lost deposits because we "had to leave early". We would do stupid things like one time we showed up in a little town in Florida - knowing nothing about it - but he had a cousin who had moved there and there was a Greek community in a tourist area with a lot of restaurants so he thought that was the best place to "look for a job" given his Greek experience. I am not faulting him. I fully appreciate the challenges of trying to acclimate to a new country and local cultures. I am embarrassed to say though that I just kind of blindly followed him around, not wanting to question my now fiancée and wanting to let him do things the way he wanted. Despite that "stellar diligence", no job materialized miraculously doing things his way.

I truly don't remember much about this time other than feeling extremely unsettled and at unease. Yanni had a habit of waiting until just before the monthly rental I had was about to expire and then say he would start looking for a job. This created a lot of tension and I was very stressed not sure what to do with my unemployed fiancée. I do remember having wine-fueled fights where I would end up screaming at him that I couldn't get married if he wouldn't even seriously look for a job. This was the clearest example of me ever recognizing a "red flag", feeling the uneasy deja vu of my "boyfriend" being unemployed, exacerbated by the fact that he was my "fiancée", given my caretaker persona. I unequivocally, unconditionally felt responsible for him.

We eventually ended up in Sarasota, Florida, my birthplace. I had no childhood recollection of it as we had moved just before my first birthday. He loved the city. He still insisted on doing things his way, just showing up at restaurants, whether they had a position or not, and trying to charm his way into one, but he was making more effort. His fiancé visa was about to expire. By then I appreciated we truly were required to get married for him to stay. I hadn't found a clever immigration loophole. I was incredibly stressed and still felt "responsible" for him but was trying to stick to my pronouncement that I wouldn't get married if he weren't employed. I silently hoped he wouldn't call my "bluff". Finally, my silent "prayers" were answered and he got a job at one of the restaurants, starting in a few days. With great relief, I signed an apartment rental for a few months, thinking things were about to get way less stressful. I felt vindicated that he wasn't taking advantage of me. Don't get me wrong, I loved him dearly but things were most definitely not going the way I wanted and I felt terrible unease based on my history.

That little blip of relief dissipated almost instantaneously when I got the call that my nephew's cancer was back and he was scheduled for another surgery. Even though he had a new job to start and I had already paid for the apartment, Yanni insisted he was coming back to the Chicago area with me as an "apparent" show of support. He didn't even bother to tell his new boss he wouldn't be working there. I knew something was terribly off but I was too distraught to think - absolutely nothing but my nephew mattered. His visa was about to expire too so I am sure you can predict what happened next....

I remember being at the apartment complex on my wedding day, sitting outside hoping the warmth of the sun would calm my frayed nerves and Yanni *singing*, as if he didn't have a care in the world. I was heart sick over my nephew and this man I was about to marry was oblivious. I knew the situation was "off" but I couldn't muster the strength or courage to do anything about it. I desperately needed the "path of least resistance" again. On our way to the airport to fly back for the surgery, we got married at city hall in Sarasota - my city of birth and marriage. I hoped it was a good sign. That hope, however, could not stop me from breaking out in laughter - laughter of hysteria - visible in our "wedding photos" - during our brief wedding vows. My second marriage, my second bout of uncontrollable laughter during vows - hopefully this one would turn out differently I remembered thinking...

After the surgery, which was deemed a success again, we continued aimlessly moving around throughout the US and Europe. Our geographical location continually changed but the backdrop of tension remained consistent. Eventually, my now husband had been convinced by the apparent success of his cousin that he should give timeshare sales in Cancun, Mexico a try. As I said, he was very charismatic and seemed well-suited for sales with his charm and confidence. His cousin's family lived next door to his family in Albania. They were like brothers but also shared an intense competitive rivalry. His cousin was apparently always letting his family know how well he was doing and always helping his family financially and with projects. I had always enjoyed my numerous vacations to Mexico, was relieved Yanni was actively pursuing something and felt "obligated" to make sure he was set up well to be self-sufficient, so we were going to Mexico. The source of that "obligation" is not so clear with hindsight...

Margaritas & Melancholy

Mexico was surprisingly not as inexpensive to live as I had anticipated from my several vacations. We were in a tourist area and Yanni was pretty adamant about having a nice place, anticipating great success, a la his cousin. He was taking the bus to work at first which made me feel bad for some reason. I had a decent amount of start up costs with pre-paying rent and deposits and work expenses. He found an Audi in Miami he wanted. We could have apparently just had it shipped through a company but he was worried about missing out on it so we inexplicably, I'll-advisedly took a little mini-trip to Miami. I can't really call it a "vacation" probably when neither of us were working.

Once he was set up, I grew increasingly restless. I really wasn't enjoying living in Mexico, vastly preferring the culture and lifestyle I had become accustomed to in Europe. I had always enjoyed my meals when I was staying at resorts while vacationing in Mexico but found I was very disenchanted with the local grocery stores I could walk to. I am a huge foodie and love shopping, cooking and eating but wasn't happy with any of those aspects. I had more or less fulfilled the obligation I had felt and decided I needed to "move on". I wasn't initially sure what that meant and I surprised myself. I was spending most of my time alone and wasn't happy. There really wasn't much to do other than go to the beach. Italy was calling me back and I heeded the call to the surprise of myself and Yanni. I had had family and friends caution me not to get married. I told my mom, knowing myself, there was no way I couldn't. I remember her telling me to go ahead and marry but get on the next flight. I hadn't followed her advice immediately, but I more or less did, taking a trip to Italy by myself. Yanni was very sad about me leaving and it was with great guilt that I left. I tried to explain that I had wanted to travel more or less after I had quit my job. That had been my initial plan when I first went to Santorini and then my subsequent plan when I thought we would be traveling together before being apprised of the limiting "details". My soul and spirit were forcefully redirecting me back to that plan.

I spent the Summer in Italy and France. I finished my masters, worked on my book "***The K.I.S.S. Plan: Mediterranean Me,***" and studied foreign languages. I was back in my "happy place" of exploration. As I recall, I was feeling more or less fine with my solitude. I had plenty of wonderful "distractions" and I was honoring my needs and desires for what truly felt like the first time. I planned to go back to Cancun and Yanni - eventually - but wasn't in any hurry, much preferring Europe to Mexico. It was a rare time that I seemed to be doing fine alone.

Just as I was starting to gratefully see glimmers of myself, it seemed like life came crashing down. I was in Geneva, Switzerland planning my next trip when I got the call - again. My nephew's cancer was back and they were planning yet another surgery. I booked a flight for the next day. I remember sitting in the hotel, practically catatonic, frozen in disbelief, sadness and the realization that I was alone and so far away. My budding comfort with solitude immediately got replaced with a sense of doom and panic.

I went back to Sonoma, California, renting vacation rentals while I waited to see what developed with my nephew and what I should do next. My nephew's surgery was delayed because of holiday schedules - the surgeon was out of town. I was doing some legal consulting work but it wasn't effective at keeping my mind sufficiently engaged and distracted. I will never forget the kindness of the "earth angel" for whom I was doing the consulting. She was always extraordinarily complimentary about my skills and my small ego warmly appreciated her. What especially touched me was when she offered the use of the company's private jet at any time to see my nephew. Her compassion was deeply comforting. As I was wrapping up my project, I got Yanni a ticket to come visit me for a few days; I couldn't stand being alone with my fear and sorrow. I still had no idea what my "plans" were when he left but nothing mattered at the moment until my nephew got well.

I was working on my book on natural health and threw myself head first into researching alternative therapies and treatments for cancer. Apologies for the crassness but I was furious with conventional medicine on my nephew's behalf. In my eyes, he had basically been butchered (his surgeries having included removing one of his ears) and burned (with extensive chemotherapy and radiation treatments) to seemingly no avail.

My heart broke for this little boy who had been battling the monster of cancer so courageously for years now. I was fixated on "saving" him. My sister appreciated my concern and recommendations even though I was the only one who was fed up with conventional medicine per se. I got him an appointment to an alternative clinic and flew back to go with them. The clinic wasn't able to do much of anything, the cancer had progressed too far in his brain. I don't think he wanted any part of going. He had more or less decided he was done with the fight - the one thing he still had control over.

I was very grateful that he was able to get a prescription for medical marijuana - he had wanted it and it was the sole redeeming grace of the visit. I hoped that "score" helped lessen his dissatisfaction with my refusal to give up. I will never forget him thanking me when I simply handed him his lunch we were getting in the cafeteria after the appointment. I will never forget how touched I was by his ability to still have that grace and politeness. My sister was also a shining example of grace. I fear I overstepped my bounds with *my* need to try to "fix" my nephew. I hadn't realized I was doing it at the time.

Everyone in my family knew how emotional I was and that I had a death phobia. I don't think anyone was upset with me, knowing my motives were out of love. My sister's ability to honor my nephew's desire to quit fighting was remarkable and a great lesson in grace and selfless love to me.

By the time, his surgeon was back, my nephew's team of doctors had decided it was too late for surgery to work - the cancer had spread too far in his brain. I couldn't fathom this - any of this for anyone - let alone a teenager who had fought so hard and had so much to live for. Hospice started coming to help take care of him. I had never felt so helpless or hopeless before. I had finally realized that I needed to take a step back and let things progress without my intervention, just my expressions of love and support. My solitude was overwhelming me. I was in full on escape mode but didn't want to go back to Europe so far away from my family nor did Mexico seem to make sense. I booked a ticket, planning to go for a week to Hawaii, one of my favorite places on earth. I wanted to be immersed in the "aloha" spirit of the culture and the soothing embrace of Mother Nature.

The morning before I was leaving, my mom called to say that my nephew had asked for all of the family to come to be with him. Nothing has ever pained me more than knowing he was gathering us to say goodbye. I cancelled my trip to Hawaii and booked my flight back to my family. The next morning, en route to the airport, I bought some calming herbs, knowing full well that I wasn't emotionally prepared for what was about to transpire. I will never forget my mom's call about my nephew - the last one this time. I can still hear, indeed *feel* the pain, in her normally stoic voice, advising me that he had not lasted long enough for us to say goodbye.

My sister and niece who are both very religious managed to get through that time in life thanks to their faith. I went to stay with them for a week and attend the funeral. I remember being in my bedroom alone late the night after the funeral, desperately wanting solace myself, having used every ounce of strength I had not to crumble in front of my family. I was always the emotionally weak one in the family. I desperately tried calling Yanni all night long. When I couldn't reach him I was petrified. I finally got a call after a sleepless night that felt like eternity. He was fine but had been in a car accident, the car was totaled and he had been temporarily jailed because the accident had been his fault. He needed money of course and we all knew who was going to give it to him.

California "Sanctuary"

I was so shaken by the death of my nephew though and the very real possibility that Yanni could have been fatally injured, all I cared about was reuniting. Christmas was approaching. I didn't want to return to Mexico but I needed an "escape" and to see Yanni. I booked us a trip to the Bahamas. Work was not going well for him yet and we wanted to be together. I couldn't deal with being alone any more so we decided he would come to California to be together and look for a job there, probably selling real estate.

I went back to California while he went to Mexico briefly to wrap things up. I was in a good financial position at the time and started looking for houses. I didn't want to be too far from my family in another country and Yanni could get a job in the US - but not Europe - so the decision was made. I distracted myself with house hunting, awaiting Yanni's arrival. This was the time of foreclosures. I found a house that was being auctioned by the bank that had foreclosed. The house was very tiny and had significant problems but was more or less habitable while work could be done. It had been the "coach house" for the adjacent huge gorgeous house.

When the bank foreclosed, they had segregated the property, leaving a huge beautiful garden with the tiny house. I had more or less grown up in Chicago and had never had the pleasure of my own garden, let alone a year long one afforded by the temperate California climate. The property spoke to me with its extremely disheveled unkempt garden overflowing with potential. It had olive trees, citrus trees, apple trees, a rose path, etc. It just needed some TLC like myself. It seemed like a sanctuary to me, something to which I had been gravitating for years. I instantly knew I had to have it.

Everyone tried to talk me out of it based on the findings of the house investigation (including structural issues, no heat, termites, etc.) and the diminutive nature of the house. I remember talking to Yanni and saying we didn't need a big house and him replying "we" didn't "mind a big house" either. I was proud of myself for proceeding despite all the naysayers. I knew it was the right thing and I negotiated my heart out as we went through round after round of silent auction bids. Between the terms I offered and the "random" last offer I made (which included my favorite number), I miraculously won the auction. I continued negotiating nonetheless and managed to get credits for things like lack of central heat although it was an obvious condition that should have been reflected in my bid.

I was pretty proud of myself and euphoric, termites and all. Olive trees had trumped pesky little bugs. Never in my wildest dreams growing up did I think I would have a house - let alone in California - with my own exquisite garden overflowing with flowers, home-grown herbs, fruits and vegetables. This was in a gorgeous part of the United States - in wine country with spectacular vistas and plenty of opportunities for Yanni to get a job in the heavily-touristed area. After years of feeling unsettled and "homeless", I was exuberant about finding "home".

I knew Yanni was handy and could do some of the work on the house but started getting quotes for remodeling/repairing the house. When he arrived, he said he wanted to do most of the work himself, except for things like electrical, heat, plumbing. I was happy to be reunited and fine with the plan. He worked on the house and garden full time, no thought of getting a job. I appreciated his hard work and talent and spending time together. I was impressed with his skills and completely fine. I even thought he would maybe get a job in the construction industry or landscaping. Between those opportunities and the plethora of wineries and restaurants, I assumed he would easily find a job after the house was finished.

All Over the Map: the Business

Apparently, our thoughts were not syncing however. Life was seriously a bit of a blur at this time and seemed to pass quickly. I honestly cannot remember how he had broached the subject but it was becoming increasingly clear that Yanni's fixation on having his own restaurant was intensifying not dwindling. He was clearly not going to try to get a job. Between loving food and wine, having owned a restaurant before and feeling "obligated" to Yanni for his help repairing the house (despite my years of funding everything), I more or less capitulated, reluctantly agreeing to the possibility of getting a small, fully equipped turn key business that would generate income from day one. I was more or less back to following the "path of least resistance" and avoiding confrontation with my husband, acquiescing to his desires.

My acquiescence opened up a floodgate resulting in us looking at restaurants all over - from Northern California to San Diego to Cleveland to

Chicago to Maui. It also included looking at huge spaces that were basically empty shells. Finally, we found a promising fully-equipped potential site in Maui. I had negotiated deals for a living and I negotiated a great lease for the space. Yanni wanted a Mediterranean restaurant however and got cold feet as we were about to sign the lease, the lease I had to guarantee since he had no assets. He was afraid the concept may fail. A space opened up in Cleveland where his aunt and family lived and we proceeded to negotiate that space. I wasn't so thrilled with that prospect. I only wanted to stay in the US if we were in California or Hawaii. I abhorred cold and had vowed to myself I would always live somewhere warm near natural beauty.

About this time in the midst of finalizing the Cleveland deal, Yanni's paternal grandmother - the one who had been so warm and kind to me - got very ill. I insisted he go back to Albania to visit her. Returning home was always an expensive proposition between travel and the gifts and financial support he felt compelled to give to extended family and friends, as well as the cost of living expenses. He still had no money so I funded that. We also decided I would meet him in Spain and we would travel around a bit. I had finally gotten the courage to tell him I only wanted to move to Cleveland as a last resort.

I had spent a lot of time in Spain, loved the country and always felt it was relatively user friendly and cheaper than its European counterparts. Yanni was focused on tourist spots given his experience in Santorini. Quite frankly, neither of us had any business contemplating a business. We had no idea what we were doing and the restaurant industry is fraught with failures. He had always had a distorted one-sided perspective of the business - he only saw the money coming in - which was a lot during the busy Summer seasons in Santorini. He didn't have an appreciation for the money going out - the expenses. His inflated ego exacerbated the situation because "failure" was not a possibility in his head, notwithstanding the reality that it is a probability based on industry statistics. I felt like I had to swap out opportunities, having more or less rejected Cleveland, and suggested the island of Mallorca, Spain where I had enjoyed a number of vacations. I knew I wanted to be back in Europe and was confident I could sell my house since I had gotten such a bargain in the auction.

So we met in Spain and started looking for a business. He didn't find anything that interested him in Mallorca so we moved on to Malaga, another area I was familiar with. He concentrated on the exclusive area of Puerto Banus. He found a lot of spots of interest and I started doing what I do best, negotiating deals. I had a sinking feeling as a couple of these started coming to fruition. I was familiar with the extremely late night hours of European tourist restaurants and bars. Yanni envisioned a restaurant and club atmosphere. I was most definitely not at a point in my life, if ever, to be enthusiastic about such a prospect but I continued with the process nonetheless. I was "saved" by a listing in Napa that Yanni had found, constantly scouring restaurants for sale. It was a much larger restaurant than I was interested in supporting but it was turn key, fully equipped and operating in a great location, or so it seemed. Importantly, I envisioned a much saner operating schedule than the venues in Spain would entail. Most importantly, it was an extraordinary deal. We agreed to pursue it, me having insisted before that it be fully operational from the get go.

We acquired the restaurant and Yanni wanted to overhaul everything and customize it to his taste. I had just guaranteed the lease with high monthly rent and started getting an appreciation for how expensive day to day operations would be, especially since Yanni wanted to offer a first class experience but keep prices moderately low. I should have refused to fund anything but instead watched nervously as a month passed by and Yanni insisted on redecorating everything, buying some new equipment and furniture and putting in a high end sound system to have a late night lounge and dance venue after dinner.

Long story short, the restaurant was a colossal fail through no fault of Yanni. These things happen a lot but most restaurants are funded through loans or investments. I was absolutely miserable not only from the financial stress but I also ended up unexpectedly more or less running the front of the house, something I had absolutely no interest in. This vantage point also positioned me particularly well to ruminate on the countless nights the huge space was virtually empty. I was funding everything and money was flowing out at an alarming rate with nowhere near enough coming in. Yanni had even less of a knack for business than I had feared and I was sustaining huge operating losses. He refused to contemplate slow business and we always overstaffed and had too much inventory. He worked extraordinarily hard, was a very talented chef and incredibly charming with the guests. I paid to have his Aunt come visit us because it was important for me to have someone in his family see what a beautiful job he had done. It was failing through no fault of his and had been the absolute worst investment of my life, despite our collective efforts.

It was obvious that I was miserable. I wanted no part of the business and feared losing my life's savings. I had sold my house, fortunately, one of my best investment decisions or would have quickly been bankrupted. Yanni's solution was to search for a smaller, turn-key cafe. He knew my restless spirit and tried to pacify my growing misery by suggesting a new city. This prompted a repeat of more or less aimless travel. I love seeing new places and was thrilled to get a break from the restaurant that was sucking the life out of me. We weren't losing money if we took a few short trips during the week to explore other places because we weren't making any money.

We looked at a number of cities again - Santa Barbara, Austin, Asheville - there weren't particular restaurant sites we were exploring. Yanni just thought maybe the competition was too steep in Napa. I was very interested particularly in Asheville and even found a home I very much wanted to buy. He dismissed it out of hand and I am annoyed I acquiesced, appeasing his ego. I desperately wanted to get out of the restaurant. I just wanted to sell it and move elsewhere. If moving were the price of escaping our failing restaurant, that was fine by me. He rejected everywhere we went though.

We returned to Napa, me deflated and Yanni seemingly clueless to my misery. I did my best to make the most of the situation, hosting charity events and doing wine dinners. Shortly after, to my extraordinary relief, we got a great unsolicited offer and I begged that we take it. Yanni agreed, apparently silently assuming we would move on to a new business venture. I thanked God that the sales price largely recouped the operating losses and planned to forever be done with the risky business, having lost two years, amassing a lot of stress and debt. Despite that failed experience and my misery, Yanni remained adamant that "his" restaurant had been a success. He wanted to move on to the next venture, knowing I would have to fund it but insisting I wouldn't have to work there at all. I realized he actually didn't want me involved with the day to day operations because he didn't want to share any "limelight" despite my active participation.

The whole time we had the restaurant, that I completely funded, risking all my money, and that I actively worked at, he literally bristled any time someone would refer to me as a "co-owner". I was the owner's wife as far as he was concerned and was referenced in such when he would do interviews without me. The interviews also always referenced the success he had had owning restaurants in the Greek islands, including Santorini. Of course, the bald faced lie caught my attention but didn't trouble me. I was used to his ego and ideally it helped market the restaurant. I remember going to a brunch hosted by a retired couple that were clients of the restaurant. The husband mentioned something to me in passing about Yanni having retired after his successes in the restaurant and wine industries and starting the Napa restaurant as a hobby. Obviously Yanni had mentioned this to him before and he had believed it despite Yanni's young age. I was the one who had been a lawyer and more or less "retired" - this gentleman only knew me as the wife of Yanni.

N*ow What?*
After we sold the restaurant, we went back to Europe for a "break" and for Yanni to visit his family. I made it clear how miserable and scared I had been - as if it hadn't been apparent day to day. Yanni still fixated on looking for restaurant ventures nonetheless. I basically told him "have at it" but I couldn't fund it. I was more troubled that he clearly still had no intention of getting a job. I just became numb to his fixation, relieved to be out of the restaurant business, determined not to fund another one.

At the time, I was more or less ok funding our living expenses, relatively happy not funding business expenses. There seemed to be a steady stream of "necessary projects" for his family though. Again, all Yanni paid attention to was money coming in, not going out. In his head, he had been a wild success and had made money and was entitled to spend my money to support these projects. The first few pulled at my heartstrings, like making improvements for better heat, hot water, new windows for insulation, etc. Then there were projects to help save them money (like solar panels to save on electricity) or make them money (like expanding their grape vineyards and putting in hazelnut vineyards). I had supported sending them money for the prior couple of years and doing something to make them self-sufficient seemed like a good idea in the abstract. Yanni always talked about wanting to fund a business for his brother as well beyond the vineyards but I ignored that one. He assured me the family projects were finished each time I funded something.

We came back from one of these Summer long trips where I soothed my soul, immersing myself in the beauty and culture of my favorite European countries. I was troubled but sufficiently engaged and distracted and thrilled to no longer have the financial stress of funding a business. We had increasingly begun arguing about Yanni getting a job though. Based on my past, I was particularly sensitive, and I knew a business wasn't likely to materialize absent my support. I had let him daydream about getting funding or investors while we were on "holiday" but expected he would get a job when we returned even if he still pursued a business. They weren't mutually exclusive of course.

Together with some of our friends, I tried to counsel him to establish himself as a chef working for someone in the area. A good friend and businessman cautioned Yanni that he couldn't survive back to back "failures" in the same town. Yanni took great issue with that characterization that our restaurant had been a failure. He dismissed the idea of working as a chef anywhere. I actually realized his ego was so big that it would likely get him in trouble in the event he and any restaurant owner disagreed. I suggested so many ideas that he would be well suited for - including sales (at the wineries or distributors or of real estate). I also offered to support him in private catering where we could control the expenses and not risk much.

We had great friends who had been frequent customers of the restaurant that owned a winery. A position in the tasting room opened and our friends suggested he "apply". It was a family-owned business of multiple interests; it was professionally run and had a Human Resources department. The friends told Yanni about the application process. Instead of following that, he showed up at the tasting room basically lording his supposed knowledge over the other employees in front of the customers. After surprisingly no job offer materialized there, Yanni considered real estate but didn't want to go through the licensing process. It was always his way or no way and we weren't making much progress unsurprisingly.

At this point my patience was wearing thin, whatever that meant.... he would go out every day to "network" for business prospects. The deja vu of an unemployed co-habitant I was supporting was not sitting well with me and my restless nature was increasingly incited. By this point, Yanni's successful cousin had moved from Cancun, Mexico to Cabo San Lucas, Mexico and was suggesting Yanni try timeshare there. It appealed to him given his cousin's success and the lack of any formal licensing type requirement so that made our decision for us.

Mounting Debt & Dissatisfaction

I knew I hadn't been thrilled living in Mexico but was willing to give it a try in a different locale. Long story short, new locale, same story. Lots of start up costs and little to no money starting off. I was stressed but knew things would take time and tried to make the most of it. I was pretty unhappy from the start though. I was frustrated that Yanni refused to accept any logistical or acclimation help from his cousin even though we struggled relocating there.

I was particularly unhappy because I was basically confined to the condo we rented given its distance from everywhere. The condo was lovely but there was a lot of construction, everything was filthy and the constant drilling, etc. increasingly jarred my nerves that were beginning to noticeably fray. We seemed to constantly lose electricity or not have water. Again, my needs are simple but they include running water on a fairly predictable schedule. I couldn't engage in any of my normal distractions. I didn't have a car, there were no distractions to speak of and the only real grocery stores were big box ones that usually didn't have what I wanted. There was a nice gym and pool at the complex but my introverted nature and lack of self-esteem were in full force. I felt completely in Yanni's shadow and even enjoying the amenities was too much out of my comfort zone. I felt very foreign, confined and alone. There wasn't anywhere nice for me to walk outside so I got a treadmill. I pretty much didn't leave the condo six days a week. We would go out on Yanni's one day off. That day always flew, consumed by errands, and then we would go out to eat. It was like I was released from a symbolic prison one day a week. I got so excited for that day but felt bad for Yanni's free time being consumed. He didn't seem to want to go out - the one thing that kept me going and I started feeling terribly guilty.

I finally felt like he was working towards something that could help support us though, which was huge for my psyche, so I continued trying to make the best of it. I hadn't had income for quite awhile and my savings were quickly dwindling. We had spent a lot of money over the prior years without making any. We seemed to have endless travel expenses, start-up costs and "family obligations". Yanni had always had a penchant for style since I had met him in Santorini. Appearances were always super important to him. He was stylish and wanted the outward trappings of success, like tailored clothes, expensive watches, pens, etc. Now he truly was in sales and wanted to emulate his cousin's appearance of obvious success with whom he maintained a fierce rivalry at least in his head. Exorbitant brand name luxury items never sat well with me - ever - not even when I was a successful lawyer. I didn't feel it was my place to question his way but I didn't want to keep funding everything. I felt guilty not being able to afford what he clearly wanted. I knew I didn't want to live in Mexico forever and hoped to buy a relatively cheap home somewhere in the US or an apartment in Europe, especially since we traveled there frequently. I desperately wanted a "home base" somewhere to visit while Yanni worked in Mexico and eventually for us to live.

For the time being, all my worldly possessions were at our friends' house in Napa. They were a wealthy couple who had bought a huge piece of property with a vineyard and a house they would eventually knock down to build a new one. They had wanted someone to be on the property so it wasn't empty so we had lived there briefly before moving to Mexico. We fixed it up to make it habitable. It was a win win situation at the time. I had been happy to not have the expense of rent and thought we would be ok once Yanni got a job there.

We had gone to Mexico instead though and, with the friends' approval, I had left my things there and went back periodically. Rent in Cabo San Lucas was surprisingly expensive especially compared to a rent free house in Napa. I had pre-funded the rent in Mexico, plus security deposit, plus bought Yanni another car etc. I did not want to keep funding our living expenses let alone the expenses of his family. I realized that, similarly to the restaurant, Yanni seemed to be clueless about all the money going out even though I deeply fretted about it incessantly. He was dismissive of my concerns and kept assuring me everything would be ok.

He said in his head we had no debt so I had started transferring some of the debt I had incurred to credit cards in his name. We were each authorized on the other's cards but they were not joint so we weren't liable for the debt on the other's cards. I wanted him to get a better sense of the expenditures and take some accountability. I was adamant not to fund any more projects for his family, particularly since he had promised me the projects were over. I couldn't work in Mexico. I was working on writing but I knew it wouldn't go anywhere fast in terms of paying for expenses. I also was adamant that it made sense to go back to Napa rent free where we both could work if his career in Mexico couldn't fund our living expenses.

My favorite thing about Mexico was the warmth of the people and the sunny warm weather. My disposition, however, was darkening each day. I was stressed and restless with no outlet. I remember sitting in the condo trying to focus on writing with the electricity going out or running out of water. There was constant construction which created a lot of noise and dirt. There seemed to be incessant drilling and jack hammering that put me on edge. I couldn't sleep and I started getting headaches regularly. My nerves were frayed. I was very uncomfortable relying on any one, including my husband, and not having any insight or control. He was terrible at keeping track of anything. He was working on commission so had no stable salary and wasn't good about keeping track of his sales so I could have some insight into future income. I was unusually stressed. I felt like I was exhibiting signs of obsessive compulsive disorder or maybe I was going through menopause. I didn't know what was wrong but I wasn't myself.

Between being more or less confined and trying to keep my emotions inside, I increasingly felt like I was about to explode. I would get up every morning and fixate on our mounting bills trying to see a path out but feeling helpless because I wasn't in charge of that path. I had no friends or family or outlet there and I was miserable. I would anxiously await Yanni's arrival at home to have dinner together. Every night after dinner, he would go out on the balcony to have wine and a cigar. I hated smoke and didn't want to join him as he "de-compressed" from the day. I had always been enthralled with our conversations before, he had been endlessly interesting to me. Now everything endlessly revolved around his work. He was understandably focused but I was feeling completely alone, "unseen" and "unheard" again. Like I said, I would anxiously look forward to our Friday night dinner dates but had started feeling guilty "taking up" what little time he had. I enjoyed them thoroughly but it wasn't enough and I was tired of feeling guilty. My relatively little ego always did fine with the relatively bigger ego or self-absorbed nature of my various partners but that was only when I was able to immerse myself in my own independent interests and passions. I was trying to work on writing but I was so "off" and stressed and feeling things were unraveling that I couldn't seem to make much progress.

I fortuitously came across a book at this time that convinced me that a lot of the nagging physiological and psychological symptoms that were plaguing me were attributable to a copper "overload", having used a copper IUD as my birth control for almost two decades. I was adamant about getting it removed the next time I was in the US. Yanni had one month off each year so we would go to Europe and I would base myself somewhere for the month while he spent most of the time visiting his family and doing projects. I missed him terribly and wished we could holiday more together but I completely understood and made the most of my time wherever I had chosen to base.

That Summer I had decided on Antibes, a lovely little seaside town in the South of France. We had day tripped there a prior Summer when we had spent months in Europe and I had instantly been drawn to its charms. I was looking forward to a change of scenery I felt I desperately needed. I was going first to Napa to get my IUD removed then Yanni would join me and we would fly to France together.

He was driving me to the airport and asked me to pick up some gifts for his family while I was in Napa. I don't remember what projects he had in mind this time. He had told me previously that the projects would be done and that's all I could fixate on. His uncle would help with the projects and he wanted to buy a nice watch for him as well as a leather jacket to thank him for his help. He commented that he would have to get his Aunt, the uncle's wife, a nice gift also so she wouldn't get upset. I was very familiar with his aunt and uncle. I was upset about the latest round of projects given our significant debt and I bristled about the gifts he felt compelled to give when I didn't spend money on myself or my family - he would even chastise me about that. I simply commented that I didn't think his aunt would feel that way, obviously questioning him about buying her an expensive gift. He brought the car to a screeching halt, a la, a prior experience and made it quite clear that he wasn't going to let me "dictate" what he did with his money.

I was shaken by the event and more stressed financially not seeing an end to the debt in sight. I had recently moved the bulk of the debt from his cards to my cards because I had better interest rates and a lot more credit. To the extent he was aware of that, I don't think he really was cognizant of it. I had just done what made the most sense financially **as a couple**. I still wanted him to pay the debt from his income. I tried shaking the incident off, hoping removing my IUD would make me feel better and looked forward to spending a month in France. I always paid for the travel and lodging expenses. I didn't know at the time but this incident of me "questioning" him was the symbolic first nail in our marital coffin....

I got my IUD removed and whether it was a placebo effect or not or my upcoming change of scenery, I felt immediately better. I bought female condoms - something I had never been aware of previously. Yanni had not wanted me to remove my IUD but I insisted, confident it was significantly negatively affecting my physical and mental well being. I wanted to shoulder the "burden" of birth control so to speak by giving the condoms a try even though they were relatively expensive, difficult to find and confoundingly cumbersome.

B*on Jour France*
We spent a few days together in France and Yanni seemed preoccupied. I always tried to speak the local language a little even though I could never master any pronunciation. Yanni had always been kind about my attempts previously. We were out to dinner and he was being uncharacteristically critical and dismissive at my attempts to order in French,

chastising me to just speak English. Nonetheless, we enjoyed dinner and wine - or at least I did and thought he had as well. He was leaving the next day.

That night when we got to our apartment, he apprised me that he needed some more money for whatever projects he had planned. I readily admit that I did not handle the situation calmly. Fueled by wine, frustration and stress, I went off. He basically said that for the most part he was paying for all the family projects with his income - more or less letting me know it was none of my business. I tried to explain that I didn't see it the same way since we were incurring exorbitant debt to fund our living expenses and reminded him that he had told me there wouldn't be any more family "projects" after the last one. He advised me that the projects would *never* be over. He also expressed his extreme dissatisfaction with the fact that his parents always told him to express gratitude to me for *our* assistance. He clearly resented any credit going to me notwithstanding that I had in reality been funding everything previously. I know in his head that he didn't see it that way. Again when we had the restaurant of course money came in - a lot more of it went out though - and he never paid attention to that side of the equation.

We were both upset and I hated him leaving after such a fight. I still loved him desperately though and assumed we would work everything out. I didn't realize at the time it was the figurative #2 nail in our marital coffin. I enjoyed my time exploring Antibes for the few weeks I was alone while Yanni was in Albania, despite a budding feeling something was "off" with him. I had quickly dismissed our fight but apparently he hadn't. He seemed very distant when we would talk each day but I assumed he was tired from working all day on the projects.

I fell in love with Antibes. I adore living "local" and was enthralled with my seaside walks and the incredible daily farmers' market. I commiserated that I wished I had found this gorgeous little gem when I had previously had enough money to buy a small home. I was feeling vastly better emotionally and physically without my IUD. That prompted me to remember what I thought was an offhand comment that Yanni had made the night of our fight. He referenced me having insisted on taking out my IUD and made it clear that he absolutely did not want to take care of anyone. Removing my IUD had been another nail in our marital coffin. I had thought he meant he didn't want to take care of a baby but he apparently meant me as well. I would have loved a baby but I didn't have some secret plan of trying to get impregnated. At my age, the chances of getting pregnant were extraordinarily low. Plus I had bought the condoms - condoms we didn't use when I struggled my first time trying them - he hadn't wanted to keep bothering trying....

We were going to be reuniting in Rome for a few days en route home. I tried spending time in Italy each year and Rome was an oft-visited favorite of mine, having become intimately familiar with her charms after the demise of my first marriage. I didn't realize things were kind of full circle again. As I noted, Yanni was very into clothes and we spent most of our time shopping for clothes for him for work, always wanting to look "the part". I felt bad about our fight and financial disagreements. Although I was feeling financially unsettled, I wanted him to get whatever he wanted.

In between shopping for clothes, we visited a pen shop. He was also into nice pens. I immediately fell in love with a periwinkle pen that coincidentally had my birth year on it and "Martini" inscribed. It wasn't very expensive - like $25 - and it felt very good in my hand. I was serious about writing and the pen made me feel better. Yanni had given me a very expensive small pen the year before for my birthday. I wasn't comfortable with something so expensive and had tried to return it in Mexico but the store wouldn't take it back. It was very small too and although I greatly appreciated it, it wasn't comfortable for writing. I had expensive brand name pens that I had gotten as gifts while working that I had given to Yanni for work since appearances mattered so much to him. He questioned me purchasing a new pen because of the one he had given me, so I didn't buy it because I felt guilty. I left the store obviously deflated as we continued our mini shopping spree for him. I was very touched because he returned later to the store to buy it for me. It was his last gift to me. It's what I use for writing and I am very grateful to have it.

Wild Fires & Angels

After Rome, we went back to Napa. Yanni returned to Mexico to work in a few days, while I was spending another week there before joining him. I wanted to spend some time in the US, shop for some things I couldn't get in Mexico and pack up some more of my belongings to take back to Cabo San Lucas. I planned on staying in Mexico for the next six months before visiting anywhere else and I wanted some more of my things with me to make me happier and more comfortable. I was taking a lot of books I was using for my writing, French language books that I wanted to study because I loved the language and thought it would be a great use of my time, some toiletries and herbs I couldn't find in Mexico, some art work, some personal gifts, etc. I was trying to embrace Mexico and make myself more comfortable and productive for my time there. And, yes, I wanted to study French while living in Mexico. That's how I always rolled. I was feeling much better in general. Removing the IUD had been the best decision possible. I was feeling great physically and was worlds better psychologically. My troubling OCD tendencies had disappeared to my great relief after my body eliminated the excess copper that had apparently been giving me a lot of physical and psychological symptoms. My month in France had been gloriously simultaneously wondrous, restorative and relaxing. Life was good.

I was still getting a bit acclimated from the trip and exhausted from packing and running around doing errands. I finished packing and loaded my car with most of the luggage I was taking back to Mexico. I wanted to go to sleep early, expecting to wake up early, re-energized and enjoy my last couple of days in the US. I remember being annoyed when I was briefly awoken by a text message alert in Spanish in the middle of the night. I figured it was a fluke and slipped quickly back into slumber. The next thing I knew I was jarred awake by a horrific pounding on the door. It sounded like someone was kicking the door in and I heard screaming. I was petrified and my heart was racing.

The property was very big and extremely isolated. There were no lights on the property and it was pitch black. Yanni had never wanted me to stay there alone and quite frankly I was extremely uncomfortable doing so given its isolated position in the middle of vineyards, no neighbors to speak of. There were wild boar, bobcats and supposedly a mountain lion to add to the somewhat ominous situation. My friends who owned the house had told me that a man had asked if he could come to the property to hunt boar that day and they had said no. I wasn't dressed and frantically looked for my robe while I peeked out the window. I saw a car I didn't recognize and thought for sure it was the hunter disgruntled and annoyed. My nervous system was fully activated and I wasn't thinking clearly.

I was in momentary freeze mode when I heard my name being called. It was my friends that owned the house and they had come to get me because the infamous California wild fires were raging again and spreading - pun intentional - like wildfire, threatening to engulf the house at any moment. I had experienced the last earthquake but this was my first wildfire. I was still more or less frozen. My friend snapped me out of it, yelling at me to grab my passport, we had to go. I grabbed what little I could and left with my car to go somewhere safe.

I was shaken and tried to call Yanni. I finally got a hold of him. He was glad I was ok but didn't seem to appreciate the gravity of the situation. But for my friends coming to rescue me, I may have been trapped there. I was so isolated, I couldn't hear any public pronouncements. The text in Spanish that I had ignored had been a public service warning that I didn't understand. "Earth angels", in the form of my friends, had saved me once again.

I stayed in a hotel downtown that was away from the fires. It was a surreal experience. The air was black and thick with smoke and we had to wear masks outside. I was hoping to return to the house to see if anything were salvageable. The area was under indefinite evacuation orders so I eventually gave up hope of returning and decided to go back to Mexico. I was still very shaken and looking forward to reuniting with Yanni. My decision was last minute and I was rushing to the airport shuttle bus station as I called Yanni to let him know I would arrive that evening. It still seemed to me that the gravity had been lost on him. I wasn't getting the solace I was seeking. I remember him asking if I could pick up shoe horns on the way...

Hello Abandonment Issues

I met Yanni at our apartment that night. I was happy to see him while he seemed distracted. I didn't get the warm greeting I expected, feeling I was lucky to be alive - again. I was also hungry though, as I always am, and there was nothing at home to eat. He didn't seem to want to go out but if there is one need I get satisfied, it's food, so we went out anyway. We went to one of our favorite restaurants in town. Yanni sent a lot of clients to the restaurant and we knew the manager well. The last time I had been there, we had taken Kathy who was visiting. She had ordered a salad but wanted chicken added so they graciously did so for a nominal add on charge. I decided to do the same and got the same thing she did.

I was disappointed when we got the bill to see I was charged for two full entrees even though I didn't order or actually receive the chicken entree. I wanted to talk to the manager about it, the one who appreciated our business and the customers Yanni always sent. Having owned a couple of restaurants, I also know that the restaurant owner wants you to be happy and speak up if something is wrong; they want happy, repeat customers, not disgruntled ones who will never return. I didn't think it was a big deal but it clearly was to Yanni - sufficient to be the final proverbial nail in our marital coffin.

At his insistence, I didn't speak up at the restaurant and we just paid the bill in full. I remember resenting seeing Yanni so jovial and grateful to the manager as we left. This was classic, Yanni. I had only seen it a few times but he would more or less go off the rails if I ever "questioned" him ever so slightly *in front of anyone*. I didn't know if it were a male thing or cultural to him but apparently such behavior was off limits. Silly things incensed him. He would get very upset if I tried helping with grocery boxes when we did our weekly shopping haul; it was like a personal affront to his manhood.

Another incident was when Kathy visited us. I was making pasta for dinner. I always made dinner at home *except* when there were guests. He insisted on showcasing his talents then. He had been at work though and I had already started dinner before he got home. I deigned to not listen to him about putting more salt in the water and Kathy and I both took note of his extreme reaction. These things sound trivial and happened infrequently since I instinctively never questioned him, particularly in front of anyone. His extreme reaction each time however was noteworthy to me despite the infrequency of the situation. He also had a habit of trying to impress everyone by insisting on trying to lavishly host notwithstanding our financial situation. One night we were out with Kathy and a lovely testa and I didn't feel like eating much because I was having some issues swallowing. He insisted nonetheless that I order a steak and I stupidly acquiesced because bizarre impressions were clearly important to him. I remember feeling foolish but vindicated when I promptly had to go to the washroom to vomit what I had tried to eat. I wanted to take my unfinished meal home but again he objected. He always wanted it to look like money was no object to him.

I also remember arguing with him about where the new thermostat should go when we had been in the midst of renovating my house. The heating technician and I wanted it where the old one had been. I didn't want to pay to repair any new holes in the walls. Yanni had a difference of opinion. Fine, but no, it was going where I wanted. I didn't make a big deal of it. I listened to his opinion but politely rejected it, explaining my side. He made a big deal of it because I dared not respect his opinion in front of another man. It was my house, my money and one of the rare times I took a stand. With hindsight, I realized how much my wanting to question the dinner bill our first night back together in Mexico had triggered him. He always wanted the appearance that he was so successful that money didn't matter. I wanted to question the bill on principle and he wouldn't stand for it.

After dinner, we drove home in silence. Ongoing silence would have been preferable to me. When we got home, I heard the most heart wrenching words I had ever heard. He managed to outdo my father's prior hurtful statements when he simply told me that he **_didn't want to be married anymore_**. This man whom I loved dearly, thought I would die married to, that I had supported and loved in the most comprehensive sense for a decade had unilaterally, without the courtesy of an explanation, a single discussion or respect for his marriage commitment, decided to dismiss me. I was blindsided and in shock. As you can see, with hindsight, I pieced his reasons together. I now know that not only was I no longer feeding his huge ego, I was "challenging" it, directly or indirectly. He had started becoming successful at work. He knew as long as I were around, he wouldn't be getting exclusive "credit" for what he did, the projects he funded for his family, etc. Just like he didn't want me to be considered "co-owner" of the business I supported, he didn't want anyone attributing anything to me. In his head, I was now detracting, not adding, value.

At the time though, I was oblivious. I was still feeling shaky and surreal from escaping the wildfires. I had just hauled a lot of luggage from the US, determined to truly embrace Mexico as home, I had just started feeling better physically and psychologically. I absolutely did not ever think Yanni would leave me **_ever_**. I certainly didn't expect to be summarily dismissed on arrival without a single word of explanation. Had he felt this way (his feelings apparently having been brewing despite my oblivion and despite him never having bothered to discuss them with me a single time), I wished he had saved me the trip.

My initial shock quickly turned into fight mode. When you have extraordinarily low self-esteem, it's difficult to challenge anyone for treating you as if you are worthless, as I felt Yanni had just done. I needed to turn to something more objective and segued into "our" debt as the gravity of "my" financial situation started to dawn on me. ***I had moved the bulk of the debt to me***, the bulk of which had nothing to do with me. I had supported him and his family, his dreams and his aspirations unquestionably for years. I didn't benefit from the projects in Albania. I wasn't financially benefiting from the start-up expenses in Cabo. I had no job, no income, no prospects. Yanni knew my assets had been dwindling at an alarming rate. I asked him what would happen with the debt and he suggested "splitting" it, something I absolutely didn't think was fair after all my years of exclusively funding everything. He wouldn't talk about it though. He wouldn't talk about anything. He refused to. He left saying he was staying the night at his cousin's house.

I went into freeze mode. I had never been so shocked, so scared or in so much emotional pain and fear in my life - not even when BS had tried to kill me nor when I had attempted to take my life. I did not think my husband was capable of such cruelty, at least as I saw it. Fortunately for me, another of my earth angels helped get me through that night I never thought would end. It was Kathy's birthday, my longest friend/ my "sister". I knew she was always up late and I reached out to her.

She quickly and accurately assessed the situation saying that Yanni loved me but he loved himself more. It reminded me of a time when we were in Cancun at a parking lot when a dog came running towards us ferociously with its teeth bared. Yanni had instinctively grabbed me and turned me around so my body was in the direct line of the angry dog as I served as an impromptu buffer. Fortunately, the dog owner intervened in the nick of time. Yanni tried to explain that he was trying to gain leverage to kick the dog if need be but I knew he had instantaneously chosen me as a shield. He had been in the military and police and his instinct had been to protect himself, not his wife. It obviously troubled me but I had tried not to think about it but Kathy's assessment brought the memory front and center to my thoughts. She lovingly acted as my lifeline that night somehow getting me through. The next day, my sister took over.

Yanni knew there wasn't any food at the house and he knew my usual voracious appetite and messaged he would bring me food. I declined. I was literally sick from sadness and felt like I would never desire to eat again. I was unbelievably distraught, dejected and confused and couldn't get my wits about me. He came anyway which pissed me off. I wasn't going to eat and I didn't want him assuaging his guilt. I asked him if we could talk that evening and he advised me he would be staying at his cousin's house again; he had nothing to talk about. After over a decade and innumerable experiences together. He coldly had nothing to talk about despite my desperate desire to.

My sister convinced me to leave, assessing the situation and telling me that I wasn't going to get anything I needed from Yanni, at least not then. I didn't know what to do but couldn't just sit there with my bubbling over feelings. It was as if a trajectory of pain had been callously hurled at me with the full force of all my cumulative surreal and hurtful pains balled into one loaded missile.....

I was beyond lost so I listened to her and knew I needed to book a flight. To where, I silently scoffed at myself, having no clue now where "home" was, my heart having just been ripped apart. I "packed" a suitcase haphazardly. I had already had a lot of possessions in the apartment and had just brought more suitcases filled to the brim for the next six months, reflective of my determination to embrace Mexico as home. I was paralyzed with grief. I couldn't decide what to take and what to leave. Nothing seemed to matter any more at that point but I was also sick of losing all of my things.

I messaged Yanni begging him again to come that evening and discuss our marriage. He refused. I begged him if we could just separate. He basically said I could look at it that way if I needed to but made it clear that I should have no hope at reconciliation. I kept asking what I had done wrong and he said absolutely nothing; he just didn't want to be married any more. Absolutely no attempt at any explanation whatsoever. In fact, he confounded my head and heart even further, assuring me I was the best person he would ever know (an oft-repeated sentiment) and that he was not only losing his wife but his best friend. "Wtf???," I silently thought without response.

To his relief, I told him I had booked a flight and would be going to Chicago the next day. The next morning after a sleepless night of trying to unpack and repack to no logical conclusion and after still not eating,

I was extremely shaken and exhausted. I couldn't believe another marriage was ending so ballistically, so suddenly, so shockingly. I have never felt more unsettled or lost. Yanni messaged asking if he could come say "good bye". His words let loose uncontrollable sobbing. I hadn't cried yet. I knew if I saw him, I would just physically and emotionally collapse and not be able to make it back to the US. I declined and shakily made my way to my shuttle bus. Of course, as these things happen, the driver was the same driver who had just brought me "home" two days earlier. He greeted me with a surprised look but comforting smile, querying, "Just you?" His words starkly described my apparent new undesired single status I realized as I quietly replied, "Yes, just me....."

As we wound our way out of the complex, to my surprise, I saw Yanni sitting in his car on the side of the road, obviously awaiting my departure. Our eyes locked in pain. It would be the last time I ever saw him...

Turkey Bound

The next few months were the worst of my life for a confluence of factors, including the obvious. In addition to my deep sorrow, I had to contend with a lot of unexpected trying circumstances I was ill-equipped to deal with psychologically or financially. I elaborate on them in the sequel. Their tenor and impact are more aligned with the topics I delve into there, like my nervous system dysregulation and abandonment issues that had just been beyond exacerbated thanks to Yanni's unexpected dismissal of me.

Suffice it to say that I eventually made it back to Napa and although I and the house were a shambles in innumerable ways, I had every intention of reclaiming myself and moving on to a new chapter. I saw a listing for a job at the Boys and Girls Club that called my name. I loved children and thought the position would soothe my soul. I envisioned using my passion for nutrition and fitness to help mold healthy little bodies and brains. The husband that owned the house I was staying in rent free was on the Board of Directors and I figured I had an excellent chance of getting the job with my qualifications and his recommendation.

His girlfriend, my good friend, had a friend with an organization that fostered Labrador puppies that were being groomed to be guide dogs for the disabled. I envisioned fostering eight puppies on the property. There was plenty of room for all of them and I had an abundance of love and affection to share. I signed up to take French classes one evening a week in town, knowing I needed to force myself to not slip into solitude. I had spent the last few months in frozen abject heartache and it was time to move on. Things were falling into place. Although my heart still desperately hurt, I was optimistically, energetically ready to master my new life and create new happiness. I was proud of myself for once that my plan was a relatively rational, stable one compared to my normal "escape", at least as perceived by family and friends.

Before any of my plans had time to materialize, however, all went to hell so to speak. It was Christmas Eve, normally one of my favorite days of the year and I had every intention to celebrate festively. I immersed myself in decorating and had invited the couple who owned the house over for dinner. I love cooking and happily shopped and prepared for a multi-course feast. I was excited about sharing my plans with my friends whom I hadn't seen for a few months. The man was particularly friendly and complimentary, welcoming me warmly and continuously assuring me I would have no problem moving on from Yanni. Yanni had always thought he was a little too forward and affectionate with me and that his girlfriend was a bit jealous.

They had told me previously that I would have at least a year advance warning before I would have to leave the house. To my utter shock, they told me over our "celebratory" holiday dinner that I needed to be out in a couple of months instead. Things had been weird since the fire, the circumstances of which I detail in the sequel, but I was blindsided again. Of course, I respected their timetable but immediately realized that none of my plans were viable any longer. I lost it that night. I tried holding myself together for the rest of the evening for the sake of my company.

I remember after they had left sitting on the floor - why I don't know - as if I couldn't even hold the weight of myself upright any more, slumped in apparent emotional defeat. I had no husband, no income, no prospects, no home and crushing debt. What would I do? Where would I go? What would I do with all my things? Where is "home?" my profoundly unsettled being ceaselessly pondered as I scanned the house filled with all of my belongings, representing my travels, my memories, my comforts, my continuity. I resented my Christmas decorations and lights, the decor that had usually brought me so much joy and happy memories now seemed like an emotional slap in the face. These things that traditionally denoted carefree mirth, celebratory merriment and family were painfully, starkly contrasted to my broken spirit and evident solitude. I had never felt so lost, so forlorn, so alone. I was clutching one of my Buddha statues in a tight grip against my chest, hoping magically for some answers.

My range of emotions accumulated with a great intensity. I was sad, I was angry, I was scared. I got up and started screaming, loudly, primally, knowing no one would hear me or answer my plaintive calls literally or figuratively. The last time I had done that was after my flashbacks. My body instinctively knew I had to move; I had to release my feelings. I eventually stumbled to bed and passed out from sheer emotional exhaustion. I awoke the next morning, a bit dazed and still shocked by the prior night's news, not ready yet to deal with it in all its implications.

Mysteriously, the Buddha statue I had been asking for answers had disappeared. At that moment though, I suddenly had the answer. I was being drawn to Turkey like I have never been drawn to anything before. I know my choice of destination often seems aimless, random at best, to others. In my head, they are divined if you will. I realized I always returned to the place that felt most like "home" to me based on past circumstances, no matter how foreign.

My plan gave me the will to move on - some direction replaced abject floundering. I don't even use Facebook but something compelled me to acknowledge my new singleness as a tangible baby step of acceptance. I changed my status from "married" to "single" on the site. To my extreme surprise, Yanni called me almost immediately thereafter, obviously upset with me for having done that. Well, isn't that special and ironic, I thought as I went to start packing to prepare for my latest round of "where's home?"

Chapter 6
Escapism Part 3: My Turkish Delights

E*arth Angels*
     I couldn't have asked for a better companion than Carol to embark with me on my next chapter of my life. We were returning to Turkey 10 years after our first visit and we were both overflowing with excitement about the adventures that undoubtedly awaited us. Cause for celebration indeed our thoughts silently synced as we eyed "Vino and Volo" en route to our gate at Chicago's O'hare airport. As would often happen between us, no need for words, as our eyes met in tacit agreement and we chose a table for a pre-flight celebratory glass of wine. "Vino and Volo" or "wine and flight" seemed like an apt description of my life, perhaps a potential title for one of my many planned books. The celebratory glass turned into a "couple" as our flight was delayed. Seemed like a good idea at the time to lull us into sleepy mode for our lengthy overnight flight.

Fast forward several hours later when we were exhausted, slightly tipsy and state side after the umpteenth delay and the imbibing didn't seem like the wisest plan. Our flight was finally canceled some time after midnight and we were told we couldn't get another flight until late the next night. Carol only had about 10 days, including travel days, for the trip and was contemplating canceling. My enthusiasm quickly waned as I grew unusually apprehensive about making the journey solo. Of course, this wouldn't be my first solo trip by any stretch of the imagination but I really wanted her companionship to usher in what seemed like such a momentous time in my life.

We had only stayed in sporadic touch after our first trip together a decade prior but we had quickly reconnected and bonded deeply after Yanni left me. She had become the truest of friends and a daily confidante and source of comfort for my aching heart and soul. I had a foreboding sense if she didn't make the journey. We were a team. She hung in there like the strong soldier she is however and, after several late night hours on the phone, managed to get us on a very early morning flight with a short layover/connection in New York. It was the first of many sleepless nights to come but we were re-energized with the trip being back on schedule so to speak.

Unfortunately we had to transfer airports in New York, however, and had an extremely tight connection especially with New York City rush hour traffic. Our nerves quickly frayed again as we watched in vain for my luggage to appear at LaGuardia airport while the conveyor belt went round and round again in a seemingly endless loop in slow motion. The chance of Carol cancelling her trip resurfaced and so did my dismay. Turns out my luggage had been off first and for some inexplicable reason had been deposited in lost luggage. We grabbed it and rushed outside, deflated by the extraordinarily long taxi line that made it inevitable that we would miss our connecting flight.

Without hesitation and to Carol's mild surprise and horror (not for the first time), I quickly procured an unlicensed cab. Reckless behavior and I are no strangers and although I don't recommend taking unlicensed transportation, but for that split-second decision, we would have missed our flight. Although we had been given our boarding passes to Istanbul in Chicago, we hadn't bothered to look at them in our giddy and sleep-deprived state. I'll never forget Carol asking me as our driver zipped through traffic en route to JFK why our boarding passes said LaGuardia. Throwing caution to the wind as I so often did, I confidently assured her we were fine, obviously not knowing if that were true. I have no idea why the boarding passes were erroneous but had we looked at them and not been in a rush to get to JFK, we also would have missed our flight. Just goes to show, some times, just "winging" it works.

Our reunion with Istanbul was almost a total blur of excitement, exhaustion, hilarity and glorious new memories to the extent either of us could actually remember any of it. I don't know if it were because of the exhaustion, the jet lag, the wine or a combination thereof but we both felt as if we were in an absolute time warp the whole time. Our flight got us to Istanbul very early and we didn't want to lose a moment of exploration, having already lost a day of our trip. Instead of resting, we opted to go out immediately after dropping our luggage at our hotel.

We were immediately caught up in the splendid cacophony of addictive sensory "overload" that is Istanbul. Fortunately we had no plan per se because it inevitably would have gone awry. An endless stream of distractions started immediately in the form of exquisite charming salesmen, whose sales tactics were largely flirtatious interactions and compliments. One particularly suave gentleman persuaded us to come to the rooftop of his carpet store to have complimentary tea with a panoramic view of the iconic Sultanahmet square with its incredible architectural treasures, the "Blue Mosque" and Hagia Sofia. We were familiar with both and couldn't resist the inviting vista nor, to my surprise, could I resist his obvious attention. Being very shy and introverted, I normally shun attention but my aching heart and bruised ego were apparently in need of some flattering interest.

The important part of the encounter for purposes of this story was when his uncle, Nuri, joined us. He was gracious, charismatic and clearly instantly captivated by Carol's luminous beauty. To my surprise, he took one look at me and instantly said that my heart was broken and that I needed to get over my heartache or I was going to get cancer. I was shocked by his forthrightness and his immediate perception of my psychological pain despite outwardly smiling and feeling happy. The gravity of his advice was not lost on me though I quickly tried to dismiss him, initially uncomfortable by his perception and his prediction. Carol believes in "healers" and was instantly drawn to the man. I chalked it up to adept perception.

We thoroughly enjoyed the rest of our time in Istanbul despite its whirlwind nature. Nuri spent a lot of the time with us, graciously hosting us. He insisted on taking us one night to Kempinski Palace, one of the grandest hotels in Istanbul. To my surprise yet again, this man who knew nothing about my history, escorted us to a swinging rocking seat seaside with a glorious view, intent on helping me "heal". He sat between us, holding one of each of our hands and instructed us to close our eyes as he began gently rocking and, to my huge surprise, chanting. Again, I don't normally believe in this type of stuff but Carol does and I believe in her so was comforted by her presence. To my extreme surprise, I almost immediately felt lighter despite my skepticism, like a weight had been taken off my heart. Rocking always calmed me and I started feeling almost ethereal. Even for days after, I felt somewhat euphoric despite my heart still having a searing ache. I had also started drinking kava tea. I didn't know how much of my transformation was attributable to the tea, Carol's presence or to my latest "earth angel", Nuri, but all I knew was that I felt better when I had desperately needed to.

Interestingly, Carol had tried to do some healing work on me our first trip to Istanbul a decade before in the form of "ancient rainbow conscious healing", a sort of "energy healing". I thought at the time it was something like reiki, that I knew nothing of other than that I didn't believe in it. I remember being very uncomfortable closing my eyes - my psyche was still in such survival mode that I was so hyper vigilant - even with my best friend in our hotel room. We had just experienced our first hamam, or Turkish bath - something Carol loved and that I had abhorred. Being naked and closing my eyes while someone washed me was way out of my comfort level, particularly at the time. I was visibly shaken. I desperately wanted to support Carol's work and was incredibly appreciative of her efforts but it was counterproductive at the time. I think I was too much in survival mode, closing my eyes and denying one of my senses made me extraordinarily uncomfortable no matter how much I consciously knew there was absolutely nothing to fear.

The outcome would be much different when Carol tried "healing work" on me subsequently, years later when apparently I was more "open" to it and ready. I think Nuri's presence - importantly in the presence also of the positive calming energy of my dear friend - was the first time a layperson had been able to noticeably calm my frayed nerves and soothe my aching heart. Nuri continued his compassion, saying he would pray for us in Friday prayers. In case you are wondering, yes, he tried to sell Carol a carpet even though he was also trying to woo her romantically. A multi-tasker - my kind of guy. Somehow I escaped the sales pitch.

My Turkish Delights

I was feeling pretty good, my budding ethereal-like mood having continued, and my restless soul immersed in the novelty of a new culture and new vistas to explore to distract me from my heartache. I was still in deep pain over Yanni but my new sensory experiences were helping lessen my fixation over him. My ***heart was deeply broken*** but my spirit remained intact. ***I was not broken.***

I was incredibly fortunate that somehow I had divined myself to the Turkish Riviera. More specifically, I had chosen a beautiful little seaside village, Kaş, as my new "home", site unseen as I previously had with Argentina. I always seem to be at my best when I am immersed in challenges. I had purposely opted for a town that, although touristy, remained very local, authentic and Turkish over neighboring towns that were frequented by many foreign tourists, where English was more commonly utilized, and where day to day to living was more "user friendly" for an American expat. I wanted to experience Turkish culture; I didn't want to see things written in English or amounts written in Euros or hear English-speaking visitors out and about. Of course, that makes things a little more trying, isolating, lonely at times but I always opt for cultural immersion, authenticity... I also had, to my surprise, forced my introverted self to book my first month in Kaş at a hotel so I would be forced to go out and interact. I knew if I had an apartment with a kitchen I would self isolate and likely quickly slip into an abyss of loneliness and self pity.

Fortunately, Carol was accompanying me for my first few days so I had the pleasure of her company during my initial acclimation. We had another whirlwind of laughs, late nights, wine and a stream of enchanting men. I was starting to get very melancholy her second to last night, not wanting to accept the reality that I would be alone again soon after her departure back to the US. Time was flying though we were making the most of each moment; the only thing dampening my spirits was the realization of my impending solitude.

We were out at a local bar for one of our last hurrahs, enjoying the music and wine. Carol started dancing, something I was very hesitant to do, not yet having appreciated that Kaş was not the least bit conservative. She is much more outgoing than I and had no hesitation dancing despite being in a bar where we were the only female patrons. I shyly tried following her lead as she even went behind the bar to grab the bartender to start dancing. The rest of the night was a bit of a blur for each of us, as we continued drinking wine, trying to delay our inevitable impending separation.

Somehow, we separated anyway, Carol accompanying one of the patrons and me accompanying the bartender with whom she had danced. Carol and I rendezvoused the next morning to "compare notes"; our evenings had been quite different. The only common factor was that she had received a rose from her companion and I had from Bilal, the bartender, as well. It was not a foreshadowing of thoughtful gifts to come; it was the only thing he ever gave me. Our evenings had been polar opposites. Carol had stayed up all night with her companion, talking until the early morning. I had enjoyed an intense night of passion. Bilal did not speak English and I most certainly did not speak Turkish, so we relied on body language. It had been an incredible experience; I had more or less uncharacteristically abstained from sex since Yanni except for an isolated incident here or there. All my pent up emotions, needs and pain from my marital separation were gratefully unleashed on this man, who made me feel "alive" again, desired again and "worthy" with his passionate intensity.

The next night we went out to a bar adjacent to the one Bilal bartended at. There was no shortage of potential suitors and we were sitting around a fire pit enjoying conversation with a few other men we had met. Turkish men are, by and large, passionate and expressive - something both Carol and I were enjoying in the carefree moment. Bilal came by to say hello and kissed me on my cheeks. I had had no expectation of seeing him again and I was touched by his gesture of affectionate interest.

Long story short, he came back with me to my room that night and kind of never left. Carol went back to the US and I was left alone, immediately feeling my restlessness and unease taking center stage again. I didn't want to be alone and Bilal apparently had no intention of leaving me alone. Despite the obvious challenges posed by our very real language barrier, we quickly grew very close. My ability to "communicate" orally, though rudimentary, had come a long way since my relationship with Mariano. I also now had a phone with translation apps that were useful, though often quite comical with poor translations that were often way off base. We managed.

When I bother trying to explain these relationships to inquisitive friends and family, I liken it to the ability to communicate with babies or animals, for whom we care deeply and interact intimately with, despite a lack of actual oral communication. I had had many encounters with people with whom I did not share a common language. It gave me a real appreciation for "listening" in the most comprehensive sense. Body language, facial cues, eye expressions, context, etc. go a long way. Honestly, sometimes I felt more in sync with some of these people than I had in other relationships, even marriage, when I knew full well I was not being "listened" to.

Bilal wasn't my only new meaningful relationship at this trying time of my life. Another "earth angel" appeared to save me from my sorrow in the form of Khalil, a Syrian friend I had connected with via social media. He was immersed in the horrors of the Syrian civil war and we soon became each other's "lifeline" if you will. Khalil's incredibly dangerous circumstances quickly gave me perspective to elevate me out of my relatively insignificant challenges. We messaged daily and extensively. These communications were some of the most positively impactful and inspiring of my life. He was a constant source of tender support, inspiration and love. Our relationship rapidly became one akin to family. We were both "alone" in many ways and heartened and strengthened knowing we mutually had "each other's back". Khalil loves books and we both talked about our writing goals. He always encouraged me to write and to heal. I am indescribably happy to say he safely made it to Turkey. He had filled my "linguistic void" with Bilal and he will always be family to me. I digress again in "earth angels"...

Back to Bilal. I don't know precisely what drew me to him so intently. He didn't literally stay from that night on. I tried going out with other men but I always ended up back with Bilal. It was obvious to me with respect to some of the other men that they were "players" and I didn't want to be "played". Even when I initially think I may want to enjoy the freedom of being newly single, I always gravitate towards monogamy. The fact that Bilal was obviously interested in an exclusive relationship quickly and clearly trumped the "small detail" of our language barrier.

I vastly preferred his company to my uncomfortable "solitude" that taunted me with thoughts I didn't want to think. Bilal's presence gave me the ongoing ability to more or less suppress my pained emotions. Our intimacy validated my worth and satisfied my oxytocin (the "love hormone") "addiction". He was very affectionate and quick to express his love for me and I equated the physical interactions with love as well. We always slept together in an entangled manner that was incredibly comforting and soothing to me. I was sleeping better than I had in several years.

I realized with hindsight that I was likely drawn to him in large part because his personality and demeanor were in stark contrast to Yanni's big, vain, hyper self-centered ego. I knew that Yanni had ***discarded*** me when I no longer was feeding his ego and I took comfort in Bilal's humility. My abandonment issues had been exacerbated by Yanni's callous dismissal of me. Bilal wasn't "going anywhere" and although with time this would come to irritate me, it was precisely what my pained soul craved at the time.

I have lived with someone else pretty much my entire life and had mastered cohabitation with my placating, pacifying persona that always subjugated my desires and needs unquestionably. I was in a tiny hotel room for a month though. This was a challenging situation because Bilal would sleep in late - and I mean late. He worked late though and I didn't want to disturb his sleep so I would leave the curtains drawn, tip toeing around the room.

My new locale was stunningly beautiful and I threw myself into exploring it and spending most of my time out in nature. I had been drawn to the incredible sea in this area when I had traveled around Turkey with Yanni many years before and had vowed to return. My prophecy had been realized though I never suspected the circumstances that would lead to that realization. I had anticipated enjoying the area when Yanni and I inevitably would return, not seeking it as a sanctuary to soothe my aching heart from his departure.

I have been blessed to see a lot of beauty in my lifetime and Kaş was definitely in the running for top spot. I couldn't believe my good fortune to have discovered this idyllic little town. The sea was the most beautiful I had ever seen with an achingly beautiful kaleidoscopic range of turquoise colors and a texture that felt like a silky hug. My walks were glorious with the sea on one side and on the other side an array of silvery green olive trees, pungently-colored citrus free trees and endless paths of roses and overflowing bougainvillea of every color imaginable. The animals are well taken care of strays and I was always inevitably kept company by many affectionate loyal dogs that would walk miles with me. The town was picturesquely terraced from high, cascading down towards the sea, the whiteness of the homes beautifully contrasted with the enveloping endless greenery. I felt like I was immersed in a postcard. The scenery was truly breathtaking.

The vistas, the soothing rhythmic waves of the sea and the fresh air were cumulatively working their magic to help soothe my soul. I was absolutely loving the food and the bustling weekly market where locals would gather amongst countless stalls of the freshest vibrantly colored produce, enjoying each others' company with traditional gözleme, a type of Turkish pancake, and ever-flowing diminutive cups of Turkish tea in beautiful tulip shaped glasses. My foodie-obsessed heart was in heaven. Notwithstanding my introverted nature, Turkish hospitality is justly famous and I immediately felt welcomed. I felt more "at home" than ever before. Unlike when I was in Mexico, I was able to follow my passions and was free to explore endlessly.

It wasn't soon after I had arrived, however, that Bilal quit his job, citing wanting to spend time with me while I was visiting as well as a disagreement with the bar owner for his reasons for quitting. This raised a bit of a red flag for me (let's call it a tiny pink flag) based on my history. This deja vu of suddenly "living with" another unemployed boyfriend alerted my intuition, something I still barely listened to and never followed. I was happy to spend time with him so pushed the flag and my intuition out of my head. We didn't really spend time together however - at least not out of bed. He was still sleeping in late - and I mean really late. All day late even though he wasn't working. He wouldn't even go out to eat. I would bring him sandwiches and cigarettes (although I abhor smoking).

I was in a new town and was happy to spend my time exploring but introverted me wanted to do so with my boyfriend, not alone. I always hated going out to eat alone. I could have used help navigating my new foreign surroundings. Presuming I was alone, men continued approaching me, questioning me about my boyfriend's whereabouts when I would turn them down saying I had a boyfriend. Having a boyfriend usually quickly shuts down a Turkish man's advances out of respect for their "brothers". I think at first people thought my boyfriend was an imaginary figmentation in my head given my ever present solitude.

I was enjoying sleeping with Bilal but I was getting really irritated pussyfooting around. I wanted to embrace life, not just him. He was the most lethargic, apathetic person I had met since BS. I had come full circle but didn't really appreciate it at the time, still shell shocked from Yanni's abandonment. I was paying for everything as usual also. I wasn't happy and I had had enough. I tried breaking up with him - the first of many times - and he started to actually cry. To this day, even with my greater self awareness, I firmly believe he was being sincere. I'm sure it comes as no surprise that I caved and we stayed together.

By this time, I had fallen in love with Kaş and didn't want to leave it or Bilal so I was staying indefinitely. I struggled finding new places to stay because it was tourist season. I moved amongst various hotels and apartments, sometimes nightly, sometimes weekly, sometimes monthly. I was feeling extremely unsettled and tired hauling my luggage around. Others offered to help me find reasonable accommodations as I was paying a lot moving around but I didn't want to make my boyfriend jealous, the one who wasn't similarly offering help even though he was staying with me and I was paying more because of that. He did eventually get a job because I told him I wasn't paying for his cigarettes any more. Sadly, that was a big step for me. I still paid all other expenses, notwithstanding I wasn't working.

Our relationship was full of disappointments for me but I was/am quite confident he was faithful so he passed my one and only real requirement. We had inevitable misunderstandings from our language barrier though and an endless stream of disrespectful incidents. Oftentimes, I would be waiting for him to come for dinner and he just wouldn't show, without even bothering to message me. He always seemed to have an endless stream of excuses. When we would go out, it was obvious I was expected to pay for everything. He would even call a friend often to join us - more or less on the pretext that the friend could help bridge our language barrier - and I always paid for everything. I knew it wasn't fair and it upset me but I just paid any way.

I hadn't figured out residency yet so had to leave Turkey periodically. I didn't want to be alone and it was off season so Bilal wasn't working. Bilal wanted to join so I let him. By "let him", I mean paid for him to get a passport and paid for all travel expenses in addition to the living expenses I was already paying for. Since it was off season and he hadn't saved any money (having spent it all, including helping his family), I started paying for his personal expenses again. Initially I had planned to go to Montenegro together for three months, a country he was allowed to visit visa free.

I enjoyed our first month together, always preferring company to solitude. I hadn't been to Montenegro and was loving seeing a new country and all the natural beauty of its regions. I was becoming more and more disenchanted though as Bilal wasn't expressing any gratitude for my generosity nor was he helping me find a long term apartment in Kaş, a prerequisite for my residency permit I intended to apply for when I returned.

My stress was growing about my financial situation and I was getting resentful paying for everything, a la all my prior relationships. I needed a break so, to my surprise and undoubtedly yours as well, I decided to cut our trip short and spend the next two months solo visiting the Greek islands of Naxos and Paros. Bilal was surprised and unhappy but I was proud I had stuck to my decision. The tourist season was starting in Kaş and I knew he should be working, not holidaying with me. I was "proud" of myself but must admit that, but for my financial challenges, I strongly suspect I would not have made that choice.

I looked forward to my return to Greece and thought I would enjoy some time to myself. As always, I loved seeing new places and made some great memories exploring the natural beauty of the islands. I quickly realized however that I was no more comfortable being alone than ever before. Indeed, I started slipping again hard into an emotional abyss. Since I had met Bilal over a year earlier, I hadn't really been left alone with my thoughts, with my unresolved pain over Yanni leaving me as well as my anger over having been saddled with crushing debt. I couldn't even get divorced because he had repeatedly failed to send me his signature page for the divorce papers I had filed. I paradoxically vacillated between anger over him not sending me his signature and hope we would reconcile. To this day, he tells me I am the best person he will ever know and that I have remained his best friend, a very sad statement.

There were innumerable instances where I had emotionally communicated with Yanni, always trying to get some sort of explanation for what happened, whatever that would have been worth. As I have noted, sober me doesn't generally have the courage to speak up on my behalf so these communications took place more often than not after a drinking episode. These communications always got ugly, my deep pain running smack dab into his defensiveness and big ego. They never accomplished anything. To this day, he never offered any explanation for ending our marriage so abruptly. I always ended the conversations sadder and more pained. I was always able to lessen that sadness and pain though by crawling into bed and getting the soothing warm embrace of Bilal who was always there and never seemed to get upset about my communications with my "husband".

Now for the first time for real, I was truly alone with my pain, something I always recoiled from. My stark solitude overshadowed the distractions I could normally rely on to keep me from delving into my feelings and emotions. This time the endless charms of the Greek islands weren't working their magic on me and I quickly realized why. I knew better than to go to Santorini, the sentimentality of it would have been like twisting a knife in my broken heart. I hadn't realized how difficult just being in Greece in general was going to be for me; there were too many similarities harkening me back to that first glorious year I had spent with Yanni in Santorini.

I was literally on an island figuratively feeling flooded by the past I had been escaping more or less from. For the first time really since my second overdose, I became plagued with suicidal thoughts again. I had promised Mike I would never give in to such thoughts and I obviously kept that promise. I was fluctuating between anxiety attacks and depression. I did my best to keep busy, immersing myself in nature and forcing myself to continue going out and exploring the exquisite islands. I continued desperately struggling with my aloneness, however, and whatever fledgling thoughts I had about leaving Bilal, because I knew I deserved to be treated better, quickly dissipated. I had seen glimpses of turning a corner when I had left Montenegro but Greece, my former home, site of the best time of my life and where I had met the love of my life, had gut punched me backwards. I was relieved when my little Greek tour was coming to an end and ecstatic about reuniting with Bilal.

That ecstatic feeling dwindled over the next few months following my return as I quickly became immersed again in his disrespectful behavior as well as my lack of self respect for myself. With awareness and hindsight, I realize that I was fully accountable for allowing myself to be taken advantage of, for not setting boundaries, for spending money I couldn't afford to, etc. My ability to demand more respect, establish boundaries or end the relationship, however, remained "obstacled" by my perspective, created by my low sense of self worth. I couldn't demand better if I didn't realize I deserved better. I remained shackled by my need for validation - something I was clearly receiving in my screwed up psyche - and "addicted" to our physical intimacy and affection. I was "addicted" to sleeping intertwined together and I was "getting off" on a heady mix of "neurotransmitter cocktails" without even realizing what was happening. I was hooked and sleeping better than I had since that Summer in Santorini.

Despite various incidents of disrespect that were becoming increasingly more commonplace, I felt better than I had in awhile. Indeed, I more or less consciously settled for the situation, choosing to confront it with my trademark energy and resolve. I became adamant that I just wouldn't get upset with Bilal any more. I knew he was faithful and I was grateful for sleeping together. My need to be loved was so high and my sense of self worth so low that I had a tendency for actually thanking people when they would kiss me - like they were doing me a favor. I could not be alone..... I just started setting my expectations low and numbing myself to anything Bilal did to bother me. Of course, that was destined to fail and only lasted so long....

rying to Rationalize the Irrational: Time to Heal (maybe)
T I won't go into too much detail about the "last straw" that finally made me stick to my "resolve" to not let Bilal live with me anymore. In part, because my resolve didn't stick. Suffice it to say, I was waiting for the umpteenth time for him when he just didn't bother to show up for dinner. As usual, he couldn't even be troubled to message me that he wouldn't be joining me for the dinner I had lovingly made while looking forward to his arrival. It and my heart grew colder with each seemingly endless passing minute. It felt like an eternity; the actual time having been distorted by my cumulative deja vu disappointments.

I was about to go on a trip to Italy for a few weeks with one of my best friends from college. I wanted to avoid a confrontation with Bilal but I didn't want our strained relationship hanging over my head while I was gone. I asked him to come get his things in my absence. He had his own key to my apartment. He expressed surprise, apparently clueless as to why I was so upset. In "optimistic resignation", if there is such a thing, I simply gave up. I was the queen of conflict avoidance and thought my absence would give us a cooling off period sufficient to try to work things out. More like give me a cooling off period. I always managed to cool off whereas he never got heated about anything; it was actually one of the things I loved about him. I was kind of like a hyper "Yang" to his zen-like "Yin", in theory, at least, making us complementary and harmonious.

I had one of the best trips of my life. Not only was I able to share some of my favorite places in Turkey with my friend, Mandy, but we had also spent an incredible time in my new favorite region of Italy, Puglia, the "heel" of the Italian "boot". It was known for its cuisine, whitewashed hill towns and endless coastline. Mandy is also a foodie and avid fitness enthusiast and we were in heaven daily enjoying hiking, exploring the towns and eating. We could spend an entire day at farmers' markets "oohing" and "ahhing" as we slowly made the rounds again and again sampling local delicacies, soaking up the fragrant atmosphere, taking endless photos of picture perfect vibrantly-colored produce, planning our meals and trying to make small conversation with the friendly, boisterous purveyors of everything imaginable. This was my first trip with her of many to come and she was an absolute delight to travel with and spend time with. As was always the case with Carol, not only was my trip one of the best in my life but it was also one of the best times of my life. "Girls' trips" were relatively new to me, neither my husbands nor my boyfriends exactly being supportive of them. It was a newfound pleasure I vowed to never give up.

After being apart for a few weeks and having a splendid, restorative trip with Mandy, I did indeed cool off, as I always did. I was really looking forward to my reunion with Bilal, my persona always ready for intimacy and endless cuddles. I had thoroughly enjoyed my glorious trip but was experiencing a bit of "withdrawal symptoms" and was anxious to get back to Bilal. He was supposed to meet me at the shuttle bus station to help me with my luggage and go out to dinner together.

He wasn't there when I arrived nor did he answer my repeated calls. My luggage was heavy and I had an assortment of cumbersome bags (including bottles of wine and other gifts I had brought from my trip). Steep hills and five flights of stairs created a bit of a physical challenge between the station and my apartment, especially after a long day of travel. I lugged all my things as had become somewhat of an arduous and comical habit over the past several years. Inevitably when one of my strong boyfriends or Yanni accompanied me anywhere, there were elevators, private transfers, etc.

My luggage struggles on my own had become a kind of badge of honor throughout my years of traveling.

I was a bundle of annoyance, hunger, and exhaustion when I finally made it to my apartment. I opened the door to be greeted by a complete stranger drinking beer, lazing comfortably on the couch, feet propped on the coffee table amidst empty strewn beer bottles and the floor covered in filth, someone obviously having tracked in mud and dirt. The two story apartment was icy cold, the air conditioner on full blast even though it was Fall. We managed to establish that the stranger was Bilal's friend despite the ever present language barrier and that Bilal was in the shower. They had played soccer - hence the floor. Bilal evidently had blown me off entirely - again.

I was furious and hurt on more levels than I could explain. I often experience unpleasant emotional roller coasters in life. I am so easily excited by the simplest things and so often greeted with unexpected, unwelcome disappointment. My joyful anticipation was quickly countered by reality. My heart hurt from the ongoing, cumulative lack of disrespect. I didn't have the energy to try to communicate my disappointment about him blowing me off in Turkish, other than giving him a pained glare when he emerged from the bathroom obviously drunk. In a baby show of self respect, as I stood hurt in the frigid apartment, I asked him to pay for the electricity for that month, most of which time I had been gone. He had never paid a penny for anything and he always used the air conditioning and heating irresponsibly, running them constantly on high even when the apartment was empty. He agreed to pay the electricity before leaving with his friend and leaving me with my thoughts and the filthy floor to clean.

Had he still been there, my growing wrath would have been unleashed notwithstanding the language barrier as I realized there were no paper towels to clean the floor because he had resorted to using paper towels after finishing all the toilet paper I had left, posing a significant risk of clogging the pipes. My needs may be simple but they do include toilet paper. I started crying, something I practically never do for myself. I was exhausted from disrespect and thoughtlessness. I felt uncharacteristically deflated, utterly saddened that I could keep letting someone treat me with such disdain and utter disregard. How could I be so excited, so endlessly enthusiastic about seeing someone who clearly did not feel the same way?

Being "greeted" so to speak with such stark disrespect was too much even for me to take. I abhor confrontations. Surprisingly, it took me until writing this book to appreciate that I abhor them because I am actually afraid based on my prior history of violence. I messaged Bilal repeatedly to please come get his stuff but he didn't. I was living in a large apartment because that was all that was available at the time. A smaller apartment in the same building had become available so instead of risking an angry confrontation with him, I put all his things outside and moved to the other apartment even though I had prepaid several more months in the larger, more expensive apartment. I apprised him of the location of his belongings but did not tell him I had moved. It took him weeks to come get his things. I listened in fear as I heard him pounding on the door of the prior apartment. He had a key and was surprised it no longer worked as the lock had been changed. He was clearly upset about that and his things being outside. I watched fearfully from the peephole in my door for him to leave. To be clear, he never physically harmed me but I was scared nonetheless.

I tried to analyze why I had kept putting up with his behavior and allowing myself to continually be mistreated. ***What was wrong with me? Why did men keep treating me disrespectfully?*** I was confident he was faithful, he was very affectionate and we had great physical chemistry - my kryptonite trifecta so to speak. Don't cheat on me, hug me a lot and show me you "love me" by wanting sex with me and you're basically golden. You get a pass with respect to all other behavior. I reveal such detail because it's insightful to my persona - both what I would and would not put up with. I had stayed with him because he satisfied my absolute deal breakers - be faithful and physically affectionate. I'm embarrassed I set my standards so low; they synced with my low self-esteem, however.

He also was my first relationship after my devastating separation from Yanni. I had known if I weren't with him that I would resort to a pattern of indiscriminate sex - fulfilling my "love addiction", which I more or less equated with sex. This was an oft-repeated pattern of many men, and although the essence of the relationship was largely sexual in nature, I was desperately trying to fill a void in my heart and my head, not my body. I did not excel in solitude and hence was rarely single throughout my life. Whenever I found myself uncomfortably alone, I would jump from one person to the next until I became involved in a relationship. This random aimlessness never bode well for a healthy relationship. My desperation to be "coupled" was not lost on the needy who quickly found me. Although my relationships were hardly stellar examples of what coupledom should look like, the pain they caused was far out trumped by my psychological crises triggered by being alone.

From outward appearances, I know my behavior often looks conflicted at best - innumerable male encounters interspersed with several long term relationships. I am a faithful, loyal person and I was always looking for my next relationship, quick to attach. Every man who had moved in with me after my marriage did so with lightning speed, more or less immediately and we engaged in intense "enviable" sexual relationships. *I mistook that intensity, that passion as a mirror of my intense, loving nature.*

My perception seemed to be intensified and validated by the feel good chemicals released by near constant physical interactions, dopamine, oxytocin and endorphins. These chemicals create bonding and feelings of intimacy. They *literally make you happy* and happy is what I needed to be to stave off my emotional sadness from my past. I was in the moment, in my body, flooded with pleasure chemicals. Practically all of my interactions with Bilal were in bed - having sex or sleeping. I was sleeping better than ever and had absolutely no fear of abandonment with him. Although I couldn't rationalize the relationship objectively, it absolutely gave me exactly what I fundamentally wanted, what I was more or less asking for, needed at that point in my life. Although I wished for more, I don't really blame Bilal. I continually tolerating his behavior and he was fulfilling my absolute needs perfectly.

Trying to have men fill my "voids" always ended tragically though, indeed deepening the voids of my soul. I had yet to appreciate that it was incumbent on me to fill that existential emptiness; it most definitely had to come from within, not from without. Solitude was not an option for me at the time though and I truly didn't want to sleep around.

I became restless on my own very quickly. I struggled to decide what to do. I knew I shouldn't tolerate Bilal's disrespect again but his absence was quickly making me incredibly melancholy about Yanni. I needed my trademark distraction. I decided to go to Italy for three months then the

US for three months. This plan synced with my pattern of moving around frequently, always wanting to be somewhere "other" - somewhere other than where I was. I had a deep, incessant, restless desire for more distractions, enabling my ongoing repressions. I loved Turkey but couldn't stay still, especially now that my boyfriend of almost two years was gone. I started missing him and my uneasy solitude was making me question myself, something I generally avoided.

I tried to keep myself busy and immerse myself in my travel plans but each day alone felt like a lonely eternity. Eventually, Bilal started coming back, having found out I moved, and, not surprisingly, I let him. One night I was waiting for him for dinner and to no one's surprise he never showed up for the countless time. I always splurged when making him dinner and made an elaborate production in his honor, preparing a multi course dinner of his favorites, eagerly awaiting his arrival with great anticipation. I was like the proverbial kid in a candy store when he would show up, lighting up and melting into his hugs to which I clung. I was hurt when he didn't show without even messaging me but it never amounted to more than that. It had actually become my expectation more or less that he wouldn't show. Pathetically, I would have been surprised if he had.

"I'm just not going to let him steal my energy," I resolutely "explained" to Carol, who compassionately and non-judgmentally listened to me about this incident and all of his other antics for the umpteenth time. We had nicknamed him "cookie boy", initially in endearment, reflective of his warm, sweet, cozy/cuddliness. It worked out fortuitously that it was also a good nickname for a temptation/an indulgence you knew wasn't that good for you, at least not regularly. Cookies also have a propensity to crumble and/or go stale.

I had gotten over my embarrassment about allowing myself to be treated this way, giving him endless benefits of the doubt. Carol and I both fully knew I would be welcoming him with open arms the next day when he appeared. I would be leaving soon anyway for my trip to Italy, I weakly tried to justify to myself. I needed his hugs - they were fuel to my soul and validation of my worth in my screwed up psyche.

But he didn't appear the next day or the day after.... Covid had hit and everyone was directed to shelter in place and he did so with his family. I was quarantined alone in a foreign country without any friends to speak of; I was sick with worry about friends and family in the US, especially my elderly parents with pre-existing conditions; I was concerned about me getting sick and trying to navigate the logistical and financial implications (without income or insurance) of illness alone in a country whose language I didn't speak beyond a few pleasantries; I didn't have Internet or news to speak of; I listened with frustration and fear every time public announcements with updates about the situation were given in Turkish, clueless as to what was going on. I was a spiral of solitary doom and gloom with no one and nothing to help break that loop.

My plans to go to Italy and the US were thwarted by the virus and my lease was expiring. Kaş is a seasonal tourist town and all apartments I was aware of were already taken (except for a tiny studio I had declined because it just wouldn't work for numerous reasons). On top of that, my residence permit was expiring imminently. I hadn't applied for renewal or extended my lease because I had planned to be gone for at least six months. I was uncharacteristically overwhelmed. My concerns felt endless and my aloneness felt starker than ever.

Covid started spreading rapidly throughout Turkey and we were quarantining with increasing frequency. Being "confined" to any extent made me feel extremely restless and uneasy. I was alone with none of my favorite occupations to distract me from my feelings I did not care to contend with. I wasn't even allowed to take my long seaside walks that always made me feel so much better. We were allowed to go to the grocery store closest to us during limited hours. I took advantage of that little leeway and walked back and forth repeatedly to the closest store, which unfortunately was only a few blocks away. That wasn't doing it for me.

My ability to continue repressing my memories and associated emotions was being seriously challenged consistently now from a lack of distractions. I had always prided myself on my subconscious' ability to repress and my endless skill at compartmentalizing to "shield" myself - at least superficially - from the emotional, physical and sexual abuses I had endured throughout life. I prided myself on my mental fortitude, my resiliency and adaptability - seemingly endlessly picking myself up and moving "forward" or so I naively thought.

Immersed in quarantined solitude, I could no longer avoid my nagging thoughts. Life didn't feel as fulfilling as I had been trying to convince myself half-heartedly that I thought it was. I started desperately missing Bilal. *"Why?"*, I wondered again to no avail, was I having such a difficult time letting go of him. *"Why*?" did I continue to put up with his behavior despite how clear it was that it was wrong?

For decades, I had erroneously thought I was moving forward, *"escaping"* my past via my successive relationships. In reality, however, I was just **repeating** my past, each new relationship a futile attempt to escape from the last painful one, each time ending in new pain and catapulting me on to the next disastrous one. I truly thought with all my heart and soul that I would die married to Yanni. I trusted him more than myself given my troubled past and issues. Nothing has shocked nor pained me more in my life than him leaving me.

Somehow I had felt I had been miraculously healing, whether from the mere passage of time or my unbelievable ability to keep moving "on". I thought my ability to open my heart anew no matter how many times it had been broken was a testament to my healing in some way. It was only with hindsight and the realizations that accompanied writing this book that it struck me that I had in a way come "full circle" if you will in the worst way possible.

The cumulative damage done to my psyche, with the most painful being the most recent in the form of Yanni's abandonment, had brought me to Bilal. We could not have been more mismatched, from the glaring obvious communication challenge to the more subtle yet no less significant myriad other ways we differed. He lacked any initiative or ambition whatsoever and had no interest in doing anything of a personal or professional nature. Our contrasts could not be more stark between my passionate, energetic, hyper persona to his disinterest in anything but his beloved football team, sleeping and sex.

He was the polar opposite of Yanni's larger than life, ambitious, driven personality and huge ego and vanity. I think that's what had attracted me to him in some ways, having been burned by Yanni's ego. Whereas Yanni had difficulty pulling himself away from the mirror or allowing room in any conversation for anything that didn't pertain to him, Bilal was not the least bit vain, superficial or into appearances. What I hadn't realized before now was that I had basically come back full circle to characteristics sharply in contrast to Yanni but akin to BS. Like BS, Bilal enjoyed spending money - mine - while having no ambition to make it. They were both incredibly apathetic. In both cases, I really felt neither "seen" nor "heard". Neither one ever seemed to do anything thoughtful for me, even something as simple as making me dinner, leaving me a loving note or bringing me a wildflower.

No man has treated me as a mere means to an end more consistently or glaringly as Bilal. I would actually say to him, "I am not your bank. I am not a whore." I could recognize the sad reality that I wasn't being treated right but still couldn't do anything about it. I thought I had been progressing on my healing journey. I was actually regressing. As the saying goes, sometimes you have to hit rock bottom. I realized that's what I had done with Bilal and hard.

So what's great about hitting rock bottom? There's nowhere to go but up. So I got up... again. I was determined to change the patterns I was repeating but still was clueless how. As I was searching for answers, I heard of a book, "Lucid Dreaming Made Easy", by Charlie Morley. I was instantly intrigued though it admittedly sounded a little "otherworldly" to me initially. I had listened to an interview of Mr. Morley by Dr. Mark Hyman, a doctor I had followed with great interest and respect for decades before he had even garnered the well-deserved notoriety he enjoys today. Dr. Hyman's "association" with Mr. Morley gave the concept all the credibility I needed.

Very simplistically put, the thesis of the book is that one can "train" to become lucid in one's dreams, enabling the dreamer basically to direct the narrative of the dream. As I have mentioned, I had always been fascinated with dreams. Mine were often disturbing and confused me but intuitively I felt my subconscious was trying to alert me. I had never really paid attention because I didn't understand their message or import. They frequently had a bizarre, often sexual or violent tone and I was cognizant of recurring themes for which I had no explanation.

Being familiar with a bit of my history now, you are likely shocked that I failed to appreciate why the subject matter of my dreams was often sexual or violent in nature, as was I with a little reflection. I wasn't consciously afraid though nor aware of my bizarre affinity with sex. These topics were things I had spent my life repressing and suppressing so the meaning of the dreams were lost on me. I shied away from any messages my dreams were trying to send me. This is the primary reason I always struggled with sleep.

The practice of lucid dreaming is used to achieve a wide array of goals - ranging from the most superficial desire to have sex with celebrities to a desire to heal a disease and a host of things in between, like learning a foreign language. Immediately I knew that, to the extent I could achieve lucid dreaming, I would utilize it to try to heal my past, the childhood sexual abuse being my exclusive focus. I still didn't appreciate the need to address the attempted murder or other physical violence. The practice sounded a little "out there" for my sensibilities but I was extraordinarily interested in the power to **heal one's self** using one's subconscious. If I could "take charge" of my troubling dreams, I thought maybe I could truly let my past go.

All my girlfriends deeply believed in things like psychics, tarot readings and the like. Although I politely respected their beliefs, I never ascribed to any of it whatsoever. I remember Kathy coming to visit me in Napa for my birthday. When she saw a psychic store she excitedly announced she was gifting me a psychic reading, confident I would thereafter be a convert. Ugh, I thought, despite the generosity. What an absolute waste of money. Worse, the people pleaser in me didn't want to upset her when I wouldn't be able to disguise my disbelief, or worse, withhold laughter depending on whatever nonsense I anticipated the psychic would spew forth.

"Ohhhhh. You know that's not my thing. Couldn't you just treat me to a glass of champagne or something?" I lovingly winked at her. She was not amused. Fortunately for me, said psychic seemed to never be present nor answer repeated phone calls from Kathy despite the ever present flashing neon "Open" sign in her window. "Can't you telepathically schedule an appointment with her?" I good-naturedly teased. Again, Kathy, not amused. She did, however, treat me to a lovely birthday lunch instead and the restaurant gave us complimentary champagne when they found out it was my birthday. Who's psychic now?

Lucid dreaming, on the other hand, greatly appealed to me because it involved the power of harnessing my own mind and energy to resolve my own issues. I always prided myself on the power of my mind to protect my psyche basically by repressing things. I have an extraordinarily difficult time trusting anyone. Lucid dreaming spoke to me because I would be relying on myself.

I was intrigued and looked up the book. I even thought I had purchased an online version but apparently had not. In part I know because I was afraid to delve into my subconscious and unleash my repressions and in part because I felt like my defense mechanism of repressing continued to work just fine. I also didn't really know what I hoped to achieve in my dreams if I did achieve lucid dreaming. I felt confident in my ability to lucidly dream productively but I needed to have a specific goal in mind to achieve it. I wasn't ready... Nonetheless, I was fascinated by the concept and it remained in the back of my mind.

Despite my evident solitude, my "boyfriend" rarely bothered to message even "hello" or check on me. I felt like I was drowning in solitude. As one of my idols, Audrey Hepburn, expressed, " I was born with an enormous need for affection, and a terrible need to give it". Even though my desire was monogamy, quarantine and Bilal's absence challenged my budding resolve. I soon began taking solace in the affection of others who weren't quarantining as rigorously as Bilal and/or had exemptions, like the police and local military.

My first encounter was a gorgeous man who spoke pretty good English and had apartments to rent - jackpot, I thought in relief. It quickly became apparent he didn't want any actual relationship per se - he had endured a marital break up with an ugly custody situation. His apartments also were a bit too far from the center of town and also more than I was willing to pay. He was affectionate though, we had great physical chemistry and he wasn't seeing anyone else so of course I took what I could get. Sign me up for my love addiction chemical cocktail please, I immediately thought.

I messaged Bilal - because I extend the same fidelity I demand - wanting to be crystal clear that we were done. To this day, I don't know if he fully appreciated what I said or just ignored it. Our language barrier was particularly challenging unfortunately when it came to communications that were more important. I'm guessing he didn't fully grasp my meaning because he periodically messaged, full of loving emojis and continued calling me "my baby" in Turkish.

Fast forward a couple weeks, I was super stressed about both my permit and lease expiring and very stressed about the financial implications, so I took the extremely tiny studio I had already rejected as "unworkable". It was about 200 square feet, consisting of one room and a small bathroom. Nonetheless, I was grateful and particularly fortunate that it was in front of the sea in the center of town. I was nervous, however, because of my need for privacy and my major hypervigilance. The studio had zero privacy, the entire front was sliding glass doors. It felt like an aquarium - any passerbys literally looked directly into the tiny living space. There were curtains of course but it was ground floor with a low ceiling and cavelike with the curtains closed. It also had no windows so if I wanted any air circulation, the door had to be left open - literal steps from the bed where I would be sleeping. It also had no kitchen or space to speak of (cooking was my therapy), no chair or table (and I was writing), no WiFi/tv (no more news or mindless distractions in my familiar, comforting native tongue), etc.

Fortunately I knew Kaş is extraordinarily safe - my issues were psychological - not based on any legitimate concern. I focused on my blessings, as I'm always inclined to, and mustered my trademark determination, knowing I would make it work. I accepted my psychological issues as challenges I would overcome. I had no other choice....

Chapter 7
The Reckoning: Shattered Glass: Time to Heal (for real)

The Answer: "Why" Do the Work

I made several trips back and forth between my new and old "homes", a couple miles apart, lugging all my possessions with me, an oft-repeated occurrence. I honestly think I was always at my best when challenged, uber focused on the task at hand and determined to deal with everything solo, never one to ask for help. I made my tiny studio as homey as possible as I always try, no matter how transient my stay may be. As I have recounted, I'm not a "materialistic" person but I have a somewhat obsessive need to be with "my things". I have a fundamental need to surround myself with a few familiar comforts. I sorely lacked continuity in my life and had had to basically part with almost all my worldly possessions. A few tiny mementos I managed to still have had become even more meaningful to me.

I had collected postcards from my travels and taped those and photos of family and friends on the bare walls as my decor and base of familiarity. I had a tiny pewter Buddha that accompanied me everywhere, resident bedside. I had some favorite bookmarks despite having had to leave most books behind and a couple of sentimental pens I was using to work on my various books. I traveled with an aromatherapy diffuser to help my mood and sleep. I had no tables so I resourcefully turned empty boxes upside down and covered them with little Turkish towels, a la my college dorm room. Essential oils, with which I'm obsessed, took center stage around the tiny room, ensuring me that whatever comfort I may need was only a sniff away. I hung some of my favorite scarves in an attempted artistic manner. Fresh herbs in strategically placed little espresso cups fragrantly completed my so-called decorating efforts. I had taken a little beat up table from outside, covered it with a tablecloth and set that up in a corner as my "office." Thankfully I was able to put my suitcases under it as there was no other space. I was happy that my exercise mat just fit in front of the sliding door, promising me that my daily routine was possible.

Fortunately, due to the quarantine, I had yet to regularly contend with people inevitably looking in as they passed by my tiny aquarium-like diminutive studio. There was a little yard in front of the building that, because of quarantine also, I had to myself save for the ever present slugs, snails, spiders and ants. The yard was unkempt and overgrown but there was a splintered abandoned picnic table where I could write overlooking the Mediterranean Sea, a dream come true I didn't even know I had. I was doing pretty well I thought thanks to the proximity of Mother Nature and the lack of people.

My move and fixing up my new "home", in addition to trying to extend my residency, gave me a temporary set of distractions that occupied my mind sufficiently to push my thoughts of healing to the background. My lifelong nature of repressing wasn't easily dismissed. I kept telling myself that things were fine and that I was basically healed. After all, I wasn't spending any time with Bilal (of course, that fact was not attributable to my resolve but to him complying strictly with the quarantine).

During the height of the pandemic, I traveled several hours by bus for my residency extension and stayed overnight only to find out the immigration office was closed due to Covid, despite me having called to confirm my appointment. I was exhausted and frustrated, being an "illegal immigrant" technically at this point, as I contemplated the long journey back with a weary heart and soul. My frustrations increased as I finally figured out after waiting for the bus on the expressway for hours in the hot sun that there were no buses because a lockdown had just been put in place, the first of many. I had to spend an exorbitant amount of money to take a taxi back. I was completely deflated having spent a lot of time and money accomplishing nothing. Why can't I catch a break, I thought to myself, no one around to commiserate with. I was ready to give up and go back to the US. I couldn't though as now I was technically an "illegal immigrant".

The next few weeks challenged my attempts to convince myself that I was healed as I traversed down a much-recognized pattern of many men and much wine. I was untethered from an actual relationship and slowly feeling more and more untethered even from the world and indeed myself. I felt like the loneliest person in a figurative sea of men. I was engaging in a self-destructive path, reminiscent of my college years and again after the demise of my first marriage.

It wasn't the silence of being alone that tormented me. It was the incessant noise in my head that it enabled that tormented me. The jarring, pounding, interminable presence of my thoughts I tried so desperately to avoid.

I was trying to keep myself as busy as possible to avoid drowning in my thoughts and creeping fears and sorrows. I lacked the "benefit" of distractions that had always been my repressive nature's saving grace. I lived alone basically for the first time in my life. I had gone from home to school roommates to marriage(s) and live-in boyfriends. I had almost always been in a relationship. Single and I did not make comfortable companions. I could easily amuse myself for endless hours during daylight. I wasn't bored but I needed affection regularly, it's like a drug for me. If I'm not physically interacting, I feel unloved since I equate sex and love. I was not able to travel, my favorite distraction; I was quarantined most of the time; and was without Internet or tv for mindful or mindless, as they may be, comforting distractions.

Despite excessive drinking and sleepless nights in my quarantine "solitude", interspersed with random sexual encounters (not everyone complied with the quarantine), I still had the gall to try to convince myself that I was essentially "healed".

I was in the midst of writing my book of travel and relationship anecdotes, " I Have Better Places to Go Than Out of My Mind," and had just written a superficially light-hearted defense of my repressive coping mechanisms to "deal with" a lifetime of traumas. Traveling and engaging in whirlwind relationships were my stalwart distractions. I was adamant I didn't need to proceed further on my healing journey despite never having fully "processed" my traumas. In reality, barely processing at all. Not only did I not know ***how*** to, I didn't appreciate ***why*** I needed to. I scoffed at the need to heal in large part, honestly, because I had no clue how. It seemed elusive to me and I didn't care to waste time futilely trying to "heal".

One morning I was trying to exercise but my thoughts couldn't escape me. Yanni had sent me a disturbing video that I couldn't shake from my head. It was from an awards ceremony for his induction into his company's "Million Dollar Club" in Mexico. This signified that he had sold at least $1,000,000 in timeshare sales. I watched with mixed emotions, the video focused on him while someone was making an introductory speech for his award. I hadn't seen him since I had left Mexico so just the sight of him was emotional. I had to focus on listening to the actual words. He said he sent me the video as a sort of "thank you", crediting me for being instrumental in helping him achieve this accolade.

The speech was full of laudatory praise, highlighting Yanni's supposed past successes with restaurants throughout Greece and restaurants and a winery in Napa, California. The speaker noted that Yanni had come to Mexico to sell timeshare as a sort of hobby, having garnered much wealth and acclaim from his prior businesses. I watched in pain as Yanni appeared humble sitting next to his cousin, while others looked at him in smiling praise. His cousin and I were the only ones aware that these alleged achievements were bold-faced lies.

He had been the love of my life and I realized that he was living as inauthentically as I had been. It made me desperately sad on his behalf that he couldn't be true to himself. It also made me profoundly sad on my behalf that my unconditional support was such that he could think that I would welcome that painful video. I truly believe he sent it as a sincere thank you to me and in recognition of my support - the precise support that had caused him to leave me because he wanted exclusive credit. Of course, it also didn't help my mood knowing he was apparently financially successful now, a fact from which I was not benefiting despite drowning in debt. *For the record, he eventually paid me half of the initial debt that he said he would but only after years of mounting exorbitant interest and fees. Plus, I had never thought half was equitable as I noted before.

My attempts to exercise in my tiny studio to "get out of my head" were ineffectual to break the incessant loop of thoughts the import of the video had prompted. I was reflecting, still silently trying to embrace my defense of my coping mechanisms, grappling with the after effects of the prior night's over imbibing in wine, feeling deep down that something was terribly "off".

My wine glass, located on a counter several feet from me, spontaneously, inexplicably shattered into countless shards, breaking me out of my "stupor" of thoughts.

I always joked that I had nine lives, having survived the attempted murder, two suicide attempts and countless reckless behaviors. I knew I hadn't really been living any of the hypothetical lives (or chapters of my life) to the fullest. I also always joked that I had a guardian angel that I nicknamed "Tipsy" who always managed to save me from any serious consequences of my questionable behavior and my life that increasingly seemed to be unraveling. I do believe in "energy" and usually exuded positive energy - but not that morning. I don't know why the spontaneous shattering occurred but it got my attention and made me chastise myself to stop trying to lie to myself.

The incident was the catalyst for some additional serious self reflection, in part related to Yanni, but in reality a much more expansive contemplation of the enigma that was I. Most recently that reflection had centered around Bilal when I finally had started to question myself, my behavior, my relationship. I knew, however, that he too was merely the source of the most recent "why" in a long string of inexplicables. "*Why*?", I kept asking myself critically. *Why*, if I were "sufficiently healed", was I still engaging in reckless behavior? *Why* couldn't I bear to be alone? *Why* did I continue to struggle terribly with sleep? *Why* did I continue to allow myself to be used financially despite being technically bankrupt? *Why* did I continue to be in disrespectful, abusive relationships? *Why* did I keep having panic attacks? *Why* was I just biding time, fully aware I was living a subpar life? *Why* did I suddenly have a nagging, inexplicable headache the past couple of weeks unusually centered in my front temple, the site of the hippocampus, the part of the brain responsible for memories?

The "Why," that was particularly nagging, was "*Why*," was I struggling so much to make progress on my various fledgling books on topics I was so passionate about?

I had endless stories to tell and had been writing for years, yet to actually finish a book. Family and friends had encouraged me to write for years. The time was undoubtedly ripe. I most definitely had huge financial motivation given my crushing financial situation and I had plenty of free time to immerse myself in writing.

So *"why,"* I chastised myself, was I immersed in paralyzing doubt, seemingly incapable of finalizing anything. I had been traveling extensively for over 15 years with a large collection of geographies, experiences, relationships, trials, tribulations and triumphs to share. I rarely met anyone who wasn't intrigued by my very un-convent-ional life. I was obsessed with wellness and sharing useful information when solicited, armed with my passionate interest, extensive reading and my foundation in natural health and fitness. I practiced what I preached (sans sleep and alcohol) and it was reflected in my health and fitness levels.

I contemplated whether my inability to finish was due to my "inexplicable" lack of self-esteem. I simply felt like I didn't have anything worthwhile to say that anyone would care to read. I had felt the same inexplicable crisis of confidence after the attempted murder with respect to practicing law, despite having excelled at my career for almost two decades. It was a primary reason for quitting my career. That lack of confidence had only gotten increasingly worse after my first divorce. I felt worthless because I wasn't fulfilling my purpose of being a means to an end. After I quit my job, I could no longer even rely on the objective "validations" of my worth (my salary and accolades).

Not only did I grapple with feelings of extremely low worth and self-esteem, however. After the crushing demise of my second marriage, I just truly didn't care any more. Historically I had been a spirited, passionate, energetic soul but I felt as if I were suffocating under a cloak of lethargy I just couldn't seem to escape from. I was squandering my life and my potential. *I knew I wasn't living my best life and I knew it was time to reclaim myself.*

It also dawned on me that writing would force me to relive so many traumatic events and feel so many emotions I had worked so diligently to suppress. *It's time to heal, however, I finally promised myself,* the symbolism of the shattered glass having not been lost on me. I still couldn't see a path out of my destructive behaviors though. Now I appreciated *why* my life needed a major overhaul but I still didn't know *how* to heal....

My decision to heal necessitated a lot of reflection. It required me to delve into everything I had mastered repressing/suppressing/

compartmentalizing. I realized to truly "feel" again, to truly "live", I needed to feel **everything**, including the pain, the fear and other emotions I had been avoiding for years. For those years, I had numbed myself into an alcoholic stupor of essential unconsciousness to be able to sleep. I was painfully fraid to sleep, petrified of what my subconscious would disclose to me in my dreams, lurid details of traumatic events I had become expert at consciously suppressing. Every day as evening approached, I would feel an all consuming restlessness, extremely uncomfortable being alone. I had mastered keeping myself busy throughout the day in solitude but struggled relentlessly at night whenever I was alone - alone with my thoughts, without anyone to "protect" me or distract me. None of it made sense to me rationally but I couldn't convince myself that I was fine, that I was safe. So I turned to alcohol and a stream of men.

There were times when I would wake up in the middle of the night, either startled that I had a sleeping companion or cognizant of his presence but unsure of his identity until I opened my eyes. It had become the norm the morning after drinking to inventory condoms to know if I had had sex with a virtual stranger or how many times. I had a morning ritual of scrolling through my texts to piece together the events of the previous night. I was so drawn to sex, it was a primary soothing mechanism, a coping mechanism, it was my "validation". Yet, I was compelled to drink heavily to engage in it because of my weird association with sex from a young age. **Why** did I care so little about myself that I was drowning my pain in alcohol and doubly risking my health by playing a kind of sexual Russian roulette with my body?

I was self aware enough to recognize the dualism at best, or the hypocrisy at worst, of writing my book on natural health, "**Mediterranean Me**", a layman's guide to achieving optimal health via natural means, a la the Mediterranean lifestyle I had been blessed to be living for several years. I was taking care of my body obsessively in certain ways while I was simultaneously poisoning and inflaming my body with binge drinking, harming my physical and mental well being with sleep deprivation and unquestionably offering up my body to a stream of random men in exchange to avoid sleeping alone.

I was embarrassed by my behavior and inevitably felt shameful. More often than not, I was also remorseful about the prior night's events, which often included emotional outbursts, triggered by ongoing disrespect from my companions, and unleashed by the un-inhibiting effect of the alcohol. Sober me couldn't find my voice to articulate my self worth and belief that I should be treated better. "In vino veritas" - in wine, there is truth. I always regretted the manner in which I chose to communicate my feelings but I generally meant what I said. I was always fearful of losing the object of my outburst (even though I was being mistreated), which made me even needier and clingier. I could no longer deny my reality or suppress the trauma catalysts for my reckless behaviors.

I had ignorantly thought that I was "healed" based merely on my knowledge of my traumas and a handful of therapy sessions. Formerly inexplicable behavior to me had became understandable once I recalled my childhood sexual abuse. I had done nothing with my knowledge and understanding, however, to change my undeniable pattern of abusive relationships. I was spiraling out of control, fearing I couldn't escape the cycle.

I had thought my mere awareness would be a sufficient catalyst to change my behavior. Deep down, I knew it was ***necessary but not sufficient.*** Despite my appreciation of the catalysts for the subpar existence I was living and my desire and relatively new determination to change it, ***I simply could not***.

Failure and I are not frequent companions and I have trademark discipline and resolve. I am blessed with a powerful, relentless mind and when I put my mind to something, I am fortunate to generally be successful. I no longer wanted to live a sub-optimal life where time seemed to be passing by rapidly without much to show for it. I ignorantly thought at the time that I could basically "will power" my way out of the subpar existence I had been meandering through aimlessly lately. I just needed to focus, I ignorantly told myself. Mere "surviving" had been the story of my life of late. Time to change the story, I resolved. I wanted to thrive and realize my potential, whatever that looked like.

Lucid Dreaming: A Brush with Self Healing

My reveries nudged me and I remembered the Lucid Dreaming book I erroneously thought I had already purchased. I realized I had pushed that emotional confrontation down the road and hadn't actually bought it. I got excited, thinking maybe it held the answer to my healing conundrum. The next time I was able to go out, I went to the village square to get Internet and downloaded it with mixed trepidation and hopefulness.

I started reading it, vacillating between those emotions - having trepidation about what more I would unrepress and something akin to hopeful elation about truly being able to let go of past traumas potentially. I had always worried about whether somehow my flashbacks were a bizarre figment of my imagination. Deep down, I knew they weren't. No one randomly starts having vivid flashbacks about abuse without a basis, but thus far I had held on to that glimmer of hope and I knew the path I was embarking on would (*Freudian" - I had intended "could") dissipate that hope.

As you recall, I also had disclosed the abuse to my mom, spontaneously, and I desperately wanted to be able to tell her I was mistaken to shield her from that pain.

In addition to reading about lucid dreaming, I started jotting down notes about my traumas and associated feelings. I've often heard of "journaling" as a therapeutic outlet to heal trauma. Until I started writing this book, I had never done any sort of real journaling per se. It ran afoul of my repressive persona. Writing about what you are trying to repress is obviously counterintuitive. Once I became determined to truly focus on healing and moving on, I decided to "journal" my thoughts in a more frequent and disciplined manner as an adjunct therapy to trying lucid dreaming. The moment I started writing, I found that memories and written words flowed, cathartically. My repressive "strategy" having changed to one of journaling and "releasing", I couldn't get the words out quickly enough. My hand couldn't keep up writing with the speed with which my brain gratefully released a lifetime of memories of painful events.

That's the thing about coping/defense mechanisms. They're so deep rooted and so profoundly powerful at "protecting" us, they are a definite force to contend with. You have to do so consciously, decisively and determinedly. Once I finally was truly honest with myself, recognized the need to heal and determinedly decided to do so, I "unrepressed" my memories with surprising ease. That's the thing about repressed memories, they are still "there". You just have to access them once you decide to permit yourself.

I could also tell my subconscious had been warming up to the idea of repressing, under the guidance/"permission" of my conscience. I have always had recurring dreams with "scary" stairs - scary in that they were endless and/or precarious or I had to pass through impossibly small passageways requiring the dexterity of a conformist or Cirque du Soleil performer. I've also always said I thought falling down stairs would likely be my demise, the origin of this feeling unknown. I've never known how to interpret that recurring theme about stairs. Soon after I began focusing on lucid dreams, I had a dream with stairs that were cluttered - not steep, precarious, scary, etc. I managed to navigate around the clutter no problem and even discovered a shortcut. I now think that the stairs represented some sort of obstacle or fear that I needed to overcome and I was heartened by the dream. I took it as a sign that I was ready to face whatever revelations and healing may lie at the "end of the stairs".

I quickly became a firm believer in "journaling" as a powerfully healing, cathartic tool. My writing was translating into real time revelations. Another seemingly bizarre recurring dream I always had was being in an "enclosed house" within a house. Like a secret space embedded in the house I was in. Literally a possible explanation of this came to me as I was writing that. My first thought was that I was longing for a safe "sanctuary" within my home, home being the site where all my abuses had occurred. Then I quickly had a second aha moment, where I felt in my stomach that the "inside house" also represented the "sanctuary" of my subconscious where the memory of my abuses had been hidden. The embedded house is always inviting, warm, cozy.....

One of the extremely useful tips Mr. Morley makes is to note in detail any recurring dreams. It's astounding to me how dreams that formerly seemed so bizarre and baseless can make perfect sense to me when I really can appreciate the symbolism and delve into the underlying meaning. I bought Freud's book on dreams decades ago based on my fascination and troubling relationship with dreams. I never found insight. I don't think I had been "ready". I also realize that I have endured an array of abuses from different abusers and I think a lot of my "bizarre" dreams are a hodgepodge collection of various abuses/abusers that only I am equipped to unravel and gain insight from.

I have had a troubling combination of insomnia, horrific dreams and very early morning wake ups for decades - since high school and the first overdose. My most troubling recurring dreams involve people trying to kill me in very imaginative, torturous ways. The dreams generally have an extended terrifying chase preceding the violence or, I should more accurately say, the imminent violence as I always seem to wake myself up just in time. I always joked that I should write for Stephen King because there is nothing conventional or mainstream about the violence.

I also realized that I never called even the most violent dreams, "nightmares". I think intuitively, I at least subconsciously appreciated that they were "messages" to help heal my psyche, akin to the "messages" bodily symptoms give us as to the source of an ailment or the insight to a cure. I had thought I wanted to be a psychologist growing up. I think the interest actually was more of a reflection of my unknown need to heal myself and my ignorance as to how.

As I tried to interpret various garbled dreams with seemingly wholly unrelated events, people and places, I realized that repressions are not neatly, rationally or chronologically filed. My dreams were like a chaotic jumble of intermingled traumas and associated emotions involving different people from all different periods of my life. This makes interpreting the dreams all that more puzzling, challenging to unravel. It required a lot of reflection to discern the meaning of the dreams but I was finally able to make some sense out of what had previously seemed completely nonsensical.

One of the many things I found very interesting about my dreams was the tendency of my subconscious to "substitute" people. For instance if something were troubling me about Yanni, I may substitute BS for him if it's too difficult to confront my husband. I had a very disturbing sexual dream with Bilal after I started focusing on my dreams and I knew my subconscious had "substituted" him for my father. When I awake I realize the substitutions but my subconscious allows me to play around unraveling my emotions in a "safer" less confrontational way.

*I wrote this chapter almost two years before finishing this book. I distinctly remember how optimistic I was during this time in my life about progressing past the undeniable ongoing effects of my prior unresolved traumas. I truly thought, having embraced the "why" I needed to heal with full force and clarity for the first time, together with the potential "tool" of lucid dreaming, that I inevitably would soon heal. I had finally realized my desperate need to heal and I thought at the time that lucid dreaming would be a sufficient means of "processing" and healing the traumas. I still naively thought that my conscious determination to heal sufficiently equipped me for success more or less with a little "dabbling" with my subconscious via dreaming. It is interesting to me to note that I was beginning to appreciate the need to engage my subconscious in my healing battle. It took me the better part of the succeeding two-year period, however, to fully appreciate the role my subconscious was required to play in my healing and to discover the way to effectuate it. That's ok though because in the end I got there.

Chapter 8

The (Slow) Realizations: Core Belief: I Am A Mere "Puppet";

Wired for Survival

When your own father has told you from a young age, implicitly and explicitly, that your only self worth is sex or money, that has an impact to say the least. Unfortunately, it took me a lifetime of abuse, an attempted murder, a couple of overdoses and a pandemic to realize the extent of that impact. That's ok. What matters is that I know it now. What matters is what I do now.

Quarantining relatively distraction less forced me to confront myself and my demons. I finally appreciated that I needed to exorcise those demons I had been masterfully avoiding to stop enabling the beliefs they *embedded* in me. The beliefs that *condemned* me to continue behaving in self-destructive behaviors and intertwining myself in abusive relationships *until I changed those beliefs.* Obviously, the first step was recognizing the beliefs. The second was changing them.

As you have now witnessed, for a lifetime, I've been grappling, unwittingly at first, with the consequences of having been sexually abused at a young age, the sexual abuse *branching* out into other modes of abuse. The sexual abuse gave *root* to the negative, limiting beliefs that more or less destined additional abuses *until I resolved them at the root.* The "means to an end" mentality that I was essentially *programmed* with is pervasive and ugly powerful. It dictated my behaviors in ways I neither understood nor desired.

It was extremely cathartic, though traumatic and agonizingly painful, to have the flashbacks to what I had repressed for a lifetime. It was necessary for me though so I could start to appreciate the consequences of the *abuse on my psyche*. Necessary but not sufficient, however. Now that I understand that abuse has made me voluntarily subjugate myself comprehensively and be reckless with my body and my finances, ***I own my behaviors and my healing.*** I refuse to play the victim any more - subjecting myself to being treated as a means to an end. ***I now realize that I, and I alone, have perpetuated the cycle of abuse in myriad forms and that I have the power to stop it.*** I do not blame myself for my abuses. I do, however, ***empower myself to stop the abuse.***

My own father had defined my worth in a utilitarian manner. My worth being a mere means to an end was programmed in my little impressionable brain at a young formative age. That belief grew more profound as a result of each of my long term relationships, particularly my marriages. BS tried to kill me, enraged at the prospect of no longer benefiting from my lucrative stream of income. Yanni basically cast me and his marriage commitment aside as soon as he started becoming financially successful.

Before my recollections of childhood sexual abuse and subsequent increased conscious self awareness, I had struggled as to why men seemed to universally treat me as a means to an end. It took me several years to realize that my deeply embedded vulnerability subconsciously screamed out for more abuse. My shyness/introverted nature, body language and all, served as a beacon to potential abusers. Subconsciously I portrayed this need to give - my money, my body - because my very worth, my essence, my ***very being*** depended on it in my messed up psyche. It was as if I were in a petrifying, perpetual existential crisis if I were alone because I had no worth whatsoever but to give unquestionably. Obviously that mindset does not bode well for creating a healthy relationship. Those inclined to abuse or take advantage perceive this vulnerability and capitalize on it.

I knew somewhere deep down (way deep down), I had a lot to offer objectively and subjectively. I needed to fundamentally and truly believe that, however, and project it. It took a lot of soul searching and reflection prompted by a lot of solitude forced by quarantining to become consciously aware of the reasons for my behaviors. It was extremely eye opening and therapeutic to me to realize that ***I defined*** myself as a means to an end because that is what I was taught/told and internalized. As long as I internalized the message that I was a means to an end, there were plenty of people waiting to treat and use me as such. Even as I write this, I oscillate between writing in past tense - the eternal optimist in me - and present tense, reflecting the reality that I am most definitely a work in progress. That's ok though because I am progressing and going in the right direction. I've learned to be kind to myself in my healing journey thanks to my greater appreciation of the trauma psyche...

I had lived life as a "puppet" - a toy to be played with at will, discarded at will. If you are a "puppet" - a mere means to the puppeteer's end or whim - you're worthless if no one is pulling your strings. My psyche needed an endless string of puppeteers "pulling my strings" to feel self worth, to feel wanted, to feel loved, to feel safe. The irony is not lost on me that the "puppeteers" were the ones actually hurting, not protecting, me. It didn't matter much if I were interested in the particular puppeteer. I was addicted to having "my strings manipulated". This is how bad it got.

I unquestionably gave my body and risked my sexual, *my physical,* health simply to satisfy other's desires at their fancy. Of course, I was satisfying my skewed need to be "valued", to be "loved", but it didn't matter whether or not I was romantically or even sexually interested. That was irrelevant. I was like an "abyss of holes", literally and figuratively, waiting to be filled.

Not only did I engage in reckless random sex, I also "stayed" with people who physically hurt me and took advantage of me. By "stayed", I mean let live with me and travel with me, all at my sole expense. I lavished gifts on these people and helped them financially. I cared that little about myself, my needs, my desires - aside from fulfilling what I believed was my purpose in life - to serve as a means to an end.

On the rare occasions, I was "untethered to puppeteers", I had suicidal thoughts because the pain of aloneness was too intense for me. By my psyche's definition, if I were alone, I was worthless, I was unloved, I was unsafe. Being alone was an existential crisis. I knew that I would never act on suicidal thoughts again because I didn't want to hurt those I loved. I still wallowed in the thoughts periodically though. I cared that little for myself, my life, my present, my future. It was only my love for others - not myself - that inhibited my execution.

I am a loving, thoughtful, passionate, compassionate, affectionate being but I profoundly felt that I had no self-worth *except* to be a means to another's end. If people weren't taking from me, I had no purpose. *What was wrong with me??? Absolutely nothing*, except my core limiting belief from childhood that I was a mere means to others' ends. That belief dictated my lifelong behavior until I discovered the way to intercede and rewire my brain. It was like I did an intervention on myself.

Writing these incredibly raw revelations is simultaneously very painful and healing.

When you are abused by those who are supposed to love you, you *equate abuse*, in all its various forms, with *acceptance and love.* You fear that if you no longer subject yourself to being taken advantage of, what little worth you have may dissipate and you will be alone, unloved. I was still perceiving myself from the vantage point of a five year old. I had been taught that love is conditional.

I had become utilitarian to myself. This skewed psyche perceives an abusive relationship as vastly preferable to being alone - a relationship to be maintained at any and all costs. If you perceive your only value as what you have to give to others, you have to give incessantly or you will be worthless in your traumatized head. It's like an addiction to subjugation. My addiction had been instilled at a very young age and it had only kept intensifying until I finally realized after decades why I needed to resolve my traumas.

It's no wonder to me why I became even more promiscuous after my financial demise. No longer having any financial means to speak of, being alone felt like an actual threat to my very being, my essence. My need to be with someone became all consuming, no matter how ill-advised or mismatched any particular partner may be; that was simply irrelevant. I had viewed my self worth as two prong - financial and sexual. Once I no longer had the ability to unconditionally, unquestionably, lavishly share my money, the only thing I had of worth to offer was my body. In my skewed psyche, I absolutely had to do that to validate my self worth, my very being. I had been *conditioned* from a young age that it was my obligation and the price of love, of bonding and of safety. If I weren't "giving", I wasn't loved, I wasn't safe. There is also a heady cocktail of feel good hormones released during sex, including oxytocin (the "cuddle" hormone) to which I had essentially become addicted.

It took me a very long time to appreciate the need to resolve my childhood traumas, which had paved the way to the physical abuses I endured at the hands of my first husband and live-in boyfriends. It took me until I wrote this book to appreciate that I needed to resolve my adulthood traumas, despite my ever present recognition of my hyper vigilance, insomnia and terrifying dreams. Childhood sexual abuse had activated nervous system responses of "freeze" and "fawn" while my adulthood physical, violent abuses had catapulted me into "fight" and "flight" mode. My last husband's callous abandonment had quagmired me in the paralyzing depths of "freeze" mode again.

Quite frankly my nervous system is dysregulated AF, firmly stuck in, and vacillating amongst, fight, flight, fawn and freeze states, at times exhibiting more than one reaction simultaneously. This is *why* I had a lifelong struggle with being alone and with sleeping. I was borderline *petrified*. This is *why* I have been a lifelong people pleaser, a fawner. This is *why* I react in such a volcanically volatile manner when triggered. This is *why* I had periodic suicidal thoughts. Fear, insecurity, low self-esteem and restlessness permeate my being. ***I am stuck in exhausting, depleting, all consuming survival mode most of the time.*** This is *why* I was living a limited life, far less fulfilled than I knew I could, that I knew I wanted to. It is not lost on me that I alternate between past and present tense, a reflection of the ongoing conflict within me.

No matter how irrational these fears may have been consciously, I was helpless to change them until I changed my underlying beliefs ***and*** until I regulated my skewed nervous system. Viewed from the perspective of ***survival mode***, quite frankly, my behaviors that may seem bizarre make perfect sense. At the risk of sounding melodramatic, I was "captive" to others - to feel loved, to feel worthy, to be safe. To stay "safe", you pacify your "captors" - you give them what they "demand".

I vehemently reject any ongoing "victim" characterization, despite the terminology I use as an analogy to describe my troubled psyche. Once I recognized the source of my behavior, it was incumbent on me to change my behavior. I am not excusing anyone's abuse whatsoever but I now take accountability of my own behavior throughout my relationships for allowing myself to be treated as a mere means and for subjugating myself. I am not judging myself; I appreciate that I was mirroring my behavior from what had been modeled to me.

I am empowering myself; my adult self has the power to stop the abuse. I fully appreciate now that *I owe me.* I owe myself to express my needs and desires, to make sure they are fulfilled and, most definitely, to not tolerate abusive behavior in any form. At times, I may still be haunted/confronted by my past but I am no longer relegated to the responses indicative of a scared child or a weak utilitarian subservient. *It's over; I am in control.* This instills profound optimism in me.

I want to clarify that, even in the midst of these various relationships, for the most part, I was happy notwithstanding the relationship issues or the often ballistic ending thereof. Post-BS, I have love and respect for my various partners. Each one of these men had a role to play in my healing journey and I am grateful for the impact each had on my life. *I love unconditionally,* expansively, empathetically and healing has given me greater insights into others' behaviors and my participation in the unraveling of relationships. I haven't let the bad moments or the eventual dramatic destruction of the relationships take away my good memories.

I also think for the most part that each of these men is a good person. I realize that they all had their own issues driving their behaviors. That does not excuse abusive behavior but it helps me appreciate that it wasn't "about me". I absolutely flinch when I hear people say we are "teaching" people how to treat us. I understand the point - no one is going to treat you better than how you treat yourself; you're teaching people what you will tolerate etc. I absolutely disagree. I agree that I should show myself self respect because I deserve it. Struggling with that because I have issues does not excuse others' *abusive* behaviors. I should not have to teach people to treat me with the mutual respect that I show them and it is most certainly not incumbent on me to teach them not to abuse me. The self respect I owe myself is to leave a relationship where I am not getting the reciprocity or worse when I am being abused, physically or emotionally.

I also am deeply aware that I am fully responsible for my own happiness.

As I've noted, I have always fundamentally been a happy person despite circumstances, challenges or subpar relations. That's because happiness is within me and always will be. No one else is responsible for my happiness. I solely am. That's an incredibly powerful and wonderful thing that no one can take away from me.

I now realize that I was not as happy as I could have been, however, had I shown myself self respect and been true to myself. I always said infidelity/betrayal was my deal breaker. I was being unfaithful to myself, my authentic persona. I was betraying my needs and desires. Again, to clarify, these realizations do not mean I am excusing my various partner's behaviors. These realizations are for my benefit, not for theirs. It's my realization that I am in control.

A lot of people wonder why I don't get angry or bitter and how I can open my heart so easily, endlessly. Quite frankly, anger is far worse than pointless. As Buddhism says, holding on to anger is like drinking poison and expecting the other person to die. Yes, these men "caused" me pain but I refuse to let them take away my happy memories and I take accountability for my behavior in the relationships as well. This is an incredibly empowering and insightful realization that I am certain will serve me well in my relationships going forward.

The time that I was my least happiest was when I was living so inauthentically with BS. I certainly have accountability for that failing to live authentically. Honestly it kind of amuses me that I can't think of too many particularly fond memories with him. I think that my primary happiness was through immersing myself in my career at the time even though it was so exhausting and stressful. Particularly when I worked at in-house corporate jobs I really enjoyed my work and it kept me sufficiently engaged and distracted from my less than stellar personal relationship. I actually was racking my brain to try to think of memorable moments. One of the things that still cracks me up to this day is when we were on our honeymoon in Hawaii. BS was always so cheap. When we would take a vacation and our hotel had complimentary breakfast, he would have me make little sandwiches so we could eat those for lunch later in the day instead of having to buy lunch. I was working my ass off as a lawyer making good money and all I cared about was to have a nice vacation. He would fixate on every penny we spent keeping all the receipts and adding up the expenses at the end of each day, making me feel guilty for trying to reap the rewards of working. As you have probably ascertained, we weren't being extravagant to start with. Along the same lines, when we were in Hawaii for our honeymoon, there was a coupon for parking which stated "turn in at exit". I still laugh uproariously to this day remembering us driving the wrong way into the parking lot exit (instead of the entrance) and arguing with the parking lot attendant because BS was insistent on using the coupon and insisting if we didn't "turn in" at the exit we wouldn't be able to use it. I don't know why I find that so hilarious but I do know it's pretty sad that this is one of my most memorable experiences of my 15 year marriage. That's all I've got.

*I realize this chapter may be a bit repetitive, long winded or disjointed. The writing is the most reflective of my healing journey though and I vehemently resist revising it. It represents my "real time journaling therapy". The repetitiveness is what was in my head as I was actually working through my realizations. Indeed, I had to stop while I was editing it because it was incredibly impactful to me. I was getting very sad and angry with the realizations of how I had been living my life. The puppet analogy profoundly resonates with me. My emotions were welling up and I was getting a migraine. I stopped editing to have a major release. I even videoed it because I knew it was going to be momentous. I hadn't quite felt that same combination of feelings since I had first started having flashbacks. My "releases" are always impactful but they are usually more of an "out of mind" experience. Even when I cry normally, it's just a release, not a consciously painful experience. This time, however, it was a consciously felt release and it was spectacularly necessary.

My head was throbbing and I felt like it was going to explode - every part of it hurt - unlike my normal headaches which are centered in one area. I started seeing the auras that often accompany migraines. I started crying - hard - something I have done *on my behalf* so infrequently throughout my life. It's funny, when people are crying, a typical response is to tell them not to. It's well intentioned but it's counterproductive. **Cry, scream, let it out.** Healing is "messy" and spontaneous. **Release yourself**, unapologetically. Don't hold it in any longer. I cannot think of any more perfect quote for this paragraph than Paulo Coelho's apt description, "*Tears are words that need to be written.*"

To my extreme pleasant surprise, my budding migraine dissipated. I always had migraines growing up but they resolved later in life. I think I was always holding the weight and pain of my unresolved traumas in my brain. They were metaphorically and in reality inflaming my brain. As I have said, I am now a huge convert to journaling/writing. I was surprised how positively impactful editing has been and I will continue to utilize these therapeutic tools. I know I said people are always surprised that I didn't get angry and I turned around and said I got angry. That's the real time healing. The stark realization of how I had been treated prompted feelings of anger in me but I didn't hold on to them; I let them out. I digress but this is relatively long winded because it was my ongoing healing in progress. I hope you find your outlets and in doing so find your true self too. I hope you *release yourself.*

As I move forward with my new determination, the philosophy major in me is reminded of the edict by the famous philosopher, Immanuel Kant: "Always treat people as ends in themselves, never as a means to an end." I find it particularly enlightening for myself that in a longer quote on the subject, he admonished us to apply it not only to others but to *ourselves* as well - "Act in such a way that you treat humanity, *whether in your own person* or in the person of any other, never merely as a means to an end, ..." Time to do Mr. Kant proud....

"Time to heal," I promised myself with steely resolve. Problem is, I still didn't really know how. What I did know, however, was that when I put my mind to something, there's no stopping me... I was now focused on healing and absolutely confident it was no longer elusive. *It was in my control.*

Chapter 9
Time to Heal (Truly): Why Do the Work; The Science

As I said, I did well academically, likely motivated by my desire to get my father's approval. I was hardly an excellent student though. I was a consummate procrastinator but an excellent "crammer". I spent countless sleepless nights in college composing papers at the typewriter (yes, I am that old) that were due the next day and countless sleepless nights in law school reading chapters of books that we would be tested on the next day. When I thusly "applied" myself, however, it worked.

I now had great resolve to apply myself to fixing my traumatized brain. I knew I hadn't successfully done so with my emotional intelligence so thought I would try to approach the subject matter - me - in a more clinical, academic way. As I said, I fortuitously had been researching the brain in connection with my book on optimizing health naturally, intuitively, *"Mediterranean Me."* I am the consummate multi-tasker and found further motivation in the fact that I could potentially reap the rewards of my research in this dual fashion, serving a purpose for each of the books.

My research fascinated me as I began to better understand - and forgive - my formerly inexplicable behaviors. Most importantly, the research illuminated a path to heal that had formerly eluded me. The science shed great light for me on how I had been living since childhood. Trauma, particularly childhood trauma, has the potential to have far-flung, pervasive psychological and physiological impacts.

Traumatic stress literally changes the brain's physiology - structurally and functionally. There are a few areas of the brain that are particularly vulnerable to being negatively impacted by traumatic stress. These areas include the amygdala (the "fear center"), the hippocampus (the "memory and learning center") and the prefrontal cortex (the "reasoning center").

Given the primary functions of these areas, it is intuitive that trauma can negatively impact our **brains** and our **behaviors**.

The amygdala plays a crucial role in establishing our fear responses. Again, from an evolutionary standpoint, this makes perfect sense. This area of the brain, the fear center appears to be larger generally speaking in those suffering from traumatic stress. The prefrontal cortex regulates emotional responses by inhibiting the amygdala function. This area of the brain tends to get smaller with traumatic stress. ***So the area of the brain which conditions our fear responses increases, while the area of the brain that would tend to "calm" these fear responses gets smaller,*** generally speaking. The third area of the brain primarily impacted by traumatic stress is the hippocampus, which is associated with memory and learning. A smaller hippocampus is frequently seen with people suffering with posttraumatic stress disorder, a condition with which I had been diagnosed following the attempted murder.

The brain will be impacted differently by traumatic stress depending on what stage in development it is in when the stress happens. The brain is largely developed by the age of *five*. It is understandable what a devastating and lasting impact childhood trauma can have on the brain during these critical formative years. This was the time of my abuse when my little brain was forming.

Some people seem to think that trauma that happened so long ago shouldn't have a lasting impact given the passage of time. Indeed, I always thought that there was a problem with me not being able to get over something that had happened decades earlier. I was ashamed at my inability to change my behavior and felt selfish that my behavior seemed to bother others. I have been admonished frequently by people, including Yanni, who thought they were being helpful to just "let it go". Believe me, those of us suffering with the consequences of abuse desperately want nothing more. Admonishing someone to just let it go reflects a complete lack of understanding of the situation. I am not chastising anyone. I was wholly ignorant of how the brain interacted with trauma too. The admonishment, however, is extremely misguided because it makes the traumatized person feel responsible/ashamed for the ongoing trauma effects without providing insight into how to 'let it go".

In cases like mine, as undoubtedly with so many, my traumas had left me with feelings of low self-esteem and self worth and the admonishment more or less made me internalize the trauma even more without addressing it. I didn't want to "bother" anyone with my troubles and was embarrassed I was letting them affect me so I was more inclined to keep them to myself and not deal with them productively. The excellent news is that it was within my power to "let it out"; I had just had to discover how.

The flippant "let it go" version, however, is dismissive of the pervasive ongoing effects of **unresolved** trauma, implying the mere passage of time suffices to erase the consequences thereof. *The exact opposite of the belief that the consequences of abuse magically dissipate with the passage of time is true, however.* The effects of trauma cannot just be magically wished away and they intensify over time if left unresolved.

Ideally, therapeutic intervention would occur soon after a trauma to help ameliorate the negative impacts thereof. Absent resolution of the trauma, the situation can easily and understandably get worse over time as the "conditioned" beliefs and responses become indelible and resistant to change, unfortunately exacerbated by additional ongoing traumas. This is the painfully ugly truth of childhood abuse. Children are the most vulnerable and when primary caretakers are the source of abuse, it's no wonder that childhood abuse has extreme potential to permeate adulthood.

According to the World Health Organization (the "WHO"), a lot of survivors of childhood abuse have "pervasive "and "rigid negative" beliefs about themselves, contending with lifelong feelings of **shame** and **worthlessness**. These beliefs translate into a greater association with: abstaining from sex or being **promiscuous**; increased **substance abuse**; eating and **sleeping disorders**; and **attempted suicide**. Victims of childhood abuse are vulnerable to a host of calamities and relationship issues from their oft-felt "desperation to be loved". *Unconditional love seems elusive, if not impossible, when conditions have always been attached to your ability to receive love,* explicitly or implicitly. *Ding. Ding. Ding for me.*

Seeing myself reflected in the grim statistics temporarily angered me. Seeing the lifelong impact of my childhood sexual abuse in black and white and appreciating the potential pervasive negative impact it can have both psychologically and physiologically pissed me off frankly. I recalled Nuri's concerned warning that I address my issues lest I develop cancer. I truly try to have a grateful and optimistic default outlook though. My research made me more motivated than ever to resolve my traumas and more deeply grateful that I had escaped some of the negative impacts associated therewith. As I said, my "strategy" was to try to "attack" my problems in a somewhat clinical manner having spent a lifetime repressing them.

Now I most clearly had the "*why*" do the work internalized and was ready to "arm" myself with the knowledge of "*how*" to do the work. I had internalized the belief from a young age ("confirmed"/more deeply embedded if you will via multiple relationships) that I was a mere means to an end. My brain had been kind of "hijacked" by my traumas and had actually changed physiologically and psychologically as a result thereof. My brain - and hence my behaviors - had remained captive to my traumas throughout my life. I needed to release myself and finally felt that I had a better understanding of me and that healing was truly possible. I needed to undo the effects that trauma had had on my brain. I needed to change my beliefs to change my brain and change my behaviors. Armed *finally* with the "*why*" I needed to heal and the belief that healing was possible, I promised myself to finally prioritize myself and figure out how to heal.

Of course, it takes concerted determined work to overcome the effects of abuse, but the great empowering fact is that they can be overcome. Blessedly, the ***power to heal is largely in your control***, once you understand how. The excellent news is that the brain has "*plasticity*", it has the potential to change. We can repair the "toxic legacy of childhood abuse" given the proper ***resolution***. As the WHO notes, insufficient attention appears to be given to the long lasting detrimental physiological and mental impacts of childhood abuse. This is a tragedy since the brain is ***capable of healing*** through "neuroplasticity". Our brains are malleable. How incredibly empowering is that?!

PART THREE: HEALING: DOING THE WORK:
BREAKING THE CYCLE OF ABUSE

"One is loved because one is loved. No reason is needed for loving."
Paulo Coelho

Chapter 1
The Turning Point

The cumulative psychological and physiological effects of the abuses I experienced throughout my life, combined with the realization that those abuses had truly altered my brain, finally convinced me. I needed to heal from my traumas in order to live the fullest, most authentic life I could. For decades, I had embodied my trademark c'est la vie attitude of "that's life", trying to convince myself that things were as good as they would get. Although I always managed to be happy and feel blessed, I was, more or less, plodding through life, somewhat haphazardly, aimlessly.

As you have now witnessed, I sort of got stuck in a cycle of repeated patterns of abusive relationships and numbing behaviors. I finally realized that I deserved better, that I wanted more. Time to finally change the absurd loop of self sabotage, sleepless nights and a half-lived life, interspersed with periodic suicidal thoughts and panic attacks, I promised myself (again) with resolve.

Yes, I was happy but I knew I could be more profoundly *happier*. Previously, I had attributed my pattern of abusive relationships to bad luck or happenstance. In reality, my behavior was largely still being dictated by prior unresolved traumas and my relationships were subconsciously modeled after my upbringing. Once I realized this, I needed to gain control and stop perpetuating abusive behavior, including self abuse and assault if you will from my numbing habits and so-called coping mechanisms.

Now I knew "*why*" I needed to heal and firmly **believed I could heal**, but I had yet to really precisely discover "*how*" to heal. The belief I needed to heal and could heal were transformative though because they were precursors. For decades, I had dismissed any need to resolve my traumas because I failed to appreciate the ongoing impact they were having on me. Even when I started gaining an appreciation of that impact, I didn't do anything about it because

I didn't believe I could. I didn't believe because I didn't understand the trauma brain. As long as I didn't believe I could heal, I didn't waste my time in what I perceived as a futile attempt. This is when I was **stuck in survivor mode**, priding myself on my endless ability to get knocked down and pick myself up.

With my new belief that I could heal, it was time to **exit survivor mode** and move into **conquer mode**. It was time to hoist the anchor of my traumas that was holding me "down", rendering me figuratively immobile. I was truly ready to move forward, to "sail on", living this beautiful life to the fullest and realizing my potential to "be all I wanted to be", enabled by my determination and the incredible limitless capacity of our profound brains.

I am reminded of two quotes by the author, Paulo Coelho. The first reflected survivor mode, "*You drown not by falling into a river, but by staying submerged in it.*" I wanted to stop drowning in my trauma; I wanted to swim. The second quote reflects my transition into conquer mode: "*The secret of life, though, is to fall seven times and to get up eight times.*" My "secret" to my healing was to use that "8th time" to figure out how to stop "falling"/getting "knocked down". I now gratefully finally felt it was within my control and that catapulted me to figure out the "how". I resolved to not just "survive" or merely traverse through my traumas but to **triumph over my traumas**.

With my new-found determination to alter the trajectory of my life, I started voraciously researching childhood trauma further in order to answer that question. The results of my research made me not only all the more adamant to stop the seeming insanity of my behavior but also equipped me to do so.

As I said, at the time, I was doing research for my book on optimizing health via lifestyle factors, "***Mediterranean Me***". **Outwardly**, I was the epitome of health, being at my healthiest and fittest. I had family members, friends and even strangers ask me for help to improve their health and fitness based on my personal success. I had absolute conviction in the intuitive advice I was writing, dubbing it the "***K.I.S.S. Plan***", as in "keep it simple, sweetheart". I was obsessed with harnessing the innate wisdom and powers of the body to achieve optimal health with simple, inexpensive healthy lifestyle habits.

Yet, *inwardly,* I was a ticking time bomb in ways, a bit of a tortured soul, and I was struggling to finish the book. I felt kind of paralyzed; it was one of the "why's" that had plagued me. I had nagging, persistent feelings of self doubt and lack of confidence. I was in "freeze" mode. The irony wasn't lost on me either that I was engaging in behaviors counterproductive to my health while espousing health-promoting habits. I was embarrassed that my reality was an insult to my very undertaking. I felt disingenuous and couldn't finish a book on optimizing health until I addressed my profoundly broken psyche that manifested itself physiologically and dictated my few - though significant - unhealthy lifestyle habits that I could no longer ignore.

I continued avidly working on *"Mediterranean Me"*, however, confident in what I had to say though not confident anyone would care to read it. I had a pretty good comprehensive first draft. The last major chunk I wanted to work on was a chapter on optimizing the brain. I became fascinated with the brain and its inner workings.

The timing was extremely fortuitous given my fledgling self-healing journey from abuse. My research on the topic led me to focus on the uber empowering concept of neuroplasticity - the **brain's ability to change,** to strengthen, to grow. This research intertwined perfectly with my research into my "trauma brain". Neuroplasticity synced beautifully with my "K.I.S.S. philosophy" I was espousing of utilizing our innate abilities to optimize our health - physically and mentally.

My research enabled me to appreciate why I was struggling to change my undesirable, often reckless, behaviors. It wasn't from lack of intelligence or discipline or desire. As noted, the **traumatized brain is changed, structurally and functionally,** by traumatic events and our responses to them. This had been an incredibly motivating epiphany that, together with neuroplasticity, made me feel capable of truly healing for the first time. I finally felt I had the solution to stop my seeming spinning out of control.

My brain had been *"programmed"*, if you will, from a lifetime of various traumas, commencing at a tender, impressionable age. Our thoughts, instilled from an early age during the critical period of brain development, create our beliefs, which dictate our behavior. These beliefs are **wired** in our brains. **You must change the thoughts underlying your beliefs that dictate the behavior if you want to change the behavior.** One of my favorite books is "*Anatomy of an Illness*" by Norman Cousins. I love Mr. Cousin's short but prophetic quote: "*Belief becomes biology*".

I had been trying to magically wish away my limiting beliefs about my lack of self worth and that I was a mere means to an end - always someone else's end. Sadly anyone's end - I not only subjugated myself to family members, husbands and boyfriends - but virtual strangers as well. I thought that little of myself. Objectively I had an inkling of the absurdity of my beliefs and behaviors but I had been clueless how to change either.

My newly-discovered knowledge fascinated, motivated and empowered me. I remember sharing my barely-contained excitement with Mike, who, as you know, was intimately familiar with all the momentous details of my life, including my family dynamics and various traumas. I was overflowing with enthusiasm from my confidence that I finally held the key to my healing. Despite having full faith in me and wanting me to be happy more than anyone, he responded that yes, theoretically I could heal, but that the journey would be akin to climbing a mountain. His assessment did not deter me one iota. The more challenged I am, the more determined I am. One of my favorite quotes that embodies my spirit is:

"*Throw me to the wolves and I'll come back leading the pack*." - "Katniss" from *The Hunger Games*

As I said, I have faith in my success when I put my mind to something but I'm careful what I put my mind to. I had only recently appreciated the need to heal and hadn't fully committed to that journey previously because I ***had no idea how to succeed***. My research on the brain and trauma gave me the missing pieces to my healing puzzle. I embarked on my journey with great optimism and determination, confident in my impending success and thrilled that I would be the master of my healing. This deeply resonated with me and the philosophy of my "***K.I.S.S. Plan***" that I was passionately espousing.

Now I fully appreciated not only that my formerly inexplicable behaviors were explicable but also that they could be altered. ***Altered by me. Self healing.*** The timing was perfect, albeit woefully late. The topic I was writing about in "***Mediterranean Me***" and believing with all my heart, soul and passion had segued me into healing from my unresolved traumas, the effects of which had plagued me for all my life, preventing me from achieving optimal health, the end game of *"**Mediterranean Me**"*.

I had intuitively known that I wasn't being completely honest with myself. I had been touting optimal healing holistically while I was overlooking my troubled psyche. Norman Cousin encapsulates well what I was feeling in terms of the wonderful innate healing powers of the body and what had been holding me back from finishing, *"**Mediterranean Me**"* with the following quote:

"The greatest force in the human body is the natural drive of the body to heal itself – but that force is not independent of the belief system. What we believe is the most powerful option of all. The control center of your life is your attitude."

I needed to overcome my limiting beliefs in order to achieve true health. For the first time, I felt truly *in control*. I could barely contain my excitement. With great optimism and enthusiasm, I switched my focus from writing about healing in that book to actually immersing myself in healing and chronicling my journey here. For the first time in my life, I was confident I would heal.

I fortuitously came across the "Holistic Psychologist", Dr. Nicole LePera, on Instagram. Her insights and recommendations profoundly synced with me, a number of her posts giving me full body "chills". I tried some of her posted exercises and they deeply impacted me. I knew I was on the right path. My gut intuition told me that Dr. LePera could provide me with insights into the missing piece of the healing puzzle that had eluded me, *"**how**"* to heal. Excitedly, I purchased her aptly-named book, *"How to Do the Work"* and dove in. This book firmly placed me on the path of healing that had eluded me for decades…

Chapter 2
The Framework: Self Awareness, Self Healing & Holistic Healing

Self Awareness

A consistent fundamental theme throughout "*How to Do the Work*" is the recommendation to become more *self aware, consciously aware.* Obviously, understanding one's self on a deep level and appreciating the source for thoughts, beliefs and behaviors we want to change can be quite enlightening and constructive. I was blessed to have clarity on precise traumas and their impacts to help guide and target my healing efforts. Dr. LePera provided the analytical framework for me to flush out my issues and their pervasive impacts in a way that enabled me to easily take full advantage of her recommendations for resolution thereof.

Dr. LePera provides suggestions for becoming self aware by building consciousness via a "grounding in the present" type exercise where you focus daily for one to two minutes on an "experience", be it something as simple as doing something like the dishes or immersing yourself in nature. The beauty is that this exercise is easily accessible to all of us and is a useful exercise for grounding in general, whether healing from trauma or otherwise.

The goal is to simply "witness" your chosen experience in all its sensory manifestations to be truly present and enable us to escape the chaos of our "monkey minds", where we typically reside. The "monkey mind" is characterized by incessant chatter vying for attention. When you're truly present, your "monkey mind" isn't ruminating about past traumas or regrets or anticipating future troubles. Basically, it's the therapeutic prescription to "stop and smell the roses". I have yet to perfect - or even come close to - meditating. This is the closest I come. I actually gently rock back and forth while I do this "exercise" - it puts me in a peaceful, almost trance-like state, akin to self hypnosis.

I now realize the positive impact these "being present" exercises have on my nervous system and my intuitive rocking is particularly beneficial. The "trick" is to make your brain feel you are safe based on what your body is doing. When you are stuck in a fear-oriented state, engaging in behaviors consistent with being safe helps counter the default state of the trauma brain to perceive danger. Consistently doing this helps to break the hyper vigilant loop. I like to think of it as "embracing yourself in the present". What you choose is completely up to you. I gravitate towards gently rocking in the yoga "child's pose". The great thing is this type of grounding exercise is pretty much accessible to all of us, anytime, anywhere.

I had erroneously thought that I had been "grounded" and "present". Anyone who knew me would have attested that I seemed to have mastered "living in the moment". Neither they nor even I recognized the extent of the overhang my past was having on my present. I was all for living in the moment but didn't appreciate the extent to which the past was still controlling me. I wasn't truly in the moment; I was just jumping from distraction to distraction.

I will forever fondly remember my interaction with a gentleman, Marcel, in Vienna during one of the lowest points of my life. It was shortly after the attempted murder, when I was apathetic about life, briefly but profoundly. I remember American friends calling me regularly to check in on me, my "mood" was so low, so "off", they feared I might commit suicide while I was so far from home. I was there on business and was invited to a lavish business dinner and city tour by the wealthy family that was on the other side of the deal. I didn't want to be alone and was very interested in exploring the endless cultural charms Vienna had to offer. Normally I would have been euphoric about the invitation. I was too withdrawn, too melancholy, too disinterested in life in general to accept the gracious invitation, however.

Marcel was my counterpart on the other side of the deal and we bonded immediately. He invited me to his home to make me dinner. I didn't find out until later that it was his birthday. I was touched by his warmth and hospitality. I felt very comfortable with him and quickly opened up about my most recent trauma. He had sensed my melancholy and "troubled" self. He shared an inspirational quote with me that was in Hebrew, the gist of which was *"the only thing you can lose and never get back is a moment."* It was like a switch had been flipped in me. Instantly, I became incredibly aware that I had not been truly "living" and incredibly determined that I was not going to let BS "control" my life for another second. I remember having discussed psychotherapy with this "earth angel" that night and he shunned it completely. I realized and tried to explain to him that "therapy" can come in many forms and that he had basically just provided very impactful therapy to me. I also experienced that night what the doctor had meant when he had forewarned me that Lexapro could cause a "delayed" orgasm. I had a profound psychological and physiological "release" of the pain I had been wallowing in.

I had to get up very early the next morning for my flight back home. I remember getting out of the shower and looking down as I was toweling myself off, seeing a stream of blood running down my leg from my pelvic region. I thought something was terribly wrong and that I was "dying" - a melodramatic reaction but it's what I felt. I can still see it visually. I had simply nicked myself shaving. It got my attention though. Just as I had felt like my childhood trauma was segregated from my adult self after disclosing my sexual abuse to my mom, I felt a delineation between my marital abuse and my present. The events were symbolic to me, like I was on a precipice between stagnating and living. I chose living that early morning...

That momentous trip snapped me out of my apathy. I also quit taking Lexapro - I literally and figuratively felt like my brain was sloshing around. I refused to live a melancholy or numb life any more. I kept living repeated patterns of ludicrous behavior and relationships though and I realized I was losing those precious moments Marcel had counseled me not to waste. My mere choice that fateful morning wasn't sufficient to change the way I was actually living. More "work" than "wishing" to be healed needed to be done. I wasn't living true to myself or the potential my life held for me. The greater self awareness I was obtaining in my healing journey made me realize that.

To become consciously aware, Dr. LePera also encourages us to meet our "shadow" or "ego" - basically parts of yourself that you may not particularly care to recognize or admit (like a jealous tendency) to help identify your self narrative, your relationship narrative and your limiting beliefs. When you have a better appreciation for your ego, you can understand how certain "triggers", which strike a raw chord with your ego, can make you potentially react emotionally. The goal is to transition from an *"**ego consciousness**"* to an *"**empowered consciousness**"* where you can make more informed, rational choices. This notion was of incredible interest to me given its potential to significantly help me "reign in" my emotions. I knew my ability to do this and stay calm would be hugely beneficial to me personally as well as to my interactions and relationships. All too often, I felt wildly out of control and desperately wanted to change this. I was determined to achieve empowered consciousness.

Self Healing

If the idea of lucid dreaming had ignited a spark in me, Dr. LePera's admonition to be an active participant in my healing was a beautiful incendiary thought that synced perfectly with me. I have trust issues (as so many of us with trauma histories do) and the idea of being in control of my healing - and not dependent on anyone else - profoundly resonated with, and comforted, me. I felt simultaneously accountable and optimistically empowered.

I am my best healer. Just as I espouse with respect to natural healing in *"**Mediterranean Me**"*, it makes perfect intuitive sense to play the integral role in our own healing. No one has greater interest in, or familiarity with, our own selves. Under the best of circumstances, conventional psychotherapy has its own limitations in terms of approach as well as resource constraints. One needs a lot of time and money to take full advantage of what conventional therapy has to offer. Taking small but consistent daily steps towards healing is the overarching recommendation for achieving profound and lasting healing. Self healing enables the daily habituation true, profound healing requires, something that is not accessible with relatively infrequent and short therapy visits. I also love the spontaneity that self healing enables. It doesn't force working on healing during a prescribed therapy appointment. I can take advantage of different healing exercises when I feel most receptive or most in need.

Holistic Healing

Dr. LePera espouses an unconventional ***holistic*** philosophy of healing that was also intuitively aligned with my philosophy. Traditional psychotherapy treats the mind only - surprisingly without any diagnostic images of the brain itself. One way to gain insight into the mind is via the body. The goal is to harness the ***healing powers of the body*** to regain balance (control "emotional activation") and build resilience. This holistic approach to healing appreciates the interconnectedness of mind, body and soul and takes advantage of that interconnectedness to heal profoundly and holistically.

The power of our mind can harm or heal the body while the power of the body can similarly impact our minds. This was in line with Norman Cousin's philosophy that had intrigued me so many years prior. I was aware of different negative physiological impacts that my traumas had had on me throughout my life. I was incredibly intrigued about enlisting my body to help heal not only those impacts but also the psychological ones. Suggestions to harness the body's healing powers include using deep belly breathing and strengthening our "vagus nerve" to help control our emotional activation. These exercises take advantage of our mind-body connection. They can help calm the body as well as instill a sense of peace and safety. I delve much deeper into this fascinating, life transforming topic in the sequel to this book, "*Soar: Pretty in Peace*".

Chapter 3
The Root of the Problems, AKA, Childhood

M *irroring Childhood*
I do not mean to be flippant or callous in my chapter title identifying my childhood as the root of my problems. Just as in adulthood I have basically always been happy, I was basically always happy as a child as well. This is true notwithstanding the abuse and the dysfunctional family unit as well as the family always being financially stressed.

The reality is, however, that we basically internalize our upbringing, repeating the behaviors and relationships we witnessed - for good or bad. These behaviors and relationships were truly the origin of my lifelong patterns. It doesn't mean I had an unhappy childhood. As I said, quite the contrary. I was always happy. I was basically left to my own devices and happily muddled through more or less. Except for the flashbacks of abuse, my childhood memories are basically of happy times, though those memories are much less vivid. It also doesn't mean I am blaming anyone or abdicating my responsibility to heal. ***I clearly own it***. Delving into childhood, however, with great self-awareness and self reflection has enabled me to alter the behaviors, the habits and the patterns I was engaging in in adulthood that I knew were not serving me and my pursuit of my fullest, most authentic life.

"Inner Child" & Trauma Archetypes
Dr. LePera provided a framework for me to gain greater self awareness and insights into my behaviors. In *"How to Do the Work"*, she describes various archetypes of our "inner child" to help identify the one(s) we see ourselves most reflected in. These include the caretaker, the overachiever, the underachiever, the rescuer/protector, the life of the party, the "yes" person and the hero worshipper. I clearly saw myself in all of these in one way or another, even the ones that may seem contradictory in the abstract. For instance, I noted I always seemed to be in trouble as a young teenager in

sharp contrast to my siblings. I realized this may have been my "underachiever" stage, acting out somewhat to try to get the attention of my parents who didn't seem to "hear" or "see" me except when I was getting punished. Later, in college, I transitioned to "overachiever" stage and finally got the parental attention I craved.

The caretaker and the rescuer/protector categories resemble my persona most closely and my pattern of always helping others at my own expense. The categorizations are not an indictment of being a helping, compassionate human being. It's the recognition that no one should categorically, consistently and automatically dispense with their own needs and desires. It is not "selfish" to put yourself first. I still struggle with this notion because of the very fact that I aligned my self identity and worth with being the caretaker and rescuer from a very young age.

With reflection and greater self awareness, I have come to realize that there is a certain level of "arrogance" that comes with this identification - almost an assumption that others need me. I have also seen in my relationships that I have enabled the behavior of "needy" and lazy people. BS in particular showed no ambition or initiative because he didn't have to. He clearly did not want to work and didn't want children because he didn't want to take care of anyone. Now apparently he has a successful career and is taking care of a family. The boyfriends who have lived with me also consistently did not work and solely relied on me. I am confident that all these people are more responsible, successful human beings without me in their lives.

Remember *I* defined my self worth as a giver from my core childhood beliefs. ***I needed the "needy" to fulfill my self-defined purpose and worth***. This realization takes a lot of self reflection and self awareness. I also am trying to use this self awareness to become a better friend. I know I have a terrible tendency of always trying to "fix" any problems or issues any of my loved ones have. I now understand that often people don't want us to "fix" anything - they just need a compassionate listener to accept and validate their feelings. Carol is a seamless master of this and I aspire to become more like her in this way.

I have also been able to use the various "inner child" archetypes to help recognize the "wounds" of the "inner child" manifested by a lot of my family and friends. It gives me a better understanding and perspective of our interactions and their behaviors, which often would incense and hurt me based on *my* core beliefs, *my* "filters", *my* perspective. This has been very enlightening and has allowed me to not take things so personally and to not react emotionally to their words and actions. Moral of the story, it's not all about us.

In addition to discussing "inner child" archetypes, Dr. LePera discusses childhood "conditioning", elaborating on various archetypes of childhood "trauma" in an effort to help us identify childhood "wounds" and suppressed emotions. Our interactions with our parents set the stage for our thoughts, beliefs and behaviors, the dynamics in our relationships and our emotional maturity or ability to regulate our emotions. As impressionable children, we tend to mirror ourselves comprehensively after what was modeled to us.

The discussion of these trauma archetypes elicited my *"ding, ding, ding"* responses as many of the archetypes immediately and profoundly resonated with me. Not everyone will have the same response. Many people may not even be aware of any particular abuses or "traumas". Dr. LePera is a proponent of expanding the definition of "trauma". Her definition is a recognition that most everyone likely has suffered some sort of negative or overwhelming experience in childhood (a particularly vulnerable, developmentally formative period of life) that has ongoing psychological and physiological impacts throughout adulthood if left unresolved.

Not everyone experiences the same level or clarity of trauma as someone like myself who remembers my childhood sexual abuse but that doesn't mean that those who experienced something less clear cut or less consistent with a traditional sense of "trauma" (like sexual or physical abuse) aren't still at the mercy of their conditioned thoughts, beliefs and behaviors. I think my circumstances (the vivid recollections and my clear cognizance of my abuses) and my clear appreciation for how they shaped me helped catapult me on my healing journey.

So many of the archetypes resonated with me - either directly, or indirectly via recognition of them in my parents. Being able to clearly identify various patterns enabled me to deal with my issues head on quickly in a way I wouldn't have been able to absent such awareness and clarity. Two archetypes in particular spoke to me. I immediately recognized my parents in the "having a parent who didn't model boundaries" archetype - my mom failed to set any and my father failed to respect the ones that should exist by default in a parent/child relationship. I also recognized both of my parents in the "having a parent who cannot regulate emotions" category.

As Dr. LePera notes, ***how we regulate and process our emotions - or fail to - is one of "the most important aspects of emotional health"***. In my case, my parents' behavior fell on opposite ends of the spectrum - with my mom "withdrawing" and using "numbing" substances and my father basically being melodramatic, acting childlike, manifesting "temper tantrum" type behaviors, always blaming others and often threatening to leave. I always joked I had inherited the worst behaviors of both of my parents and now I saw it in black and white. I now had clarity to deal with my tendency to emotionally overreact - instead of thoughtfully responding - and/or engage in numbing habits. I also felt less shame over my reactionary tendencies, having a greater appreciation for the source thereof.

The fact that I recognized my abysmal emotional regulation/maturity and lack of effective coping mechanisms literally excited me. My tendencies had always perplexed me. I abhorred feeling out of control, at the mercy of my emotions, and often felt shame and remorse for the way I handled myself. For the first time in my life, I felt confident that this was in ***my control*** and I knew that changing my "ego consciousness" that ***dictated*** my emotional (over)reactivity to a more ***"empowered consciousness"*** would be positively life-transforming for me - ***psychologically and physiologically*** - and my relationships ***with everyone*** - not just romantic partners but with family and beloved friends too. I was ready to fiercely ***conquer*** my consciousness "*krav maga*" style. The ***"Naked Conqueror"*** *in me* was ready to ***"Roar"***...

Beliefs

I am reminded again of another quote by the brilliant Paulo Coelho, "*You are what you believe yourself to be.*" As I noted, a milestone in my healing journey was gaining a better understanding of how our brains work. We are basically ***wired for survival***. This, understandably, is particularly true for those who have suffered childhood abuse. We often form ***core beliefs*** in childhood that essentially ***automatically dictate*** our ***behaviors*** throughout adulthood ***unless*** we change them.

We must *override our subconscious*; this was the piece of the enigma that was my life that I had always been missing. As I have noted, I credit Scott Robinson, aka "The Brain Guy", with initially helping me understand the interplay between our subconscious, our beliefs and our behaviors. He brilliantly, enthusiastically makes incredibly useful information easily accessible to the masses. He changed my life by helping me solve the trauma puzzle.

Core beliefs - which are often negative and limiting - come from "practiced thoughts". We are not our thoughts although we often equate them with our very identity. We can *change* our *practiced thoughts*, which in turn will *alter* our core, *limiting beliefs,* which will *change* our *behaviors*. By analyzing the various themes or patterns that underlie our thoughts, we can identify our core beliefs.

I was easily able to identify my core belief which has not only severely limited me but also had set me on a formerly inexplicable pattern of lifelong behavior where I clearly allowed myself, my dreams, my goals, my needs and desires to be cast aside in favor of others. My old belief was that I was a mere means to others' ends. I am actively working on changing that belief and the pattern it destined by wholeheartedly embracing the fact that I am not a means to an end.

Your "shadow self" or "ego" is reflective of your perception of your self worth and often contains deeply embedded *limiting* beliefs. These are beliefs and traits about yourself that you're likely not proud of (like low self-esteem, a jealousy tendency, uncontrollable anger, etc.) and often aren't fully cognizant of, absent conscious reflection. When your ego feels threatened or "triggered", there is a high probability that you will have *an uncontrollable compulsive tendency to react emotionally* regardless of your intention or determination. *Ding, ding, ding* I thought as I read excerpts on this in Dr.LePera's "*How to Do the Work*", having recognized myself all too well.

This often leads us to instinctively "act out" (like arguing, yelling, criticizing, basically throwing a child-like "temper tantrum") or, on the other spectrum, withdraw or detach. As noted earlier, different parts of the brain are responsible for emotional control (the prefrontal cortex) and for negative feelings such as fear (the amygdala). I remember reading about childhood brain development for my youth fitness certificate a few years ago. I gained appreciation for not judging little children's temper tantrums or attributing responsibility to their parents because **the child is truly incapable of emotional regulation** before the "reasoned" prefrontal cortex has been developed.

Those with **trauma brains** are similarly challenged with respect to emotional regulation when the **"reasoned" regions** of their brain **shrink** and the **"fear" center** of their brain **grows**. Obviously exhibiting either extreme (be it temper tantrum-like behavior or withdrawal) from an inability to emotionally regulate does not bode well for a calm, reasoned resolution of whatever the issue or event is that "triggered" you.

Becoming consciously familiar with your ego and resulting "triggers" is the first step to enable transition from an instinctively emotional **reactive** state to a state of empowered consciousness where you can more rationally, consciously choose your **response**. I found this concept of empowerment consciousness extremely appealing. I have many triggers and am painfully, embarrassingly aware that I can react ballistically when I feel threatened/ hurt. Inevitably, I feel remorseful and shameful after the heated interactions this results in. Even if I have objectively good reasons to be troubled by the issue at hand, I know my highly reactive emotional instinctual reaction is clearly counterproductive to resolution thereof.

In my case, I readily admit that I have frequently exacerbated the issue, having more often than not been drinking too much when I engage in ego reactions. It's a lethal combination of feeling particularly sensitive and vulnerable, combined with the intoxicating effect of feeling I'm entitled to speak up on my behalf - sadly something sober me generally struggles with. I often "joked" that I should have some sort of breathalyzer device for my mouth and devices, rendering me incapable of communicating when I'm feeling incendiary/incapable of controlling my emotions when I am triggered.

My major trigger is crystal clear and centered around **my core limiting belief that I am merely a means to an end.** To be "loved", I need to "perform" sexually and/or provide financial assistance/bestow "gifts" **in pursuit of others' happiness**, while **betraying** my own needs and desires. I need to "buy love" with my body or money. The source of this twisted sense of self worth isn't difficult to ascertain. As you recall, my father had inextricably intertwined sex and love in my head at a young age and clearly articulated to me as an adult that no man would ever want me for anything other than sex or money, a repugnant belief he had instilled in me throughout my life. I had a ceaseless habit of offering up both without hesitation regardless of the circumstances or my financial wherewithal or lack thereof. There was no shortage of men who thusly "took advantage of" me, sexually and financially.

I am actively working on replacing my negative, limiting core belief with much more positive ones: "I am not a mere means to an end. I am the be all and end all. I am worthy and loveable simply by being me. My self worth does not come from what I give others - sexually, financially or otherwise".

This is probably the most difficult part of "doing the work" for me, changing my lifelong core belief that I am basically at others' disposal and whim. It is a very sad belief that has instructed my behavior throughout my life. It was instilled in me at a young age, with the message being reinforced to me throughout my life. *I now take accountability for the belief.* I still struggle with thinking otherwise, even though I know objectively that this is ludicrous and no one should consistently or automatically subjugate themselves to another. Uprooting the seeds of ugly limiting beliefs planted in childhood takes determination and habituation but it's undeniably doable and undoubtedly worth the effort. For me, it means the difference between merely "*surviving*" from my traumas and "*conquering*" my traumas to truly live life authentically and limitlessly to be "all I want to be". The stakes are high and I am more than ready, more than willing and more than able. *#nevergiveup*

Of course, this doesn't mean there won't be times when I compromise or put loved ones' needs before my own sometimes but it should not *define* my worth nor *dictate* my behavior on autopilot. For the most part, I have been used in relationships because that's what I projected my worth to be. I unconsciously attracted the very type of disrespectful narcissistic people who would take advantage of my low, utilitarian self-esteem. "Givers" have to be vigilant because "takers" will always take. I find it difficult to accept this because that type of personality does not sync with my notion of how people should be.

With the benefit of hindsight, it's much clearer to see how people have used/treated me as a means to their end. I wasn't aware of it whilst immersed in. The most glaring examples are my husbands. BS tried to kill me, enraged and homicidal at the prospect of losing my stream of income - *not me*. Yanni cryptically told me he no longer wanted to be married as soon as he started earning a decent income, after I had supported him, his aspirations and his family for over a decade plus had transferred his debt solely into my name. I have had other relationships in between the marriages and after the second marriage that were defined by me being taken advantage of as well, some of which I have detailed, but there were many more.

Behaviors: Bonds & Coping Mechanisms

We model our relationships after what we witnessed in childhood, adopting behaviors and relationship dynamics we grew up with, ***regardless of whether or not they were healthy or ideal.*** If your parents had a mutually loving, supportive and respectful relationship, you're more than likely going to as well. Whereas, if you had parents with basically a codependent or otherwise unhealthy relationship, as most childhood trauma survivors had, you're likely to end up in unhealthy relationships yourself.

We are basically ***destined*** to ***mirror*** the relationship dynamics modeled to us during childhood because they are familiar and "relatable"; ***we associate love with them. We may find these relationship dynamics to be undesirable in the abstract or from a rational perspective.*** It doesn't matter. Indeed, we ***undoubtedly*** also ***witnessed*** our ***loved ones suffer*** in these dysfunctional relationships. From an evolutionary standpoint, to maximize our chances of "survival", our brains gravitate to the familiar. Historically, our ancestors had a greater likelihood of survival if they were in "predictable" situations and knew how to "survive" based on prior experiences. The brain prefers to conserve energy and opts for running on autopilot by default whenever possible.

It's neither rational nor seamless. You're likely not even aware of it, because you were immersed in it; it was "normal" for you. I always felt bad for my mom, yet to me she was my strong hero. This absolutely does not make sense to me nor is it a pattern I consciously care to repeat. Yet, I did so over and over. My mom was basically modeling self-sacrifice and martyrdom as "love". Although I internalized this, it wasn't until after my flashbacks and a lot of self reflection, that I realized I was following in her footsteps. ***I was*** *clueless I was doing this.* To *heal*, I needed to be *consciously aware* of that and *change* my underlying *core limiting beliefs*.

Trauma Bonds

Dr. LePera advises us to "do the work" by identifying our trauma bond (or, as in my case, bonds) to become consciously aware of them. The concept of trauma bonding made perfect sense to me when all of her trauma bond categorizations resonated with me - two in particular profoundly so - lack of boundaries and emotional regulation or maturity.

One category is when a parent does not model boundaries. Unfortunately, both of my parents failed to do so. My father consistently overstepped fundamental boundaries that should exist by default in a parental context. He did this primarily in a sexual, financial and "confidante" context. Obviously, being sexually abused is a glaring transgression of a fundamental boundary. There was also a lot of pornography in the house growing up. I remember Playboy and Hustler magazines being pretty much out in the open when I was a young child. As I write this, I feel nauseous and my skin crawls as I can vividly recall them on the bottom shelf of the coffee table in the living room. Stacks of them. Usually the latest Sports Illustrated Swimsuit issue (which always made me feel self conscious) was at the top, as if somehow anyone could think that made the pornography less obvious.

My father always teased me about my breasts being so small. I remember pictures of me outside topless at a young age and sleeping topless in the Summer until probably about nine years old in the living room. He always joked I would never need a bra; I could use a rubber band and two bottle caps instead. I literally feel my nerves activated as I write this. I feel repressed anger boiling up, an "uncomfortable" gnawing in my gut, and tears welling ever so slightly in my eyes. My heart is racing and I start instinctively rocking as I feel irrationally "fearful".

When I was a teenager, the stacks were "hidden" in my father's underwear drawer. Mind you, my sister and I were tasked with doing laundry and putting it away in his drawer. I was always simultaneously repulsed and intrigued. I was fascinated with sex from a young age. It wasn't until after my flashbacks and subsequent analysis that I appreciated that I felt "threatened" by pornography. As I was discussing my traumas and recollections with Mike after my flashbacks, he remarked that I always had a unique view of pornography. I always felt the women were in control. After all, they had what the men wanted. I was repulsed by men's desire of it, particularly if they were in a relationship. To me, it's cheating and calls into question the fundamental link I have between sex and love. To this day, I instinctively bristle when anyone mentions pornography. It's as if it represents an existential threat to me and my self worth... The mere word triggers me. Women are objectified in it, as was I. I felt like they were in control though whereas I felt like a vulnerable child who had no choice - hence the simultaneous intrigue and repulsion.

My father also always had me "draw his bath" as a teenager. Recall that I have recurring bad dreams of bathrooms and flashbacks of abuse in them. I also remember my father recounting to me as a teenager his lack of sex with my mom and her anger about his "infidelity" - no context or explanation given – just a stark disclosure I listened to in horror, fervently wishing I had never heard. I remember my skin crawling one time when I was visiting my parents as an adult (after my flashbacks). I was laying down trying to drown out the sounds of what seemed like the ever-present sounds of my parents fighting. My mom left - as she often did - to go secretly smoke. My father, who always assumed I would "take his side", came in, sat down on my bed, put his hand on my bare thigh and complained again about the lack of sex.

Mind you, the argument had nothing to do with sex; he always went off on a tangent whenever there was discord. Despite my unease with such monologues, I silently felt vindicated as I always questioned the veracity of my flashbacks given the deep pain I felt I caused my mom by disclosing them. Still I just wanted to cover my ears and make it stop as he went on and on about the lingerie he tried unsuccessfully to interest my mom in. He seemed to attribute her lack of interest to the attempted sexual assault my mom had experienced by my grandmother's boyfriend as a teenager (the man in who's care my parents regularly entrusted me and my sister to as young children). It was almost as if he were excusing my mom's lack of interest in sex. I never knew what he was seeking from me but I had no interest in being his confidante in this regard at all. He also always told me I was the most beautiful little girl - something I was flattered by - pre-flashbacks - and deeply uncomfortable with post-flashbacks.

My father also had countless lengthy conversations with me complaining about my mom and endlessly telling me their financial woes. My mom was forever telling him not to discuss such topics with me but he did with great regularity, prefacing each disclosure with the admonition not to tell my mom. My parents always helped and treated my brother and sister and their families financially and otherwise. I had to pay rent to my parents while still in school from jobs I worked in school and on school breaks. Even though I had to pay my way through school with scholarships, jobs and loans, my mom said the first thing I would do when I came home on college breaks was go through the refrigerator and cupboards to make sure they had enough food.

As you may recall, I didn't have enough money or loans to pay for a semester in college and was panicked that I would have to quit my education. It was a very traumatic time for me. My parents basically nonchalantly told me I would figure it out. Always left to fend for myself... As I noted, "miraculously" someone paid my tuition for that semester - "earth angel", Mike. During law school, I would charge gift cards on a department store credit card, then buy something nominal (like a pair of socks) because back "in the day" they gave me the balance of the gift card in cash and I could use it to buy groceries. Lots of ramen noodles in my dorm room on a hot plate throughout law school. My parents managed to go out drinking a lot while I was in grade school and high school while my sister and I took care of my little brother, nine years my junior. Horse racing and casinos were always a favorite past time of my parents, even when my father wasn't working. They did not help me financially through school but took my brother to Las Vegas with them and my brother and his girlfriend on a trip to Churchill Downs, the famous horse race track, during that period of my life. You may recall I loaned my parents money to pay off a second mortgage - they had obtained it to pay off gambling debt. I was mortified later on when I had to tell BS they asked me to overnight a few thousand dollars to them because they had to pay off their gambling debt at one of the casinos again and they needed the money immediately.

I share these things in detail because objectively I think it's crystal clear why I always had (*first time I ever wrote that in past tense) subconsciously valued my worth in terms of sex and money and why my relationships centered around that notion. It wasn't until my father had actually told me that no man would ever want me for anything other than sex or money that I had an inkling that these core limiting beliefs about my self worth had been instilled in me from my years growing up. From an early age, I was always expected to take care of myself without assistance or even much compassion; I was to shoulder the actual and psychological burden myself. Nonetheless, once I started making money, there seemed to be a tacit agreement that if anyone needed "help", I was to give it.

While my father consistently overstepped "boundaries" that should have existed by default between a parent and child, my mom constantly subjugated her own needs (her time, energy and emotional resources). She failed to set any limits/boundaries in her codependent relationship with my father, endlessly seeking to satisfy his needs (at the cost of her own) and pacify him in any conflict.

As I have indicated, I had always revered my mom as my hero. My best girlfriends and my niece did too. I remember a grade school assignment where we were tasked with designating a hero. Without hesitation, I immediately chose my mom. It was a rookie mistake to openly admit that my mom was my hero. I wasn't sufficiently sensitive to my father's bizarre jealousy at the time to realize my choice would upset him. I would never make that mistake again.

Although there is no one I love more than my mom, after my flashbacks my perception radically changed. What I had previously viewed through child's eyes as strength and independence, I saw as weak and dependent. It was the first time it was apparent to me though that I had modeled my relationship behaviors after her - always being the caregiver, the provider, the subservient one in a clearly codependent relationship. I no longer thought of her as a strong independent hero I wanted to emulate but at best as a martyr and worse as a victim, neither of which I cared to be. My mom is still incredibly strong in my eyes and I attribute my tenacity and strength to her. Whereas, however, she used that strength to stay, I now choose that strength to move on, to *conquer*, not merely *survive*.

The other categorization of trauma bonding that particularly synced with me was when a parent can't regulate their emotions. I am very aware of the childlike emotional reactivity exhibited by my father on one end of the spectrum and the withdrawn responses engaged in by my mother. I've often joked to myself that I inherited the worst "coping" behaviors of both of my parents. I engage in numbing behaviors a la my mom, including drinking, and my father's hyper emotional reactivity, which I frequently manifested post over imbibing in alcohol. I also, perhaps ironically, utilized relationships and sex as a numbing agent. I have this "bizarre" craving for sex when I am particularly sad or ill - its association with love having been cemented in my brain at a young age.

Once you are aware of your relationship patterns - which fortunately, from a healing perspective, I clearly was - you can consciously try to make different choices. With respect to my parents' failure to model boundaries, I was keenly aware of my failure to set any boundaries whatsoever. I almost never said no, even when I desperately wanted to or needed to for my own well-being - physically, mentally, emotionally and/or financially. I was too afraid to say no for fear of losing the person asking and felt profoundly guilty and sad in the rare instances I tried to assert myself. I would read articles on the subject which posed the question whether you ever felt bad or guilty about saying no, thinking, doesn't everyone???

I was taught by my father that love was conditional and taught by my mother that self-sacrifice is love. Particularly when you are a vulnerable child, you equate love with being safe and being cared for and you lack the faculties for objective, rational analysis. Seen through the lens of love modeled to me in childhood, my historical behaviors make perfect sense. My norm was betraying my authentic self - my wants, my needs, my goals. I unquestionably catered to everyone else, including virtual strangers sometimes, and always to people who consistently had hurt, disrespected and took advantage of me.

My needs didn't even register in the hierarchy of importance. It is objectively ludicrous to me that one would lead his or her life in basic "servitude" of others' needs. Yet, that is what I had spent my life doing, having *internalized self-denial* as *love* and aligning my *life purpose* with being a *mere means to an end*. I was a slave to love. I desperately wanted to be loved, to be cared for, to be safe so I steadfastly followed what had been programmed in me from a young age as the way to achieve those fundamental desires.

These realizations simultaneously sicken and shock me. It would be unfathomable to me that anyone would basically choose to live his or her life in "servitude" to others' needs. It also shocks me that it could take decades to even realize that reality but for it happening to me twice, indirectly and directly, via witnessing my mom and modeling my life after her. Ironically, my chosen role model, my mom, was also the woman for whom I felt a profound sadness, always feeling like she was more or less miserable and had squandered her life. She always told me she had made her choice and was willing to live with it. With my new conscious awareness, despite my relative happiness and life well lived, I wanted to choose differently. I knew it was long overdue for me to ***stop modeling*** her behavior.*

*This last paragraph is the most reflective of my self awareness as well as the most painful paragraph of the book for me to write. It makes me sad, sad for my mom, sad for all the parents who live their lives like she has and profoundly sad for all the children who follow in their footsteps, particularly those who have endured ongoing childhood sexual and physical abuse. Time to heal. Time to break the cycle.... Again, I'm the lucky one. I'm blessed. I'm breaking my cycle, determined for the rest of my life to be the best of my life. My fervent hope is for all those who have experienced childhood abuse to truly heal and do the same.

Coping Mechanisms

A lot of us who have endured traumas have mastered maladaptive "coping" mechanisms. These mechanisms do not heal the underlying traumas. Indeed, they are more or less designed to avoid addressing the traumas and absolutely to avoid feeling the painful emotions associated therewith.

To work on achieving emotional maturity, it is useful to analyze the "coping" mechanisms that were modeled to us by our parents. Unfortunately, I was modeled a full range of ***counterproductive, indeed, destructive*** "coping" mechanisms ranging from one end of the spectrum to the other. In my case, as I have noted, my father would "lose it", with the slightest provocation. He would act like a child having a tantrum - yelling and forever blaming others, more often than not using me as a scapegoat. He seemed incapable of taking any responsibility or accountability and did not have the emotional maturity to respond to anything in a calm manner. When he wasn't actually blaming me for whatever was happening, he would change the subject to something completely unrelated and irrelevant instead of processing or addressing what was actually happening. I could tell he was experiencing the smallest of stressors physiologically too and he forever made me feel at fault for his inability to cope. He has a history of cardiovascular disease and was forever telling me I was going to give him another heart attack. It wasn't until adulthood that I fully appreciated why I always felt I was to blame and why I was a serial apologizer who felt responsible for everyone else's feelings and emotions.

My mom, on the other hand, would pacify by superficially accepting all blame (not believing she was actually at fault) and self soothe with numbing substance abuse - alcohol, cigarettes and prescription pills. I honestly cringe now when I witness my mom doing this, fully realizing how long I internalized this behavior I had modeled after her. These were painfully stark reminders of my mom betraying her authentic self, something I had witnessed throughout my life and had spent a lifetime doing as well.

I "inherited" the worst of the "coping mechanisms" from each of my parents, alternating between reacting explosively like a wounded child a la my father and self soothing a la my mom with alcohol (and/or, in my case, "intimacy" - the very act that would **validate** my twisted sense of **self worth**).

The Result: "T3": Trauma Brain, Body & Bond: A Holistic Approach

With my relatively new self awareness and insights from self reflection, I was easily able to diagnose myself with "TB3" - my shorthand for trauma brain, trauma body and trauma bonds, reflective of the pervasive holistic impact trauma can have. Given the vernacular to identify and categorize my issues helped me understand them and approach them head on. I recognized the parental behaviors I was modeling with glaring clarity. It was as if a light had been shone on the dark issues I had been contending with all my life. Unveiling these things seemed to give them credibility and show me a path to healing. It was comforting and inspiring. It's like the relief one gets when they can replace an undiagnosed medical condition with a diagnosis of a particular condition that they can actually treat. Having a diagnosis enabled me to address the ongoing issues and understanding the sources thereof provided me the guidance for targeted self therapy.

Although I was already aware of some of the more obvious physiological and psychological manifestations of the impact of my various traumas, Dr. LePera's categorizations (physical; psychological/emotional; and social) and breadth of symptoms were eye opening. I was keenly aware of psychological symptoms, symptoms that were so apparent, I had been diagnosed with post-traumatic stress disorder after BS attempted to kill me. I was all too familiar with a number of the symptoms in the various categories. I delve into the physiological manifestation of trauma in detail in my sequel, *"Soar: Pretty in Peace: Rewire Your Magical Mind to Live Happily Ever Now"*. Suffice it to say for purposes of this book that I had suffered from innumerable physiological symptoms throughout childhood as well as throughout my first marriage. Although some (like insomnia and bizarre troubling dreams) continued thereafter as well, for the most part *a lot of the ailments* seemed to *"magically" disappear once I was* no longer living with my parents nor living with BS. Another ding. ding. ding. epiphany for me.

The category that surprised me the most, as I had never thought of this in terms of a "trauma body", was "social", including attachment and emotional issues. These symptoms were significantly present in my life. I had attachment symptoms of consistent *fear of abandonment,* extreme *clinginess* and *incredible difficulty being alone*. As I noted previously, as a child, *I made my mom promise me she wouldn't die before me.* I clearly associate my mom's absence with bad things happening to me. As I also noted, I was an unusually clingy child, panicking if I weren't physically attached to my mom. As an adult, I felt the dread of night approaching like a suffocating cloak if I were alone. I was fearful of the approach of bedtime and what my mind would reveal to me if I slept. My unease was exacerbated by the deep discomfort I felt being alone from a trifecta of reasons. Solitude meant I had no distractions from my thoughts/emotions, no "protection" and no intimacy that I required to feel "loved"/"safe".

Physical intimacy/sex were borderline "addictive" to me. I craved the oxytocin released during sex, an intensely powerful craving that didn't always result in the best choices. I would become very restless and my skin would feel like it was starting to crawl. I would drink to numb my feelings but generally the alcohol would not have the desired calming, sedative effect unless I drank to great excess. My hyper vigilance was powerful and I would actually become more energized as the night unfolded, diligent in fulfilling my "guard" role whenever I was alone. My desire to sleep was a primary motivating factor for sleeping with men. I felt "safer" when I wasn't alone. As unwise and ill-conceived as it may seem objectively, even the presence of virtual strangers made me feel better. I would often "disassociate" during sex, a classic adaptive measure from trauma where the mind and body "disconnect" as a way to avoid cognition of what is taking place. This is the reason so many trauma victims have spotty or incredibly poor memories. It's particularly twisted that I felt the need to resort to random engagements - from which I would frequently disassociate - to try to cope with my unease at being alone. I think the disassociation reflects the obvious conflict even in the mind of a young child when you realize ***the very act you're groomed to associate with love is the very thing that is traumatic.***

I also experienced emotional symptoms of a trauma body which I previously disclosed, including social anxiety and an absolute lack of boundaries; it is noteworthy that some trauma victims exhibit an opposite tendency of overly rigid, inflexible boundaries. It wasn't until I was finishing this book that I remembered a childhood incident that captures the essence of my social anxiety and low sense of self. My sister (who is a mere two years my senior) and I used to take the bus to grade school together when I was about 7. I engaged in a daily non-negotiable habit of running through the entire day's itinerary, including each class, as well as any upcoming tests or projects, and even recess and lunch. It was incumbent upon my beloved sister to reassure me on an individual basis that each and every one of these things was going to be ok in particular and that nothing catastrophic in general would happen to me that day. I also remember that I volunteered at the school library, going through the books to identify any "check out" index cards that had been mismatched with the books. The thoughtful librarian was so expressively complimentary when I would find any errant mismatched ones that I actually started intentionally mismatching them to get her kind praise when I "discovered" more mismatched ones.

These incidents may seem trivial but are indicative of my need for "parental" reassurance and validation vis-a-vis my sister's loving indulgence of me and the kind librarian's recognition.

I think it is extremely insightful to see in black and white the great breadth of symptoms that can reflect a "trauma body". It really speaks volumes about the ***pervasive, extensive and long-lasting impact*** trauma has on us, ***not only psychologically but physically*** as well. To me, this fact highlights the importance of treating trauma ***holistically***, recognizing and addressing the ongoing effects it has on one's mind, body and spirit. Even though I had first hand experience with so many of the symptoms, and appreciated how they could all result from my ***unresolved*** traumas, it was initially shocking to me to make the connection for such a wide ranging and extensive list of them. It intensified my resolve to truly heal once and for all to escape the wide-ranging, deleterious consequences of m6 unresolved traumas.

Since childhood, even before I had flashbacks of my initial trauma, I always intuitively said (mostly silently to myself) that it was as if I had been an abused child based on a confluence of physical, emotional and social factors. I largely kept this intuitive thought to myself. I remember my father rebuking me harshly when I voiced it once in front of my parents. I have super intuition and a powerful gut instinct but historically didn't have enough self belief to give them any credibility, let alone have them influence my behavior. I now have a great appreciation for the gut and brain connection given the science behind it.

Dr. LePera's elaboration on "trauma bonds" hit particularly close to home for me. Basically, a "trauma bond" is when you are in a relationship based on an emotional addiction to stress from your upbringing in a stressful/chaotic environment. In the abstract this sounds illogical if not outright unbelievable. After all, isn't "stress" what we're all trying so hard to avoid? Your brain seeks the comfort of the familiar though as well as the "happy high" from the chemicals released during a stress reaction.

A whopping ***95% of our brains' "operations/thought processes" are governed by the subconscious,*** which is ***neither logical nor rational.*** Our subconscious protects us from perceived threats and gravitates towards the *familiar* because it is known and predictable *even if the familiar is painful, sad or scary.*

When we are stressed, our bodies release more of the stress hormone, cortisol, as well as the *"feel good" neurotransmitter, dopamine.* Dopamine is also released when we have *sex* or eat foods we crave, contributing to feelings of *pleasure* and of *satisfaction* as part of our *reward system.* This makes it much more understandable how we could crave the physiological responses to stress. If it's *familiar and feels good*, it doesn't seem so counterintuitive.

Rationally we know that chronically-elevated levels of cortisol are "bad" for us but they can also create an energizing high of sorts - like a "cortisol roller coaster" to use Dr. LePera's vernacular. Think of that "scary high" from riding a roller coaster or the exhilaration some feel from skydiving or engaging in extreme sports. It makes them "feel alive". Something a lot of trauma survivors crave. The concomitant release of "feel good" dopamine serves to exacerbate that craving. The brain sort of predisposes us to seeking dopamine. It is irrelevant whether the activity that promotes the release of dopamine is health promoting - like exercise - or health-depleting - like chronic stress. Throw in the feel good hormone oxytocin (the "cuddle" or "bonding" hormone) released during sex and you have the perfect set up for an *addiction.*

Although objectively I would've said that I shun stress and erratic relationships, I am very aware that I tend to be very restless - almost feeling bored and numb - in

mutually respectful, promising relationships. With hindsight, I feel I sabotaged many of these. I didn't seem to have the same attraction to respectful, thoughtful, financially independent boyfriends. Something seemed to always be missing and "off". The situation was unfamiliar to me and it didn't sync with the type of relationship that had been modeled to me as "love". I was uncomfortable being unsure of what I had to offer to the relationship since I wasn't subserviently filling some need. I struggle appreciating what I have to offer if I am not "being used".

My low self-esteem and sense of worth is painfully exacerbated by my fear of abandonment. This dictated my attraction to the particularly needy. If I were fulfilling the "needs" of someone especially "needy", it made me feel more "indispensable". Nonetheless, I kept getting "dispensed" with, possibly making me subconsciously seek out even the "needier". This is of course a recipe for disaster.... Feelings defy logic but understanding the inner workings of the trauma brain made what seemed absurd rationally or in the abstract completely explicable.

With hindsight and reflection, I realized that what I just described is why I was so attracted to Bilal and had such a difficult time being apart from him. I would light up and become incredibly energized whenever I would see him, the memory of his most recent transgression instantly fading as I welcomed him with open arms. We were "co-regulating" giddiness when we were together; I felt euphoric getting my "fix". This relationship was my most glaring manifestation of being used sexually and financially, which sadly was the very thing that unwittingly and profoundly attracted me to him.

We were mismatched in every other way. He actually reminded me most of BS in terms of absolute apathy and lethargy. All he wanted to do was sleep and have sex (or accompany me on all-expenses paid trips, dinners, etc.). He would come in the middle of night and we would be up until very early in the morning. I would let him sleep all day the next day while I went about my routine, comforted by the fact that he was there and I could freely go get my cuddles and oxytocin, my "drug", at will. He was my addiction so to speak and I couldn't get enough of him...

Chapter 4
The Solution: My Therapeutic Prescription; What I am Doing to Heal

So..... I was fortunate enough to be able to clearly identify my "problem" once I engaged in self reflection and became increasingly - painfully - consciously self aware. In my case, my traumas were pretty clear cut and representative of a pattern. Remember it took an **attempted murder** and therapy to trigger my memories of childhood abuse though. Once my lifelong coping mechanism of repressing was trumped by the need to actually heal, however, all the elements I needed to start healing started falling into place. They were present but still lay dormant more or less until I could no longer ignore or accept the ongoing patterns of abusive relationships or the self-inflicted harmful habits.

I needed to believe I deserved better before I could get better. I am crying writing this - in small part because I realize the sad statement embedded therein - but in greater part as a reflection of my recognition of how truly blessed I am. Throughout my entire life, there was always someone who believed in me and helped me see the reason to go forward when I didn't believe in me and didn't care to go forward - be it my grandmother, a teacher, a chance encounter, various "earth angels", inspirational strangers, Kathy, Mike, Carol and now Barış. Even in my darkest moments and in my loneliest hours, I was never "alone" and someone always "appeared" to show me the "light". My good fortune is not lost on me. I know I am one of the lucky ones, oh so lucky. I digress in gratitude and angels...

Back to the healing.... My "problem" was that I had a *"trauma brain"* that was quagmired in *limiting beliefs* and ongoing *psychological pain and anxiety* that was creating a *limited life*, far less fulfilled and profoundly happy as it could be. I had ongoing *negative physiological effects* of having a *"trauma body" embedded* with the physical manifestation of my traumas and pain. I also engaged in less than mutually respectful relationships because of my limiting beliefs and because of my ***addiction to trauma bonds***. I was ill-equipped to deal with my TB3 self (trauma to the third holistic degree) with my ***lack of emotional maturity*** and frequent episodes of ***emotional reactivity***, my frequent reliance on ***numbing substances*** and activities and my periodic slipping into the abyss of ***"freeze" mode***.

The origin of my problems was rooted in my negative ***limiting beliefs*** from childhood, the lack of ***boundaries*** modeled in my childhood, the ***behaviors*** that had been modeled for me in my childhood, and the ***maladaptive coping mechanisms*** and ***lack of emotional maturity*** that I had witnessed in my childhood. I had a ***traumatized wounded "inner child"*** that needed to be ***"reparented"*** and needed to feel ***safe*** and ***at peace*** and an incredibly ***dysregulated nervous system*** that needed rebalancing.

I'm the self aware adult now and it's incumbent on me to change the limiting beliefs; establish and maintain the boundaries; cultivate emotional maturity and replace destructive coping mechanisms with productive ones; make sure my "inner child" is "seen", "heard", loved, safe and at peace; and realign my skewed nervous system. There is no one in a better position to effectuate that comprehensive therapeutic holistic healing than myself.

So, this is what I did and am doing.....

Be Present: Get out of the "Monkey Mind"

I regularly engage in grounding exercises to help cultivate a more present me, immersed in the sensory experience of the moment. This is very calming and soothing and induces a feeling of peace. It is also very effective in stopping my past from dictating my present. There's the saying, "you only live once". I prefer "you only die once". We have the opportunity to live - ***truly live*** - each and every moment we are blessed to have, *provided we are present*. We are human *beings*. Try to simply "be" as a regular practice. The only moment you can truly live is the present moment and if you are stuck in the past or fixated on the future, you lose that moment.

As you can tell, I'm obsessed with quotes, particularly inspirational ones I take to heart. Remember the positive impact my earth angel, Marcel, had on me when he had jolted me into that transformative realization that I was losing moments? I also love the following wish by Jonathan Swift: "May you live every day of your life." I remember giving my mom a bookmark with that quote. She has always been a voracious reader - an "escape" for her. It's her favorite bookmark. The quote really resonated with her. It may sound silly but it almost seems to represent a secret "pact" between us, a reflection of the reality that she hasn't achieved that wish but that she and I know I am fully capable of realizing it, for the both of us, symbolically if you will.

My favorite way to be present is to immerse myself in nature, ideally first thing in the morning with the sun shining. I am beyond blessed to live on the stunning Mediterranean coast with endless natural beauty and a temperate climate. I loved standing barefoot in my little garden (benefitting from "earthing" or "grounding"). After I took in the visual beauty with deep gratitude, I loved shutting my eyes and heightening the awareness of my other senses. I could feel a pervasive sense of peace throughout my body as I felt the cool, often slightly damp grass under my feet and the solar embrace of the sun on my face; I brushed my palm along my prolific herbs, rewarded with a heady waft of thyme; and I enjoyed hearing the melodic morning greeting of the various birds welcoming the day. I also used this opportunity to take in slow deep, belly breaths, "tasting" the crisp freshness of the refreshing sea breeze air.

Nature is healing and affords an infinite array of immersive sensory experiences to incorporate into this daily routine. I find this a very calming yet energizing way to commence each day, grateful to set a tranquil tone for the remainder of the day. If it's raining, I like to do something as simple as full on contemplating a piece of citrus, paying attention to its texture in whole form, thoughtfully zesting it to utilize the potent pungency of its zest, deeply breathing in its energizing, uplifting fragrance and tasting the sweet nectar of its beautiful sticky citrusy elixir. This experience never disappoints me and I silently express gratitude for this sensory experience which uplifts my mind and spirit and provides nutrition to my body. You get the point. This might seem silly but I urge you to try it; it is an incredibly easy way to simultaneously find calm and energy while starting the day in a spirit of gratitude.

I am happy to be an extraordinarily sensory person; I truly feel these things throughout my body. I physiologically *feel gratitude*, often with tears of joy welling up in my eyes. Experiment - find "your thing". Honestly, doing something like the dishes (an oft-repeated suggestion for grounding) doesn't have the same profound impact on me but simply *immersing* yourself in *a sensory experience* for a couple minutes each day can have a very calming effect. *It takes you out of the monkey mind and into your body.*

Change the Limiting Belief: Awareness & Affirmations

A core and fundamental part of my healing has been changing my prior negative belief that I was a mere means to an end. I had to believe and internalize that I did not deserve to be treated in this utilitarian manner. I had to convince myself that: *My needs, desires, and goals matter as much as everyone else's* and, indeed, to me, should matter most. *I matter.* I deserve to be *seen, heard and loved simply for being me*.

I had the most profound and conscious releases (and relief, physiologically and emotionally) when I began reciting affirmations along the lines suggested by Dr. LePera. Initially I tried using her suggestion verbatim but parts of it didn't sit well with me. I didn't like the saying that it was "no longer ours to carry" because I didn't want to give validation to the thought that it ever was. Nor did I like the acknowledgment of my abuser's issues because even though that insight/belief can help me better understand whichever abuser I was referring to at the time, this was a deeply personal exercise and I did not care to feel compassion for anyone in those moments except for myself. For the first time I was truly exposing and acknowledging my deep hurt and fears and I didn't want them diluted in any way whatsoever.

Affirmations are most effective when you truly believe in them and when you have a lot of passion behind them. My healing has definitely benefited from that intense belief and passion. I was also fortunate to be very cognizant of the actual incidences of the various abuses I had endured throughout my life so that I could pinpoint my feelings and target them contextually. Not everyone is really even aware of the precise nature of their traumas nor do they necessarily believe what they are stating in their affirmations. I think the fact that I was fully aware and passionately believing what I was saying significantly helped my healing proceed extremely quickly *once I finally began* (at now 55). It was as if all the decades of unrepressed pain, anger and resentment accumulated into this intense, deeply cathartic expression that I unleashed with ferocity and gratitude.

The part of Dr. LePera's affirmations that impacted me the most was when I would say I no longer need to "*perform*" or "*betray*" myself for love.

Those two words still chill me every time because they captured the essence of my behavior in an extremely stark, raw and painful way but also in a very healing, cathartic and enlightening way.

Of course if I am in a loving relationship with someone to whom I am attracted, I want to have intimacy and sex. This affirmation however starkly revealed to me that that wasn't at the heart of what I had been doing. I had been "*performing*" for another's validation and/or pleasure, regardless of my interests, needs or desires - those simply don't matter. It was great if they coincidentally coincided sexually but it wasn't a prerequisite. That word, "perform" nauseated me, it captured what I had been doing in a painful but healing way.

I had a similar reaction with respect to the word "betray". I had never thought of my behavior in this way before but it poignantly captured how I had been treating myself all along. For example, I betrayed myself in my first marriage when I worked incredibly hard and subjected myself to a lot of stress staying in an unfulfilling career and foregoing motherhood instead of working for a charity and having children as I desired. I betrayed myself when I supported my second husband's business aspirations in the most comprehensive sense despite being extremely uncomfortable with the risk and being miserable with the responsibilities I had to fulfill there....

My very first affirmation was so intensely impactful something prompted me to video my second and third. The simple affirmation catapulted me *hard* along my healing journey. It was so raw and intense, had it not been happening to me, I would have assumed it was acting. I could tell it was quickly working its magic on me as succeeding ones were less "emotional", having been blessed to have quickly and deeply released so much on the first few ones. As crass as this may sound, it was akin to the intense relief one feels, despite the discomfort, of violently throwing up when you are really ill. I was "vomiting" toxic thoughts, feelings and pain.

I kept tweaking the base affirmation to fit my very particular circumstances and needs. As I noted before, I had a history of very violent scary dreams and it took me a long time to associate them with the violence I had endured (including the attempted murder). I remain intrigued that I always automatically choose the word "dreams", not "nightmares". I believe I always realized as troubling as the dreams were that they were helpful "messengers", useful to my healing. I think I had the delayed association because I wasn't consciously aware of the ongoing impact of the various violent incidents I had experienced. I really had never tried to "process" the attempted murder or subsequent incidences of physical abuse.

Also obviously the very nature of childhood sexual abuse is a physical assault, although I had never appreciated it that way before. Indeed, I initially wrote a "softer" "affront", always in protect others' mode instead of calling it out for what it was - an assault. I also did not remember being hypervigilant until after the attempted murder but my best friends from high school have told me that I was always very jumpy and easily startled. Even though I wasn't consciously scared from any of those incidences of physical abuse, they cumulatively clearly continued to plague me subconsciously and physiologically. I remained in a hyper vigilant stance and couldn't sleep. *I am thrilled to say that after the very first set of affirmations I did on violence, I have not had a single violent dream.* It is unbelievably amazing how impactful cueing your nervous system with body work that you are safe and verbally affirming the same is. Similarly to the affirmation I was using vis-à-vis my childhood trauma, the initial couple of affirmations on violence produced dramatic releases which quickly tapered off.

For someone who was entirely dismissive of affirmations all her life, I quickly became a hard-core believer of the incredible healing power of affirmations. Nothing else helped heal me as quickly or deeply or has been as integral to my holistic healing. I am now beyond grateful for their incredible healing power and regularly utilize affirmations to help me in any area of life I desire.

The affirmations were incredibly empowering. They were completely within my own control. For the first time I was directly, consciously confronting my demons/ my abuses. I was also simultaneously guiding my subconscious to reprogram my core limiting belief that I was not lovable - or safe - if I weren't fulfilling my "purpose" of being a means to an end. I am extraordinarily grateful for having discovered free tools that I have at my disposal that I can use to calm my nervous system, alter my beliefs to loving ones and create the foundation for the life that I want to live.

Change the Behaviors: Don't Accept/Don't Project Limiting Belief

I know objectively that my worth is neither my sexual performance nor my financial support but habitually entered into relationships that seemed to indicate otherwise. As long as I believed I was a means to an end - even subconsciously - that unfulfilling habit would continue ad nauseum. This makes perfect sense. I was unwittingly projecting my value as such, attracting men who would capitalize on that perceived twisted sense of self worth *and* I got the validation that I needed.

By changing my beliefs about myself, I stopped *projecting* my worth as a utilitarian one and stopped allowing myself to be treated in such a manner. It was high time for some *savage self love* and *self respect.* I no longer wanted to/needed to be an obsequious "servant". I no longer wanted to be the "caretaker of the needy", a la my beloved mom. I was becoming my *own hero.* I was no longer in a *subconscious loop of insanity* that was beyond my control. I was *self aware* and able to make rational choices. Instead of seeking validation by giving sex or financial benefits, *I* became the *only validation I needed*, becoming resentful if anyone tried to take advantage of me. I had been able to cast this type of behavior in a different light, enabling me to distance myself from one-dimensional users. I was no longer satisfied with living a sub-optimal, inauthentic life dictated by leading a life of figurative servitude.

The sexual "use" was clearer for me to recognize. I still struggled a bit (ok quite a bit) at first because of my clear association between sex and love subconsciously and the validation I was used to feeling. With self awareness and cognizant reflection, however, I was able to identify those who only wanted to use me for sex. I wasn't at a point in my life where I was interested in casual sex so I would no longer accept it. If someone didn't want a relationship with me on my terms that gave me sufficient motivation to turn down sex, even when I still wanted sex. I knew I needed to say no to heal. By internalizing my belief that I was not a means to an end, I no longer felt the sick, *twisted* "obligation" to engage in sex merely based on someone else's desire. That notion repulses me and thankfully I no longer feel compelled to give in nor guilty for saying no when I want to.

With respect to the financial "use", it was relatively less clear for me to see because I am a compassionate, generous, helping person at my core. When I did recognize that someone was using me financially, however, it was easier to say no. My belief that I was worthy for me - not for what I could offer financially - made it easy to avoid relationships where it was clear that the other person didn't similarly recognize my worth. My struggle was with respect to people I care about who seemed to need help. If someone needs help, I desperately want to help them. I still wanted to despite having significant financial challenges myself. It was difficult for me to come to grips with prioritizing my needs even though I clearly recognized them.

The realization that helped me the most - especially to distinguish between anyone I should help and should not - was to stop taking care of others who could take care of themselves. I initially saw this as advice by the hypnotherapist/embodiment coach, Atarah Valentine. He has a brilliant way of succinctly capturing a lot of the realizations that had slowly come to me through my healing journey. I find his easily-digested snippets of wisdom extremely practical and insightful; he's like my modern day Dalai Llama in that respect.

I had always had a screwed up perception of who "needed" "help". Those who could take care of themselves - like BS or Bilal - shouldn't be looking to me for financial support - they were fully capable and did not "need" me. My conception of "help" was incredibly distorted as well. Yanni wanted a restaurant and refused to work towards that goal. The fact that he wanted a business "compelled" me to risk every penny I had to fund and support his desire, notwithstanding my wants. The restaurant business is so risky and those who are not independently capable of funding a restaurant venture usually raise money from investors and/or get loans. Indeed, I had done these deals when I was a corporate lawyer. Yet, I had unquestionably funded a restaurant for Yanni and guaranteed the long term lease with huge monthly rent, as well as all other liabilities. I was scared and miserable. I had funded all sorts of "projects" for his family that were "needed" even though they had been living all their lives just fine before I came into the picture. I should not be funding someone's aspirations. I would even buy boyfriends cigarettes even though I abhor the habit because I felt bad they couldn't "afford" what they "wanted".

Utterly ridiculous and by no means could I afford any of it in the most comprehensive sense. I share these embarrassing behaviors to give insight into the unbelievably profound control our childhood can have over our adulthood unless we intervene. Once I could break free from the belief that I was a means to an end, I could see my prior ways for the absurdity they were. I was more or less "prostituting" (for free) myself or "buying" love through gifts and financial support even when I was financially challenged.

Establish Boundaries: Communicate What is Unacceptable

As you can undoubtedly see, I still struggle despite working on changing my underlying beliefs. I view boundaries as a kind of "stop gap" measure to keep my behavior aligned with the life I want going forward when my new beliefs seem to waiver/be insufficient. For instance, as a boundary, I will never fund anyone's business aspirations again (or buy them cigarettes for that matter).

Before reading Dr. LePera's, "*How to Do the Work*", **I never ever even entertained the possibility of setting a boundary.** Boundaries were completely "in conflict" with my core limiting belief that I was a means for others' ends. Conceptually people couldn't walk over me; I was letting them step on me like a doormat. As we know, I viewed my purpose as being basically subservient, sexually and financially. Setting boundaries would be completely antithetical to me fulfilling that purpose.

My father did not respect any boundaries - the ones that should exist by default - and my mom set no boundaries in terms of what she would tolerate. It was glaringly obvious that she didn't establish any boundaries in terms of her time, energy and resources, always being obsequious, trying to pacify my father's needs even when it was clear to me that she was being insincere and resented it. Hence, my inextricable association between self sacrifice and love.

Setting boundaries has been extremely difficult for me since I have never set any nor were any modeled for me. I would always say "yes" to whatever anyone wanted or needed. As I said, generally no one even had to ask. I was easily manipulated and provided without having to be asked. I remember waiting for one of my therapy sessions, browsing through a book by Sigmund Freud, interestingly, we share the same birth date.

Freud apparently was way more self aware than I, stating that Taurus, our birth sign, is a notorious **serial giver**, susceptible to being "**used**". Freud gave a useful admonition to at least start by not offering help to others, as opposed to waiting to be asked. Upon reflection, I quickly recognized how easily I always let myself be manipulated. The deeply compassionate, empathetic side of me incessantly offered/insisted on helping when people consistently shared their various "needs" and desires with me. My father and BS were masters at this. I could definitely see the surprise in the reactions of people who were used to easily manipulating me when my behavior started to change. By following Freud's admonition, manipulation has become so much more transparent and obvious to me. I now know that no one can "take advantage" of, or manipulate me, without my acquiescence and I'm trying to be vigilant about my accountability in the equation. By realizing when someone is manipulating me, it has helped me recast my view of that person from someone in **need of help** (that my good heart is compelled to help) to someone who is unfairly, surreptitiously trying to **use** me. It has made it much easier to not give that person what they **want**.

Writing this book has also made me realize that I am borderline **petrified** of "conflicts" with others based on my history of traumas and physical abuses. Part of my problem setting boundaries is the deep-rooted, underlying subconscious fear of creating conflict. Historically, as a child, I was forced to do things as the price of love and safety and as an adult, I was physically harmed a number of times when people didn't get their way. As a child, "conflicts" with my father inevitably were melodramatic, resulting in extremely uncomfortable situations at best where I was always made to feel responsible, bad and guilty. This is in large part why my mom avoided conflicts with my father at almost all costs. It's human nature to avoid feeling bad and setting boundaries equated to feeling bad (if not actually scared) as far as I was concerned.

As I am trying to achieve greater respect for myself, I am trying to view boundary creation as a simple expression of my needs and what I will and will not tolerate. I'm all for expressiveness/open communication and it helps me to view boundary setting in that context. Now I appreciate that establishing boundaries has the potential to avoid conflicts by clearly enumerating my needs. This in and of itself is still difficult for me as I am not a personally-centric person. I always view things from others' perspectives, needs, etc.

Setting boundaries should not create "conflict" and if it does, I now consciously know that that is not a sustainable relationship. My "boundary" is basically an admonition not to "use" me/objectify me or take advantage of my default kindness and generosity. If anyone does, I view it as disrespectful and rude. I am a very respectful and polite person. It has helped me to see this behavior I formerly tolerated in terms of disrespect and rudeness because I know I do not want to be with someone who is disrespectful or rude. *I had needed to change my beliefs* before I could begin to appreciate others' behaviors as such.

I am happy to say that I have successfully started establishing boundaries even if I am still uncomfortable doing this. I know it will get easier. I am now empowered to not be treated as a means to an end. I now say no to *unwanted* sexual advances and romantic interactions. *Yes,* I am embarrassed to say that I would actually engage in *unwanted* sexual advances and romantic interactions before. I was "*programmed*" to give my body freely. It was as if I were in some sort of "sexual servitude", obliged to acquiesce, my desires being wholly irrelevant. *I also associated sex with love and/or being safe*, which provided an additional compulsory reason for my acquiescence.

Now I also decline requests for money or things I have to pay for. Historically, this was shockingly challenging for me even when I had no financial wherewithal whatsoever. I even had virtual strangers I barely knew ask me to buy them expensive things. I realized that somehow I was clearly projecting my core belief in this regard too even though I had not been cognizant of it. I had let men *treat me like a bank*, asking me for money or to pay for things at their whim, absent any reciprocity, absent any expression of gratitude, sincere or otherwise even.

The absurdity of acquiescing to being treated in this manner is clear to me now and makes it relatively easy to behave differently. The crucial takeaway, that bears repeating, is that *I could not judge the behavior for what it was* - being treated as a mere means to an end - *until after I changed my belief* that I was a mere means to an end. *Change your beliefs, change your behavior, change your life.....*

Cultivate Emotional Maturity

I was painfully aware of my inability to regulate my emotions when triggered, modeling my father's instinctual emotional overreaction interspersed with my mom's numbing habits. As Dr. LePera describes, the challenge is two-pronged. We should strive to adopt healthy soothing mechanisms to deal with or neutralize whatever is emotionally inciting us and learn to develop tolerance to stressors. This can help us develop emotional maturity and resiliency so we can experience strong emotions without "losing it" and endure stressful challenges without having ongoing negative emotional and physiological impacts.

To "do the work", we need to cultivate coping tools to help our ***bodies*** return to ***homeostatic balance*** and ***"get out of our heads"***. Otherwise, our minds inevitably prolong and exacerbate the "hurt". Dr. LePera elucidates several positive soothing mechanisms we can try to help us cope with stress in a beneficial - instead of harmful - manner. Different people will likely gravitate towards different self-soothing mechanisms. Some are more passive (like taking a bath or reading), while others are more active (like dancing or exercising). Some mechanisms, like exercising or cuddling, can help soothe via the release of positive hormones, like endorphins and oxytocin, respectively. You can engage in activities that will help calm you and make you feel better instead of numbing activities, like substance abuse. Some mechanisms are more expressive and geared towards helping you "release" the stress, like screaming into a pillow or writing about your feelings. It is extraordinarily ***empowering*** to me that if we can attain ***emotional maturity***, we can gain ***control*** and refrain from ***self inflicted*** ongoing emotional and physiological ***suffering***. I'm working on achieving the power of emotional maturity that has largely eluded me throughout life.

Chapter 5

Putting it Into Practice: Just Breathe, Jumping Jacks & Jasmine

We truly are our own best healers. No one can be more intimately familiar with our own unique traumas/stressors, family dynamics, history, egos, triggers, etc. No one else can possibly give us the conscious self awareness necessary to attain the insights necessary to guide our healing. You cannot change something if you are unaware of it and no one but you can make you self aware. No one else can dictate the particular soothing and coping mechanisms best suited to help you on your ongoing journey.

My research armed me with the understanding, framework and practical suggestions to catapult me on my healing journey. I customized my healing to best suit me and am happy to share some practical tips with respect to what has been useful for me, especially with respect to cultivating emotional maturity, adopting productive soothing and coping mechanisms and increasing my resilience to stress.

Get Out of Your Head

Experiment to see what works for you to give yourself whatever "space" and time you need to calm your nervous system down sufficiently to enable you to **respond** from a state of **empowered consciousness** instead of an **autopilot emotional (over) reactionary** state whenever you have an "issue". Personally, a "cooling off" period of separation is usually counterproductive for me. I think this is primarily due to my abandonment issues. If I don't quickly get the reassurances I need, I am primed to go into "fight" or "flight" mode. Working on diffusing the situation is certainly more productive than metaphorically arming for battle or running away.

What is most effective for me is deep breathing while gently rocking back and forth with my eyes shut to cue my nervous system that I am **safe** and am at **peace**. This helps me pivot from intense, instinctual survival mode *reactions* of "fight", "flight" or "freeze". I am truly shocked and grateful as to how effective something so simple can be. Obviously, engaging in this exercise also cues your counterpart in any situation that you are refraining from an autopilot emotional reaction.

Another favorite tool for me is to inhale calming essential oils. This is incredibly effective for me and I delve into the topic in greater detail in the sequel, "***Soar: Pretty in Peace***". Diffusing oils is a scientifically proven way to diffuse the situation, pun intended. If a particular situation is too inciteful or challenging for me and deep breathing and oils are insufficient, I like to do jumping jacks to release nervous energy and focus on my body. I used to have a stationary punching bag that I absolutely loved to use as an incredible outlet for my emotions and highly recommend that. I was immediately drawn to using a punching bag instead of being used as one... It felt very empowering! Some of these suggestions may seem silly or out of place at first whilst in the middle of a "situation", but, trust me, they seem far less silly and are far more productive than guzzling wine or lashing out seemingly out of nowhere at someone you care about.

My absolute favorite way to "get out of my head" is to cuddle/hug. I find comfort even in something as simple as embracing a favorite stuffed animal or rocking with a pillow. Actual hugs are certainly the best. I am extraordinarily fortunate that my current boyfriend, Barış, is very in tune with me and has been instrumental in my healing journey. I discuss Barış in greater detail in the sequel. He has been with me since before I figured out how to heal and has been an incredible partner in that journey.

When I am "triggered" and starting to "lose control", Barış' go-to response is to hug me while having me sniff my oils. Even when I have been in my simultaneous "fight" and "flight" mode (that historically ended with me being physically hurt with Marlon and Mariano), he has gently persisted. I am grateful that he listens not only with his ears but with his heart. He recognizes when I am triggered, is loving and mature enough not to take it personally, get defensive or combative, or, God forbid, in my case, leave. Instead, he gives me exactly what I need - loving reassurances. His name is Aşkın Barış, which is Turkish for "Love Peace". How great is that? I can't make that stuff up.

Get Over Yourself: Awareness & Perspective

The foregoing tools help to give me the pause I need to ground in the *present* and get *perspective* as well. Buddhism suggests when we are having a dispute with a loved one that we pause to contemplate the other person not being around anymore. When I am calm enough to remember to envision this, it is a game changer for me, giving me perspective and immediately diffusing the situation. It's impossible for me to be angry when I think of a loved one being gone.

I also reflect whether my "*ego*" is being *triggered* and whether I am likely *misperceiving* the situation; misperceptions are a primary cause of suffering per Buddhism. I have named my "ego", "Jasmine", which helps me analyze my emotions and feelings more objectively. My "pause" also affords me the opportunity to reflect whether the other person is also likely approaching the situation in a particular manner as a result of his/her own triggers and ego. Triggered egos create volatile, incendiary situations that can quickly spiral out of control, creating a situation that is absolutely counterproductive to resolution of the issue at hand and the health of the relationship in general.

At this point, following a pause to ground myself, calm my nervous system and reflect on the situation, I am more *present* and likely to *respond* from a default position that the other person is likely not trying to hurt me. My prior default position from my *past* was a defensive one. I anticipated that painful history was about to repeat itself, I was "on guard" and ready to do battle or retreat. The reality is that your loved one - be it your romantic partner, a friend or family member - is not likely trying to hurt you. Starting from that default likelihood has been incredibly helpful to me to stop from automatically going down a dark path of painful assumptions that unleashes an ugly, reactionary backlash triggered by my past abuses and fueled by my pained ego. This reaction can quickly get out of hand, particularly when your counterpart is experiencing the same thing and your respective pain and angst from "triggered egos" and misperceptions from the past feed off of each other.

Replace Destructive Coping Mechanisms with Productive Ones: Attitude & Gratitude

Historically, I engaged in destructive, maladaptive, injurious "coping mechanisms", a la my parents. Whenever I was experiencing very strong emotions/triggers, I would feel so restless and my skin literally felt like it was crawling. I had to fight, flee and/or numb my overwhelming emotions. I would drink to excess or take prescription anti-anxiety pills and/or (usually "and") engage in random sex. It still takes a lot of energy and discipline for me to opt for healthier choices instead of slipping into old negative patterns. I have a huge motivating factor though now that I understand the process. Also, for the first time, I feel equipped with the necessary tools to ensure a happier, more productive outcome.

As I already noted, both deep breathing and inhaling/diffusing essential oils are a couple of my immediate "go to" coping mechanisms. Getting out in nature and immersing myself in my senses is incredibly therapeutic as well. Exercise is an excellent way to ground myself in my body, release nervous energy and relieve stress - guaranteed. Writing has been unbelievably cathartic for me as has what I call "friendapy", or "friendship therapy". I am blessed to have Carol, the truest of friends, who allows me to express my feelings endlessly, listening compassionately without judgment. It's amazing how much better I feel simply "venting" to her, even if I am just leaving her messages; it's like taking the lid off a pressure cooker and letting the "steam" escape. I know I will be "seen", "heard" and loved. "Friendapy" has been a Godsend for me.

A stalwart coping tool for me is practicing gratitude, something I have regularly done for as long as I can remember. After BS tried to kill me, I intuitively continued to do so even though I didn't "feel" it when I was silently reciting to myself. I distinctly remember sharing this change in mindset with a National Geographic journalist in Argentina who had traveled as a photographer with the Dalai Lama, my spiritual icon. He expressed his clear belief how important it was to continue my practice regardless of my feelings and that helped motivate me to do so.

My silent and lengthy recitations of gratitude have a profound impact on me, physiologically and psychologically, often eliciting tears of gratitude and causing tingling throughout my entire body. I'm confident that this habit has significantly helped me to have perspective and stay grounded, calm, positive, happy, energetic and resolute despite whatever adversity or challenge I face. Focusing on our blessings keeps us grounded and in the present and crowds out potentially competing negative thoughts. Our thoughts literally rewire our brains so we need to be very careful what we allow ourselves to repeatedly think. It truly fundamentally matters. Your repetitive thoughts become your reality. I find this incredibly empowering. With habituation and passion, we can retrain our brains to create the reality we desire.

I have an even greater appreciation for my daily gratitude ritual after having researched the brain and gaining an appreciation as to why it is effective. It remains an integral part of my healing, something that I had done instinctively and intuitively way before I realized the need to heal. It is likely a large part of why I seem to have a trademark optimism in me that despite how bad things may seem at times, I am always grateful, optimistic and hopeful. I often rely on my gratitude recitation to help calm me or get me back to sleep if I am troubled or wake up throughout the night.

I've also kept a journal of little things that make me happy, like inspirational quotes, photos or clippings of things that evoke simple pleasures, kind words of others, etc. Inspirational people and their words of wisdom never cease to bring comfort and hope to me. "The Art of Happiness" by the Dalai Lama has been my spiritual guide since the demise of my first marriage and ensuing tumultuous hurtful relationships. His practical wisdom has given me helpful frameworks to analyze events and relationships and help me to be calm, centered, grateful and happy. I like to include snippets of sage advice that "speak to me" in my journal. These things soothe my soul and calm my "triggered" self.

Writing is a new coping tool for me and an incredibly useful outlet. Just as I had historically shunned affirmations, I had always rejected journaling as a release, ignorantly thinking it would more or less be an act of wallowing. Quite the opposite though. I have had an unbelievable amount of revelations as I have been writing this book. Facing my traumas and abuses head on has been incredibly therapeutic. Writing has enabled me to recount my traumas as a "story" so to speak to be left in the past where it belongs. It has helped make the traumas *history* in the truest sense instead of an ongoing story of my life. As I have described, exposing the "light" on my dark moments of abuse, via writing or talking, has made them feel less scary and less ominous and has made me feel less alone, less hopeless...

Build Endurance

There are a number of things we can proactively work on to help increase our resilience to stress in general and make us more capable of enduring the inevitable stressors of life. This can have a hugely positive domino effect. The more traumas we endure, the more we are apt to more readily produce more cortisol in subsequent stressful situations. If we can master dealing with stress better, we can help to modulate cortisol levels. As noted earlier, we can become "addicted" to our stress responses because of the various chemicals released. If we increase our resilience to stress, we can help train our nervous systems, making it less likely they are in a skewed, dysregulated state. You want your "baseline" to be calm and composed.

Building endurance relies on a lot of the techniques I have already highlighted.

Strategies that are beneficial to maintaining that desired relatively calmer baseline include engaging in breathwork, immersing yourself in nature, grounding yourself in your senses and the present, engaging in meditations or praying, resting, reciting affirmations or mantras, and enlisting compassion and support. I have actively and regularly utilized most of these different strategies. They have been extremely helpful, not only to help me get through particular stressful moments but also to fundamentally calm my nervous system in general. Cumulatively and over time, they have made me feel like my "fight or flight" sympathetic nervous system is less actively engaged in general. I am also better equipped to get myself back in the ideal default "rest and digest" state of my parasympathetic nervous system when I am stressed or "triggered". I write more about these important issues in the sequel, *"Soar: Pretty in Peace"*, which is primarily focused on positively regulating the nervous system to address the negative impacts of past traumas and to become more resilient to future traumas.

Reparenting

Most of us have experienced some sort of childhood trauma that has left a "wounded inner child" in us that didn't feel "seen", "heard", "loved" or even like they could be childlike. Dr. LePera suggests four areas or "pillars" to "reparent" ourselves. In other words, having the opportunity to treat yourself the way your "inner child" needed but your caregivers weren't able to. This one is very practical. Two of the reparenting areas are: emotional regulation (this includes witnessing emotions, breathing and letting the emotions pass); and loving discipline (keeping small daily promises to yourself like stating your needs and saying no to things you don't want to do). We've already touched on these subjects indirectly.

The other two reparenting exercises were things that I was already instinctively doing in an attempt to take care of myself and generally be happy. These last two areas are: self care (things like exercising, cooking, connecting with loved ones and spending time in nature); and childlike wonder (doing things that are spontaneous and playful and give you joy). I have instinctively done a number of these things for as long as I can remember. They are my simple pleasures and make up the bulk of my normal day. I was happy to see that things I was already regularly doing were useful for trauma healing.

Nervous System Regulation

Our nervous systems are often "dysregulated" from repeated onslaughts of stress and/or prolonged durations of stress. Unresolved trauma creates dysregulation within the nervous system and the longer it goes unresolved, the more deeply embedded that dysregulation becomes. Traumas that are left ***unresolved*** become "***embodied***" in our bodies physiologically. This is why it is important to take a holistic approach to healing. We can help resolve our psychological traumas by engaging our bodies therapeutically.

As noted above, Dr. LePera highlights a wide range of ways stress can negatively impact our nervous systems. I was able to quickly assess my level of nervous system dysregulation from my repeated and prolonged traumas, immediately recognizing most if not all of the dysregulation symptoms in myself. Suffice it to say, for this book, that my assessment was that my nervous system was completely "whacked".

In "*How to Do the Work*", Dr. LePera enumerates useful daily practices to restore balance to your nervous system.

As I was writing this book, I knew that stopping the ongoing cycle of abuse I had endured throughout my life was, obviously, a huge part of my healing. I couldn't truly ***move on*** though until I addressed the cumulative damage that had been done to my nervous system from my lifetime of abuses and traumas. I often felt the impact of my taut, frayed nerves from my history; despite stopping the actual abuses, it often felt like the smallest of things could still cause my nerves to unravel. I still had a ***limiting overhang*** from that history I was determined to break free from. I hadn't really appreciated that not only had I been "battered" and "bruised", not only had I become exhausted and depleted from always having to be "on guard", adaptable, strong and resilient, but so had my nervous system. It too was "broken", in a state of disharmony, the ongoing impacts of which I couldn't/didn't want to ignore. I was also still incredibly shy/introverted and also knew I still had a lot of work to do to tackle my abandonment issues.

I had come so far in my healing but I wasn't done. I had waited a lifetime to heal and realized I didn't want to do so in a half-assed manner, so I dove head first into addressing my whacked nervous system. I became fascinated with the nervous system and my ability to heal myself from my classic instances of abuses more profoundly as well as better equip myself to deal with the inevitable traumas and stressors we all face. I was confident I would no longer be "classically abused" but I wanted to take my journey one step forward...

I chronicle this latter part of my healing journey in the sequel, "*Soar: Pretty in Peace: Rewire Your Magical Mind to Live Happily Ever Now*". This book is about **getting control** and **stopping the abuse**, becoming "primed for peace". I'm thrilled to say, I "stopped going to the circus". The sequel is about **balancing my nervous system** and actually **finding peace** to enable me to realize my full, authentic, unlimited life.

Chapter 6

Testing 1, 2, 3.... : Testing Empowered Consciousness

& the "Triggers"

The Power of Perspective & the Empowered Consciousness

With hindsight, my new awareness and healing progress, there are many historical instances where I realize I had emotional incendiary arguments with people that I love based on *my* ego "issues" *and theirs*. I truly believe that my healing helped me improve not only myself but my relationships as well. I now better understand my loved ones and engage with them in a much calmer, enlightened manner. This will be an ongoing project as I navigate through it but it gives me great optimism going forward in my interactions which often unfairly suffered from the effects of my history of abuse. I never want to hurt loved ones but I realized I often did so based on my instinctual, "survival mode" reactions *dictated* more or less by my history of abuses. Healing has given me an unexpected beautiful gift of greater perspective and compassion, enabling better relationships from my ability to respond to situations with *empowered consciousness* instead of *emotional reactivity* with all the negative "fall out" that accompanies it.

For example, I know I feel extraordinarily threatened historically if my romantic partner didn't *need* me sexually or financially, because to me that meant I had no worth. Lack of fidelity is my one deal breaker in a romantic relationship and I wholeheartedly believe that no one has ever cheated on me. I view infidelity as an existential threat to my very being, my worth, my identity. After the demise of my second marriage, a college friend had a tendency of suggesting that my husband had cheated on me. I was already in deep pain over him leaving me but I was confident that he never cheated on me. I should have simply told her that I was confident he had been faithful, that it was a super sensitive subject that was off limits. Instead we had seriously heated spats over it a few times. I now realize - and she basically acknowledged at one point - that infidelity was her "issue", her sore spot, her former husband having confessed to cheating on her.

With my greater self awareness, I also now realize why I reacted so emotionally instead of just dismissing her comments as meaningless pure speculation and conjecture on her part (and nothing to do with my husband or me per se). In my head based on my definition of my self worth, she was questioning my very identity and value. We love each other dearly and of course she wasn't doing that. In her head, all men cheat and she was just throwing my husband within that erroneous assumption. She didn't mean to strike a raw chord with me - repeatedly... Assuming all men cheated helped her ego and to process her story. She wasn't saying anything negative about me.

It took my healing and that reflection though to understand the situation for what it was. I abhorred these arguments. They really challenged our lifelong friendship because the topic was very emotional and incendiary for both of us for different reasons based on our different experiences and perspectives. I do not bristle whatsoever if someone talks negatively about my husband having taken advantage of me financially. He clearly did and in my skewed psyche that historically meant I had worth. My friend's repeated insistence that he had cheated on me implied the exact opposite to me - that I was worthless. Of course, this was absolutely not her intent or belief. Appreciating our respective perspectives enables me to diffuse the situation and prevent an incendiary, hurtful argument.

Recognizing someone else's "filters", "projections" and issues helps me not only interact in a more compassionate understanding way but also helps enable me not to let my energy get stolen from fruitless, pointless discussions. I am not a very vocal opinionated person. Normally, I have no problem not engaging with someone pointlessly over topics we are in disagreement over. I know how I feel about things and I don't need to try to prove a point or be right for the sake of being right. I prefer to preserve peace. It wasn't until after I had progressed in my healing though that I was able to be more circumspect and respond calmly to things of such a great personal nature like a discussion about my husband's fidelity. I am now better equipped to interact thoughtfully even with topics that are so emotionally charged based on my ego and triggers *and* the other person's ego and triggers.

Another example is Mike, obviously one of my longest and dearest friends whom I know also views himself as the "caregiver", the "rescuer/protector". I found him very distant and painfully much less interactive after the demise of my second marriage and my financial situation. It hurt terribly because at first, it felt to me like he was being dismissive, basically ignoring me and not giving me the compassion I wanted so desperately. He had been there for me every day after the attempted murder. How could he "leave me", I wondered in disbelief and dismay after I experienced the worst pain of my life. Surely, he no longer cared....

I now realize based on my healing and my reflections that he likely struggled with not being able to absolve me of my pain. I believe that he did somewhat "distance" himself from me because he wasn't able to fulfill his self-defined worth, his very purpose from his perspective. I know no one loves me more or wants better for me than he does. I truly think he feels my pain as I feel my loved ones' pains. The distance I perceived was not from lack of caring or compassion whatsoever but from his "ego issues". This more understanding, informed analysis enables me to feel less "abandoned" and hurt and to share my feelings with him, clarifying my need for compassion - not solutions. This awareness and communication has deepened our lifelong bond even further.

Another example is with my dear sister. I used to spend a lot of money on her and her children, financially helping her and treating them to lavish gifts and trips. Additionally when my nephew was ill, I spent thousands of dollars on travel and other expenses to be by her side and support her. For a long time, I was incredibly hurt because when I was visiting one time from out of the country she said she didn't know if she could "justify" incurring the expense of the gas money to take the 90 minute trip to visit me. At this point, she was a lawyer. I was quite pained, thinking how little she must care for me despite all the money I had previously spent vis-a-vis her and her kids.

It wasn't until recently that I was able to analyze the situation differently. Decades before, my sister's husband had left her and her two young children in the middle of the night, abandoning them, including financially. My sister wasn't working at the time and struggled. It's one of the times that I had helped. Between that experience and having grown up financially challenged as we did as children, I know this instilled a certain fear in her and a Spartan-type budgeting mentality. I assumed from that one little likely unintentional remark that I meant so little to her that she couldn't justify a nominal amount to see me. I am quite confident now that it had to do with her bruised/frightened financial psyche and was absolutely no reflection on me or her love for me. I should have talked to my sister when she made that comment instead of being silently pained for years. I now have the perspective and awareness to better deal with any similar situations in the future, saving myself a lot of heartache. My sister and I are wildly different in the most comprehensive sense. Writing this book has made me appreciate her "earth angel" status throughout my life. She has always "had my back" and I am extraordinarily grateful that our bond is closer than ever.

My final example is when my mom had casually remarked that she should have left my father decades earlier. As I recounted, this pained me unbelievably for years especially with my abandonment fears. Like I said, she clarified that she would have taken my sister and me with her. But for my "ego" and issues, I would have never made the grossly wrong assumption that she was callously going to leave us. I suffered in silence unnecessarily for years before I finally asked her about it. Previously when I thought someone was doing something hurtful, I didn't have the courage to question it because I didn't think I deserved better.

I now appreciate the power of communication and perspective more than ever. As Buddhism says, a lot of suffering is caused by misperceptions. We **owe** it to **ourselves** and **our loved ones** to openly communicate instead of harboring insecurities and uncertainties in silent suffering. This new perspective has been a huge unexpected blessing for me from my healing journey. Based on my appreciation for my "ego", as well as others' egos, I am far less likely to assume the worst/take things personally and be hurt, or lash out from pain and/or "withdraw" and resort to numbing substances.

Testing the Triggers

My easiest test cases to challenge how well I was doing healing were those with men to whom I was not attracted or with whom I wanted more of a relationship and it was obvious they only wanted sex. Yes, as noted, sadly my psyche was that f—ked up where I would have sex with someone I did not want to have sex with or with someone who clearly could not meet my needs.

One instance of the former was one man to whom I had never been attracted and who relentlessly pursued me after having had sex with a dear friend of mine. The thought of having sex with him repulsed me in multiple ways, yet I still struggled to say no based on my underlying belief that it was my "obligation". The extreme discomfort I felt saying no to "giving my body" in this circumstance helped me realize the ludicrous nature of ever saying yes - or having difficulty saying no - when I did not want to have sex for whatever reason. I was no longer going to let that sense of obligation instilled since childhood dictate what I would do with my own body - really nothing more fundamental than our right to say no in this case.

My real test came when I made myself say no to test myself with a man I wanted to have a relationship with. I had been out of the country for several months. Not only had I not seen him but had barely interacted with him in my absence. After I returned, he asked if he could come over one morning. I had more or less just finished reading Dr. LePera's "*How to Do the Work*". For some reason because it was morning, I naively thought he had just missed me and wanted to spend time together. He came at noon with a bottle of wine, which to our mutual surprise, I declined to drink - only because of the hour.

He said he wanted to cuddle which I was more than fine with, thinking we would cuddle and catch up, having not spoken in several months. He immediately proceeded to try to have sex. When I asked him to slow down, he basically told me he had to leave very soon to do some work. He became pretty physically assertive. I still primally, instinctively wanted to have sex - very much; I really liked him. His assertiveness and my realization that he clearly was just using me for sex motivated me to assert myself verbally and physically. I basically had to fight him off; he even commented how strong I was, I was resisting so much and for so long. He eventually stopped and left in a huff. The experience shook me. I realized how sad it was that I gave myself so willingly that I honestly could never before consider the possibility of me being raped by someone I knew because I never would actually say no, regardless of what I wanted. As sad as it may be, I was extremely proud of myself, having not allowed myself to be used, notwithstanding that I had wanted sex too.

These types of events actually disgusted and saddened me. I now finally appreciated the origin of my lifelong habit of unquestionably, obligatorily giving my body. It sickens me recounting these events. Although I was proud of myself and my evidence of healing, it troubled me that it took such extreme cases to say no - and even then uncomfortably. The extreme nature was not lost on me and served a healing purpose, making me realize that it was never my obligation to do something I didn't want to - **no explanation, apology or guilt needed**. "No" is a complete sentence and I was ecstatic I had finally found my self worth and my voice to be able to start saying it....

PART FOUR: PROGNOSIS: HOW AM I DOING?

*"**Stop** going to the circus."*
Me

Chapter 1
Signs of Healing: Measured Responses, Measured Wine & Boomerang Love

*F*iercely Overcoming the Negative Limiting Core Belief

I realized I had to change my belief instilled since childhood that I was a means to an end before I could stop the ongoing pattern of disrespectful and abusive relationships. I have been working on replacing that belief with the belief that "I am the end". I am now deeply and painfully aware that allowing anyone to treat me in a utilitarian manner is ludicrous and was the cause of most of the pain and heartache I had endured throughout my life. Not only was it ludicrous. It had also turned out counterproductively, as I was discarded once I no longer served another's purpose.

This is a harsh reality for me. I could have saved myself a lot of suffering had I "done the work" much earlier in life. That's ok, I'm glad I finally got where I needed to be. I hope though that I help shine a little light for someone else. I hope someone can learn from my "lessons". I am intentionally not calling them "mistakes". You do what you can, what you need to, when you need to. I think that childhood abuse and trauma in general are starting to get the attention they deserve. I fervently hope that it takes others less time, less trauma, and less abusive relationships to get where I finally landed.

I have plenty of non-romantic relationships in which I am given true, unconditional love and I am cognizant that I should not accept anything less in romantic encounters. I am trying to internalize this validation that I am loveable and loved and continue daily affirmations to override my conditioned belief that I am merely a means to an end. ***I am not a means to an end. I am the be all and end all. Love me for me - simply me - or kindly step the f—k aside.*** These are my new ***savage self love*** and ***self respect*** mantras more or less, now that I have finally found my ferocious power to *roar*...

Empowered Consciousness & Emotional Maturity

Disavowing myself of my prior limiting core belief has paved the way for me to change my behaviors since beliefs guide our behaviors. I recognize there will be periodic, and importantly, *temporary* setbacks from a lifetime of traumas and conditioned trauma responses. I am fully, consciously aware of my traumas and conditioned responses, however, and have the tools I lacked for decades to *respond* to challenges and triggers *consciously and rationally* instead of letting my *conditioned emotional reactivity* dictate my behavior. Of course, there are times when I slip, but I feel more *empowered,* more *in control* than ever before. *I am not responsible for what has happened to me.* Now that I am aware though, *I am fully responsible for my actions* instead of relegating myself to autopilot programmed subconscious behaviors. There are several indications to me that I am firmly on the path of healing and growing.

Boundaries

I have begun to set boundaries. Honestly, this has been the most difficult for me because I was profoundly conditioned that I was a means to an end. Saying "no" is extraordinarily challenging for me but I have started saying it nonetheless. Not only did I feel terrible and selfish not automatically subjugating myself but I also struggled subjectively with my self worth given the fact that I felt I wasn't worthy of love if I weren't giving something of tangible value. I consciously know that anyone worthy of me will love me just for me and that it isn't healthy or productive for me to be with those who don't *value me simply for who I am, not what I give.* It's still a radical notion to me but I know now how sad that is and am determined to embrace and internalize my new positive thoughts.

I struggle though between unfairly filtering people's behavior through my lens of pain and not being so "naive" and "unguarded" that I continue to repeat disrespectful, abusive patterns. My very essence is to be loving, open and trusting. I fervently resist being otherwise even though to do so would inevitably save me a lot of pain. To not be my natural self, however, would also mean that I miss out on a lot of love, passion and happiness. My compassionate being would rather risk helping someone who doesn't actually need help than withholding help from someone who truly needs it. I refuse to let those who abused me close my heart or make me bitter or distrustful. I just need to be more circumspect.

I have realized setting boundaries on the things that are real deal breakers for me gives me a clear delineation so I don't have to worry about "red flags" or be on constant guard. The boundaries reflect what I will and will not accept so if crossed, no further analysis is necessary. I try to gauge the "reciprocity" of my relationships now. If they aren't mutually respectful and reciprocal, they are unbalanced and enable exploitation.

Reliance on Numbing Substances

As Dr. LePera has aptly described, trauma is like a gateway drug. This is a rare and enlightened perspective that resonated deeply with me. Another sign of healing is my healthier relationship with numbing substances. I absolutely stopped relying on any prescription medicines (like Xanax or Valium) to "get through" a night, my "go to" after Yanni left me, and cut down on my wine consumption. The prescription part was easy for me fortunately and I stopped regularly relying on pills years ago.

Honestly, drinking less alcohol has been more challenging for me. I am normally an "all or nothing" type but I enjoy wine. It's the only type of alcohol I drink regularly. I was extremely relieved to discover that although I had a psychological "reliance" on alcohol that I was not physically dependent. I am in control and I have given myself limits in terms of frequency and amount. I use a measuring cup that I got from my mom for baking which makes me feel like we're in this together. I'm setting boundaries on myself so to speak.

I am very focused on continually improving my health as I age. I have the clear motivation to avoid numbing substances and a subpar life and now am in control to do so. I am fully aware that "drowning" my sorrows was an attempt in futility and just made the situation vastly worse. I am being vigilant about avoiding drinking to *numb* myself vs. drinking to enjoy myself. Historically, sadly from an early age, I was trying to drown my "thought demons". Now, I confront them. I am more enlightened and make better choices generally. I have used a number of natural substances to cope with stress, anxiety over solitude and difficulty sleeping with great success. I engage in daily rituals and pastimes to help me self soothe and increase my tolerance to challenging situations.

Relationships & Sex

Love is not a subset of sex. This was a huge realization for me. I don't attain love from the mere act of sex, notwithstanding I had lived my life as if this were a truism. Sex is a subset of love - a wonderful intimate expression of love for me. It is a huge sign of my healing to me that I no longer inextricably intertwine sex with love.....

Monogamous sex is the sexiest for me now. This is extremely telltale for me given my historic behavior from my skewed psyche. I am thrilled that I have been "checking myself" for some time now and not engaging in random, indiscriminate sex. I am a monogamous person at heart. Historically, I would go through periods of sexual interaction with multiple men. Even if I were in an exclusive relationship, I needed a "back up" plan when things weren't going well with a relationship. My initial reaction to relationship issues, that had my triggers at heart, was to explosively break it off and immediately seek comfort in the next man "in line" so to speak. My daily affirmations have helped me avoid this merry-go-round of men approach to soothe my pain and my determination to no longer engage in reckless sexual conduct provides further motivation.

Actually, I'm having the best sex of my life and, quite frankly it's always been great. This came as such an incredible unexpected surprise to me and not just because of that fact alone. It's because it's a huge reflection of my healing. I realized that previously being basically used as a mere object of desire subconsciously turned me on; it was validation of my twisted sense of self. Since I had mistakenly associated the mere act of sex with love, the more men I had, the more I felt I was loved on some level even when it felt shallow. I always said I felt like the loneliest person in a sea of men. I felt empty, unfulfilled. Now I am enjoying sex as an intimate expression of deep, true, mutual love - not as a means to an end. It's the most beautiful gift. Monogamy is the hottest for me, not only igniting my body but my soul.

I am extraordinarily grateful that love is limitless. I have an endless supply no matter how many people I loved and no matter how many people did not show me the same unconditional love I bestowed on them. ***Love is my superpower***; it is my reason for being. It is my purpose and I mean love in the most comprehensive sense, not just romantically. Love for friends, family, nature, animals, life in general, and, yes, now myself. Love is the greatest expression of one's soul and I am a master at expressing it.

Love is also the greatest healing "medium" for me. Healthy relationships are integral to profound trauma healing. I no longer needed anyone to "validate" me or make me "whole". I wasn't "incomplete" but I did want someone to "complement" me. I hadn't needed anyone to "save" me either. I was the leading lady/the heroine of my story. I needed to progress on my healing before I was ready for true love. I am so grateful to have found that in Barış. Barış' and my co-regulation is off the charts in the best way possible. I always said "misery loves company" but "happiness loves company" too, so choose wisely. I've always been an incredibly expressive, loving, affectionate, basically happy person and I have finally met my match. It's like we're our own little good vibes tribe.

As you undoubtedly have concluded, I love inspiration and symbolism. From the beginning, Barış lovingly called me his princess. I felt like I was a princess of love in a fairytale. I was the self heroine who triumphed over evil trauma and a half-lived life, uniting with my "prince" to *live happily ever now*. It was coincidentally fortuitous that his name is "Love Peace". What more could I dream for? We even dubbed our apartment "Chateau Amour". Feel free to embrace my rose-colored glasses or ignore them if too sappy for your personal taste. I've earned them though and obviously I am not blind to the often harsh realities of life. I've always been happy, positive, energetic and loving but for the first time, I have an equal counterpart in that regard. So, yes, I am reveling in that...

So many people have expressed surprise that I can love so easily and openly having experienced various extremely painful things in pretty much all my relationships. Others have expressed that they would be too bitter, too mistrustful to open their hearts again. I love though. That's who I am. I love with an unconditional all consuming love - to me that is the only way to love. There is no such thing as unhealthy or toxic love. There are unhealthy attachments and toxic relationships but love itself is, and always will be, true and beautiful to me. I never regret loving.

So many people have hurt me but I refuse to let them take any more from me. No one will ever close my heart or dilute my spirit. No one can diminish my essence. Unfortunately most of my relationships have largely felt like a one way street in terms of love, support, thoughtfulness, respect, caretaking.... Barış is a beautiful exception to that. I am blessed to be enjoying what I have dubbed *"Boomerang Love".* Barış has shown me how huge and simultaneously exciting and peaceful mutual true love can be. Our respective love, passion, respect and thoughtfulness is returning to the other with the same spectacular intensity and ferocity and gloriously "boomeranging" back. I am proud of myself for never letting the darkness in my life darken my soul. I am grateful to have been thusly rewarded for my seemingly infinite capacity to love. I am blessed.

Sweet Dreams

One of the most significant signs of my healing and for which I am beyond grateful is my ability to sleep relatively well. I admittedly still struggle at times with nighttime restlessness and lingering feelings of unease but have vastly improved in this area and continue to do so. I know I will get better and am actively working on this, the details of which I elaborate on in the sequel, *"**Soar: Pretty inPeace**."* It makes sense that undoing the cumulative harm to your nervous system from a lifetime of traumas takes time. If you are used to being on "high alert"/ on "guard" your whole life, not being vigilant can seem uncomfortable and cause its own unease because it's so unfamiliar. Once I get to sleep, however, I am sleeping more easily, more peacefully than ever before. As I have indicated, I struggled with sleep for my whole life. For decades, I would wake up at 3 or 4 and often arose then because I knew I couldn't get back to sleep. I know how incredibly important sleep is for our psychological and physical health and this is a huge triumph for me. Now, even if something wakes me up, I can get back to sleep. The "call to prayer" from the mosques in Turkey are as early as 4:30 am and always wake me up. It is miraculous to me that I can fall asleep afterwards, not fearful of what I will dream at this normally dream-intensive time. I am also not having dreams that are violent or sexual in nature. Finally, I have been able to nap on those rare occasions I choose to. Previously I would start having panic attacks and not be able to sleep no matter how exhausted I was. There could be no greater, more tangible sign to me of my healing than being able to sleep in tranquility.

Physiological Signs

I've always loved uncontrollable laughter but cry relatively little in regards to myself. I can shed waterworks for others but rarely for myself. I find myself laughing more, crying tears of deep gratitude and joy and sighing frequently. Laugh, cry, sigh....These are all great means of letting your traumas out and releasing nervous tension. I have also finally been able to release the knot of tension I have always carried in my shoulder. It was the primary ongoing physiological embodiment of my unresolved trauma. It also connected to my optical nerve and historically caused me to frequently have a migraine in the works. My posture was always terrible, a reflection of a kind of shielding myself/going inward as a sort of protective cocoon and a reflection of my low self-esteem. I know my horrid posture, which I have had since childhood, has exacerbated that shoulder knot. I am actively working on my posture and becoming more confident, more "open". I feel so much better without the constant knot reminiscent of all my prior traumas.

Confidence

I have lived my life seemingly paradoxically as an "overachiever" to garner my father's pride and to support others financially and an "underachiever", dismissing my achievements and contributions to pacify the relatively largely self-absorbed or larger ego of my husbands, respectively. It's time to live ***my*** life for ***myself*** on ***my*** terms.

I have never worked harder on anything, nor been prouder of anything I have done, more than this book. I am proud of my courage to share the ***raw, intimate, vulnerable*** details of my life, most of which I was not proud of. Understanding myself from the insights I gained in my healing journey gave me that courage to share. I hope my healing in some small way may help another on his or her own unique path of healing. In particular, I was the poster child for avoiding healing, opting instead to continue to repress and suppress. I hope the seemingly absurd way I had been living my life sheds some light on why it is important to resolve trauma. There are endless resources to help heal once you understand you need to do so. I have shared some of the resources and tools that have been impactful to me. I hope sharing gives others some insights and inspirations on their paths to discover what uniquely works for them.

I normally shy away from attention and think I have nothing worthwhile to contribute. I hope that by sharing my story, I may help in some small way shed some light on the crisis of childhood abuse and the need as a society to prioritize and address it. I profoundly hope we stop the suffering in silence of children and the adults they become. I hope we collectively *ferociously roar* in this regard. I am proud to serve as an example of the happy, fulfilled life that is possible notwithstanding a *history* of abuse. ***I'm done being a survivor***. That's why I have self-dubbed myself, "***The Naked Conqueror***", reflective of my intimate chronicling of my triumph over trauma. I'm happy to put a qualifying "*ex-*" before "survivor", just like before the husbands.

Absent my healing and my budding confidence, I would never deign to think I could be of any help or an inspiration to others. I know marketing this book will be a huge challenge to my shy, introverted self, plagued by a life of low self-esteem and self worth. I'm up for the challenge though and I have given myself the ongoing challenge to grow. I have sprouted now - shout out to Carol - and I am only going to continue growing...

Chapter 2
(mis)Perceptions in Practice

I have incredible discipline when I put my mind to something. Realizing there could be nothing more important than my health has caused me to prioritize my healing and channel my resolve and efforts in a much more productive way than ever before. Healing does not mean I will never be "triggered". I am self aware enough to realize that I tend(ed) to analyze the present through my traumatized past and this can frequently create "trauma drama". This is unfair to the other person and to myself; it inevitably creates new pain.

As I admitted, it's challenging to control my triggers because there is a barely imperceptible line between being triggered irrationally and allowing myself to continue to be used. I am aware now and that is half the battle so to speak. Now when I encounter a potentially triggering event, I make myself pause and reflect. This helps prevent me from automatic, intense, emotional, caustic reactionary outbursts that previously accompanied my assumptions that I was being taken advantage of or about to be abandoned. I now ask myself whether the other person's general treatment of me is consistent with the assumption I am making based on my past painful traumas.

As I have noted, my healing has given me a beautiful gift of awareness that is incredibly useful for my relationship interactions. I touched on this briefly before but want to share how this has worked for me in practice because it is a huge testament to my moving forward.

Recall that Buddhism sagely cautions that ***misperceptions are the source of a lot of unnecessary suffering***. Although this quote had resonated with me since I first read, "*The Art of Happiness*", by the Dalai Lama, I hadn't done much with it frankly. My new increased self awareness enabled me to use this wisdom in a very practical way. Now if I have a potential issue with someone, I try to be forthright with the fact that *I* am feeling a certain way based on *my perceptions* and sharing those perceptions with the person in an effort to get the clarifications/reassurances I am seeking. It's a recognition that often I am misperceiving the situation.

This enables me to broach the subject of whatever is making me feel uneasy or upset in a non-confrontational way, without triggering the other person or making him or her feel responsible or defensive. It makes us take responsibility for how we *perceive* the situation, recognizing that we may often be misperceiving it based on unfairly filtering it within the cumulative context of our issues, our egos, our triggers, our insecurities and our past traumas, etc. This is a much more productive way to address the situation than jumping to the wrong conclusion and immediately, instinctively lashing out in pain and creating a combative, contentious environment counterproductive to peaceful resolution. Communication is so critical and can save so much unnecessary drama and pain.

No one is perfect; people make mistakes; relationships require understanding. Whenever I'm feeling insecure for instance with Barış because of something he does or doesn't do or says or fails to say, I pause and reflect on the way he generally and consistently treats me. That reflection enables me to quickly realize that my assumption/perception likely isn't warranted because it's inconsistent with the loving, respectful way he treats me. I have always needed constant affirmations of love. Barış has been the most expressive person I have ever been in a relationship with - romantic or otherwise. He consistently expresses his love for me in word and deed. Sometimes, I start to feel insecure if he is busy and I haven't heard from him for a while. I definitely still have abandonment issues and Barış is very sensitive to that. I hope to get to the point though that I can internalize his expressed feelings and not be overly needy. The onus is also on me to respectfully share my feelings and needs. I cannot expect him to cater to my unspoken, often irrational feelings.

My sister just told me a very telltale story about the overhang impact our childhood has on our relationships. Apparently, my father used to make a production about going around and making sure all the windows and doors were locked before we slept to demonstrate his "protection" of us. I didn't really remember until she brought it up - likely because that was ironic to me since it has always been within my home that I have been abused.

She, however, spent years going around in a huff checking to make sure the doors in her house were locked, very troubled that her husband wasn't doing that. To her, it signified he didn't love her. Of course, this wasn't true and she caused herself a lot of unnecessary suffering by not communicating her feelings to him.

Deep breathing is a great way to "pause" before *responding*. It's important to practice this regularly to be able to calm your nervous system when you feel your sympathetic "fight or flight" system being activated. Having an agreed "cooling off" period may also work well for others. As I have noted, it does not work well for me. I realize in part because of my abandonment issues. If something that is troubling me isn't immediately resolved, I start to already feel "abandoned". I am such a passionate intense person, I need to dive right in and get to the heart of the matter. I do realize that if I can't deal with a "cooling off" break, I owe the other person my respect to not lash out and give voice so to speak to my pain. I need to articulate what I am feeling respectfully with the realization that my perceptions are, more often than not, inaccurate. Another useful exercise is to experiment with trying to align your perception with the reality you want. As Scott Robinson, "the brain guy", wisely counsels, your perceptions become your reality. Makes sense to focus on the most positive ones possible!

Most of my "issues" and "triggers" (and Barış' as well) have at their core, the need for reassurance. We're feeling unloved or are mistakenly feeling the other is going to abandon us. These situations call for calm reassurances, loving words and hugs - not lashing out at each other from respective deep levels of pain and insecurities. If you are in a truly, loving and mutually respectful relationship, you can find effective, loving means to deal with the inevitable issues and disputes. Having disagreements is part of a healthy relationship. The important thing is how you work through them and how you are there for each other.

Fortunately for me, given my intense persona, Barış doesn't insist on a cooling off period. He knows what I need. When I am deeply triggered, his "go to" response is to hug me, cuddle me…. Historically, I have gotten in to simultaneous and paradoxical *"fight" and "flight"* mode. Let me tell you, I readily admit it is ugly and scary. I call the combination *"fright"* mode. As I shared, I was in that mode when I ended up physically hurt by Marlon and Mariano.

I was also in "fright" mode a couple of times in the midst of my healing journey with Barış. He has issues with "control" from his childhood, when his dad would punish him severely if he didn't keep him apprised of everything he was doing, where he was going, etc. I love so deeply and in an all consuming manner. I always want to know what my loved ones are doing, how they are feeling, what they are thinking, etc. He would be going out and I would ask where or to do what, and he would only respond that he was "going out". He would be with friends and message that he would be home "soon". When our definitions of soon didn't sync and each minute felt like an eternity to me while I waited up for him, expecting him to be home "soon", I was livid by the time he got home. My insecurities and abandonment issues added incendiary fuel to my emotional fire each moment I waited, certain he was being disrespectful. I would immediately lash out accusatorily when he got home.

During one of these incidents before I was aware of his childhood issues, he said something about my "controlling" ways which made me lose it even more. Lose it to the point that we both feared for my physical well-being. I think I reacted so visibly, so explosively because I was in the midst of my healing journey and thought I had been completely wrong about Barış. I was certain my heart was going to be broken again. He was trying to calm me down, trying to hug me, help me slow my breathing. I was in fight mode, my heart racing, my body trembling. I felt like I couldn't breathe, sobbing and gasping uncontrollably. My fight mode quickly turned to flight mode. I was adamant I was leaving, not able to contain the emotions inside me. He continued trying to calm and comfort me. He was trying to encourage me to sniff my calming oils and holding me in a tight embrace. I was desperately flailing against his efforts, particularly in light of my history of physical abuse, at times in the context of trying to escape some sort of confinement. Nonetheless, he kept holding me, trying to soothe me with loving words and it eventually worked. He told me he wanted to change - he wasn't used to being in a long term relationship - but that he couldn't overnight.

We were supposed to go on a trip that next day. I was exhausted, forlorn and adamant that we would not go, annoyed that he had disturbed my sleep and peace. He said we would still go and asked if we could sleep together, him holding me, saying it may be the last night he could smell my natural scent. His words and hugs calmed me down sufficiently to agree. The next day was awkward until we got into another dispute in the other town - that took us 10 hours of bus rides to get to. I wanted to understand why he had called me "controlling". He wasn't ready to discuss it yet which incensed me again. I asked if he wanted to go back home while I ferried to Greece - my m.o. - "escape" mode. He said this wasn't him, he didn't do long term relationships or live with anyone.

I was crushed, beside myself. I thought he was breaking up with me. This time instead of lashing out, I retreated, walking a short distance away, seriously thinking of going to Greece instead of enduring a miserable long bus ride going back. I kept thinking how could he be breaking up with me over the last night's events when he constantly told me he loved me more than anything and that I was the meaning of his life. I was crushed but proud of my mini retreat - something I would have been incapable of pre-healing progress. I loved him dearly and didn't want to say anything hurtful out of pain.

After I managed to calm myself down sufficiently to talk calmly, I rejoined him. My assumption had been way off base. I said something about what an awful bus ride back it was going to be since he dumped me. He looked at me in shock and asked how I could possibly have thought he would break up with me when he always said he loved me more than anyone, would always love me and that I was the meaning of his life. I smiled in profound relief as he explained he was trying to apologize that he wasn't used to being in a long-term relationship and he was trying to navigate the nuances. Then, he started telling me about his childhood issues and his visceral negative instinctual reaction to being questioned, "controlled", etc. He said he wasn't used to anyone caring about him or worrying about him - as opposed to controlling - and how much he appreciated my love and concern. He had just been reacting to it with his filter of his past traumas. I was sad for him about his childhood but was so relieved that we weren't breaking up and so happy to understand each other better.

Knowledge of each other's pasts was helping each of us react to the other in a more sensitive, rational, calmer, informed manner. He also mentioned that our language "barrier" caused some of our misunderstandings. His English was so good and he was so quick to understand me that frankly any language barrier had escaped me. I didn't realize that he didn't know as much English as I thought given how smoothly our communications went. He always listened to me so intently, so thoughtfully and with love. Sometimes he was understanding me - not all the words - based on context and I didn't appreciate that he was embarrassed to tell me when he didn't understand everything. I immensely enjoyed the rest of our trip together. For the first time, I was living with someone who treated me with mutual love, respect, thoughtfulness, admiration and adoration. Score 1 for healing!

PART FIVE: REFLECTIONS & HOPES

"They tried to bury us. They didn't know we were seeds."
Dinos Christianopoulos

You are not Alone
One of the worst things about abuse is *feeling* like you are alone. Like you are suffocating incomprehensibly in solitude in an endless loop of incredible confusion and pain. Like something is wrong with you, "off". Particularly if you endured childhood abuse at the hands of a primary caretaker, you likely confided in no one. If the people who are supposed to love you and take care of you hurt you, to whom do you confide? Whom can you possibly trust? These are questions that are too conflicted, too overwhelming for a little mind to comprehend. Indeed when you are abused by a caregiver, it's difficult to understand the gravity of the abuse or the incredibly evil nature of it. It's what you know. It's your own little world. It's what's being modeled to you as "normal". You know you are terrified and that you don't want any part of it but you don't have the faculties to appreciate the "abusive" nature of it. You have nothing to compare it to and you are extraordinarily conflicted.

So what does your wise brain do when it's confronted with something too horrific, too terrifying, too much to handle? It often makes you "disassociate" so your mind doesn't have to consciously endure what your body is suffering and you frequently repress it. You are in survival mode. It's no wonder that survivors of childhood abuse have little to no memories from childhood. These powers to "disassociate" or disconnect and to repress seem like almost superhero powers at the time, enabling you to get through the petrifying event(s). When you are too confused, conflicted or scared to divulge the abuse, it exacerbates the harm and makes it less likely you will confide in anyone, seek help or even remember. These likely circumstances are obviously and sadly counterproductive to healing...

Unfortunately there is also often a stigma associated with the abuse itself, whether societally, or self-imposed. When we know something is "wrong" and has to be kept a secret, we feel shame, if not outright guilt. It's extraordinarily difficult for a child to comprehend that he or she is not responsible for his or her "participation". We generally don't benefit from an exculpatory "no", which can translate into an erroneous but incredibly uncomfortable feeling of being voluntarily complicit. This adds a great deal of confusion to the situation.

Even if we manage to escape feeling shame with respect to the abuses themselves, we have likely engaged in different "survival-type" behaviors or coping mechanisms which make us feel weak and out of control. We are ashamed by our natural tendencies to avoid pain. Addictions and substance abuse are coping and numbing behaviors. There are a number of things I have divulged throughout this book of which I was not proud. I understand them now though and that gives me the courage to share them in hopes of providing insight into the traumatized psyche to those who have also been abused as well as to those who struggle to understand us. Throughout my life, I was often an enigma to family, friends, strangers, even myself. My relationships, my numbing behaviors and certain decisions (like quitting my job and endlessly moving) were irrational to them, indeed, often reckless.

The overriding tendency to remain silent with our "shameful secret" is incredibly counterproductive to healing. We individually and collectively need to *"roar"*. ***Healing does not happen in silence.*** Exposing abuses to the light of day so to speak, whether to a friend, a therapist or even a journal, for instance, helps to make it less "dark", less scary and helps pave the way to healing. Sharing your abuse with another helps you to be "seen", to be "heard", to have your feelings validated and to receive compassion. Talking or writing about how you feel also helps prompt the kind of self reflection required to become sufficiently aware to identify underlying negative limiting beliefs, unhealthy relationship dynamics and maladaptive, often destructive, coping mechanisms.

Childhood abuse is an urgent worldwide crisis with lifelong significant consequences absent intervention. We need to stop allowing it to be a taboo topic. Just because society is uncomfortable with it or doesn't have all the answers is no excuse to let children - and the adults they become - continue suffering in silence. We need to give the issue the priority it deserves and the resources necessary to address it.

I'm emboldened by the increased attention this topic is getting. I absolutely loved the fundamental shift in perspective from "what's wrong with you?" to "*What Happened to You?*", in the seminal book by Oprah Winfrey and Dr. Bruce Perry. It's this shift that can lay the groundwork for healing unresolved trauma individually and societally. I came across that incredible book while I was finishing writing this and appreciated how they had captured the essence of the problem within the extraordinarily insightful title itself.

I hope more and more people become comfortable sharing their experiences with abuse. *We have been silent for long enough. No more.* Writing this book has been extraordinarily healing to me although I had shunned even journaling my whole life. I thought it would keep me in a psychological loop of profound pain. It has been extremely cathartic instead, helping me to "let it out", to truly "release". We need to spread the message that *healing is possible and no one is ever alone.* No one should ever suffer in silence, in solitude.

Unfortunately, we are remarkably numerous but that gives us the power to help each other with a unique understanding and empathetic perspective. *Healing from trauma should not be a luxury*, reserved for those with the resources to get professional help. There are so many things we can do to *self heal* for free. Indeed, we are our own best, and holistic, healers when we have the necessary guidance to heal. I hope the tools integral to self healing continue to get the exposure they deserve. I hope by sharing insights and resources of our own healing journeys, others will find inspiration and useful guidance on their own unique path to healing.

Perspective

This book is a labor of love - for myself, as well as for any other trauma survivors I fervently hope in whose lives I may make a small difference sharing insights into *why* and *how* to *stop the insanity*. "Healing" undoubtedly will feel and look vastly different for everyone. I do not purport to have the answers for anyone. I hope I may motivate others, like myself, struggling to appreciate the need to address their traumas. My unresolved traumas had been limiting me from living a truly authentic, fulfilled life. My wish for everyone is to break free from the shackles of their past abuses.

I will forever be "colored", to some extent, by my traumatic experiences, but they never defined me and *no longer control me*. Their impact will always be "there" "somewhere", akin to scars. I am, gratefully, an eternal optimist, however, and am self aware enough and sufficiently distanced from my traumas, that I can appreciate the "good", if you will from *traversing* through my healing journey, necessitated by those traumas. My healing has made me an even more passionate and empathetic person and empowered me in a way that a different life never could have. Receiving compassion has been extraordinarily healing for me and I am forever grateful to my friends for their ceaseless willingness to listen lovingly to my troubled heart and mind. I humbly hope that I can similarly be "there" for others.

I no longer repress/suppress my memories but I also certainly don't dwell on them. I do, however, still compartmentalize to a large degree to be able to coexist with my father. I do not normally refer to him as "father" but intentionally chose to throughout this book for that very reason - as a sort of linguistic separation if you will. Since I was a teenager to this day, I have never felt comfortable alone in my father's presence - not so much due to the sexual abuse per se but because I am always on edge, awaiting to be blamed/scapegoated for something or be in trouble for doing something to upset him/trigger his health issues.

I used to appreciate the buffer of my mom's presence but, particularly over the past several years with heightened awareness and sensitivities, I significantly struggle being around them because I abhor how my father treats my mom a lot of the time. I find it impossible to keep my mouth shut and always try to defend her. He actually said once in "jest" (not the least bit funny to me) that he never thought my mom was a bitch when I was around - implying I am "bitchier" for having come to her defense. Notwithstanding the fact that my mom gets extraordinarily defensive on my behalf in my relationships, she clearly does not want me to speak up on her behalf as it makes things worse in her opinion. She can't pacify him while I am calling him out on things. It makes me very uncomfortable being around them and that saddens me terribly. I can't "fix" them. All I can do is no longer follow their examples. I fervently hope with my healing and new self awareness and appreciation for others' issues that I will be better equipped to deal with these interactions. Time will tell....

In case you are wondering I have absolutely no desire to "confront" my father. This is an extraordinarily personal decision and I know people differ on the topic. No one in my family is aware of this book. When I started looking into lucid dreaming, a couple of my friends thought I wanted to use it to confront my father in my dreams. I am confident in my ability to lucidly dream if I apply my mind to it. I did it a few times. My primary reason for wanting to lucidly dream was to "validate" the nature of my flashbacks. I was holding out hope that somehow I had gotten it wrong. In particular, I was hopeful I could tell my mom I had gotten it wrong.

It didn't go down that way, however. I got the confirmation I was looking for from my subconscious once I was clear what I wanted from it. This is before I had progressed so far with my healing. I didn't feel the need to "unrepress" anything more; it's not a place I care to dwell. I still find the concept fascinating. Dreams have always fascinated me. As I noted, I never even referred to my terrible dreams as "nightmares" because I intuitively realized they were useful messengers trying to send an alarm to alert me that I needed to address my unresolved traumas. They have served their purpose.

Rethinking Terminology

As I have shared, it took me decades to realize *why* I needed to heal and even longer to discover *how* to heal. I had always been frustrated with the advice to "*process*" my traumas, in large part because I didn't have a clue how. It seemed so elusive to me. I didn't even know what the f—k that meant. I would actually get annoyed when well-intentioned people would advise me to do so. Truly annoyed when people would tell me to just "let it go". Like they didn't think I desperately wanted to???? I thought everyone had some grand insight that I was missing out on.

Well-intentioned people would tell me to "process", to "sit still" with my pain and my feelings. It implied to me that there was some magical set flow chart or formulaic methodology or something that I just needed to "plug" my various abuses into and miraculously I would be healed. Or if I just sat long enough in excruciating emotional pain, the pain would simply, magically disappear. To me, it implied there was some defined process akin to the steps of processing grief from death. Death is natural and an inevitable part of life and does not involve a "perpetrator". It's something everyone must deal with. Abuse is unnatural, abhorrent and not inevitable. Death is something we more or less have to "accept". Abuse most certainly is not something we should ever accept.

I was not only lost about "processing" but also about what to process. The actual abuses themselves, as far as I am concerned, are not the focal point of the resolution. That terminology of "processing abuse" is primarily what confused me for so long and why I shunned addressing the various abuses. To me, it implied focusing on the abuses per se or ruminating about them - things that cause you to more or less relive them. Like fixate on them to understand them. They are inexplicable, shocking, irrational, inexcusable. I knew I could never "process" them in a way to comprehend them so it made perfect sense to me to repress and suppress them. The brain does not have a concept of time. If it is "triggered" by these things, it reacts as if it truly is happening again. I had absolutely no interest in dwelling on the abuses, which I could never make sense of. This is not healing for me.

This seemed idiotic to me, like "wallowing", further quagmiring myself in the traumas, giving them ongoing influence over my life, or *so I thought*. What happened, happened I told myself. I took a c'est la vie approach, priding myself on being "resilient" and adaptable, repressing/suppressing and "moving on", or *so I thought*.

In reality though, *by not resolving* my history of traumas, I was *giving them the ongoing power to determine my beliefs, dictate my behavior and control my life* - the exact opposite of what I thought was happening. I wasn't "moving forward"; I was *quagmired*, repeating the same patterns of abuse given my negative core belief that I was a mere means to an end. That hideous belief destined me to repeat the same soul-sucking, destructive, ruinous patterns.

Before I came across Dr. LePera, I had never read any books on trauma and abuse; to do so would have been inconsistent with my repressive strategy. After I had finished my first draft of this book, I started reading a few books on trauma and was surprised at how much they synced with me. I tend to do things the hard way. I now realize that I could have benefited significantly from reading these books earlier and hope that others may find them insightful as well.

In one of these books, "*Waking the Tiger*", the therapist Peter A. Levine beautifully captured a synopsis of how I had been living based on my failure to resolve my traumas: "Unresolved trauma can keep us excessively cautious and inhibited, or lead us around in ever-tightening circles of dangerous reenactment, victimization, and unwise exposure to danger." The "dangerous reenactment" certainly characterized what I had been experiencing as you have now witnessed. The "excessively cautious and inhibited" reflects what I had been feeling as living a suboptimal life, kind of paralyzed to really advance my life in any meaningful way.

I always felt like I exhibited completely contradictory behaviors at times - overly cautious some times and reckless other times. The fact that Mr. Levine captured each of those extremes as being the potential consequences of failing to resolve traumas resonated with me deeply. I often manifested seemingly contradictory behavior based on which nervous system "tool" I was utilizing in my survival mode at the time - for instance "flight" and "freeze" are on opposite spectrums. My tendency to oscillate amongst the different survival mode mechanisms undoubtedly confounded many an observer of me, whereas they made sense to me, being intimately involved with what I was feeling at the time.

I also vastly prefer the term, "*address*" over "process" for resolving unresolved trauma. I finally figured out how to "*address*" the ***ongoing negative effects*** of my abuses and behaviors modeled to me in childhood by becoming aware and dealing with my issues at the subconscious level. I needed to be "doing the work" to ground myself in the present, become self consciously aware to understand the beliefs, behaviors and patterns I was doomed to repeat and to reach a place where I felt safe, worthy, at peace and loved.

I, like many others who have survived abuse, also often bristle at the ***characterization*** of ourselves as "victims" or "survivors". These terms aren't any more useful to me than "processing" abuses. Both "definitions" are technically true to a certain extent. A "victim" is a person harmed by an event in simplistic terms. Yes, of course that is true. It has a tendency to denote passivity and/or helplessness, however. None of those connotations apply and I resist them vehemently. A "survivor", simplistically, is someone who manages to get through something so horrific that there was the potential to die, metaphorically or in reality. This term is preferable to me insofar as it connotes strength, courage and personal accountability and credit. I am much more than a "survivor" though; it merely denotes escaping some horrific circumstance or event.

"Victim" and "Survivor" give too much "control" to the acts perpetrated and the perpetrators thereof, something we understandably recoil at. We adamantly refuse to have ourselves or our lives be more or less defined by, or even characterized by, the abuses or the abusers. My abuses may have "colored" my life but the perpetrators do not get credit for "molding" me into the person I am proud to be. I and I alone define me. I am strong, courageous, adaptable and resilient because of me, not because of my traumatic abuses. I am in control now. I zealously take full credit for these traits of which I am fiercely proud and I fervently plan to utilize them in my quest for the rest of my life being the best of my life...

My refusal to give defining power to the abuses I have endured or the perpetrators thereof has led me to the term I referenced earlier, "The Naked Conqueror". Instead of "victim" or even "survivor", this term resonates with my experiences and my preferred way to analyze them. The "Naked Conqueror" is not just reflective of my intimate exposure of my healing journey and success; it is a more comprehensive reflection of my persona.

"Naked", reflects my raw spirit, my passionate being, my exposed affinity for intimate, sensory experiences. It is a reflection of my vulnerability - not in the oft-considered helpless sense - but in the sense of my sensitive, expressive and empathetic ways that are personal traits for which I am grateful. It also represents a profound part of my healing. Knowing that I am worthy enough to admit when I need help and accept it is unbelievably huge for me. I am incredibly happy to finally feel I am worthy enough, courageous enough to share my vulnerability.

I dismissed "Naked Survivor" because I haven't just "escaped death", in my case, both literally and figuratively; I emerged victoriously, triumphantly. I also rejected "Naked Warrior" because it implies an ongoing battle. I no longer need to be on "the offense" or "the defense"; it's time to move beyond the demons with which I have battled and embrace myself and life with all their limitless possibilities.

"Conqueror" reflects not only my healing victory but is generally reflective of my determination, my perseverance, my gratitude and my endless optimism. It is my trademark ability to **overcome**. These essential qualities instill a pervasive belief in myself that I can always handle whatever life may throw at me. Traversing through and overcoming my abuses is attributable to those traits but they did not originate from my abuses, they came from within me. I have maintained these fundamental attributes **despite, not because** of my moments of abuse. I am eternally grateful for them as they have served me well in life in general and make me the fundamentally happy person I have always been blessed to be. Now that I have finally found my path to healing, I can put down my "sword" and "shield" and utilize my virtues to live the **rest of my life as the best of my life**.

AFTERWORD: AKA, "FORWARD"

"You've seen my descent, *now watch me rise.*"

Rumi

No matter what rosy picture I tried to continually paint of my childhood, I knew with my newly discovered awareness, that my **childhood** was not conducive **whatsoever** with the types of beliefs or behaviors I wanted for the **rest of my life.** To date, my childhood "programming" had created a life filled with trauma drama, abusive relationships and a seemingly unshakable belief in my essential worthlessness. After Yanni abandoned me, I also realized I had been living a subpar life. I was living for him, not me.

I am deeply and gratefully indebted to Scott Robinson, aka, the "Brain Guy", and definitely one of my "earth angels". Mr. Robinson's insights helped me understand the need to address my issues at the subconscious level. I was truly astonished that almost 95% of our "processes" are operating at that level. It was a lightning bolt moment when I started following him. It made me appreciate that I couldn't change the behaviors and patterns I wanted to without addressing my subconscious. He lit a healing spark in me.

Healing had eluded me for decades because I lacked that crucial insight. *I wasn't consciously in control.* My subconscious and its deeply-embedded beliefs were running the show. If we have programmed **subconscious negative beliefs**, they inevitably **dictate undesirable outcomes.** The realization that I could change my beliefs and therefore my behaviors was one of the most momentous events of my life. Not only did I have the *power within me* to resolve the ongoing effects of my traumas. I could also use this knowledge to accomplish pretty much anything I wanted to... Seriously mind blowing information. I highly recommend following Mr. Robinson for incredible user-friendly life transformative insights into your magical mind.

To me, "neuroplasticity", the ability to "change" your brain, is a beautiful blessing that *everyone* can benefit from in extraordinary ways. As I noted, healing should not be a luxury. Fortunately, neuroplasticity is accessible to all of us. This power to alter our brains for the better holds the key to transform your mind, your body and your life. It is my new fascination and obsession and I explore it further in the sequel, "***Soar: Pretty in Peace: Rewire Your Magical Mind to Live Happily Ever Now.***" Neuroplasticity allows us to change the Army slogan, "Be all you can be," to the incredibly empowering, "Be all you ***want*** to be."

My healing has come with many blessings. My newly-discovered appreciation for neuroplasticity is an unbelievable gift and I plan to make the most of it. I also now have the self awareness and compassion that enables me to more calmly and lovingly interact with my loved ones. I have a more profound appreciation for authentic, unconditional love, friendship and kindness. I have a deep gratitude for "earth angels" and the everyday simple things in life. I have "flirted" with death literally and figuratively (a soulless apathy) and do not take my life nor its countless blessings for granted.

For me, this book is a story of optimism and inspiration. I hope it is for you as well. I'm living in the present like never before, no longer "stuck" in my past and no longer having my future "dictated" thereby. Although historically there have been relatively isolated incidents of abuse and dark moments, that's all they were at the end of the day, thanks to my ability to finally address them and release them.

I was always able to persevere and I was always pretty happy during the time between these moments. The abuses could not dilute my essence. I think the fact that I have been more or less fundamentally happy all my life is a testament to happiness being our underlying default state. Those dark moments - at the hands of others - may have temporarily challenged my happiness but my ***happiness is from within me*** and always accessible. This is a ***profoundly grateful*** realization. This is why and how I persevered. This was always my foundation.

No matter how many times I got knocked down, I always returned "here". No one could, or ever will, take this from me. No matter how many times I felt like I took one step forward and many steps backwards, I ***always*** knew I would take that step forward again. This is why I always felt like I had "nine lives". Even when I was more or less relying on others for validation of my worth, somewhere, deep down, I believed in myself. My incredibly open, vulnerable heart may have belied otherwise but I always knew... I always knew I could return to myself....

I always knew that betrayal in a relationship was my one deal breaker, yet I had been ***betraying myself*** throughout my life without appreciating it. I now - *finally* - realize that the times in my life when I wasn't as happy as I could be were the result of me not living authentically. I am a very genuine, authentic person vis-a-vis others but I had been denying myself that same respect and courtesy. I dismissed my needs, my desires, my goals. Now I know. ***I. Owe. Me......***

My low points in life were the result of not living **my** life the way *I* wanted to because of my subconscious belief that I was a mere means to an end. No one should live his or her life "for" anyone else. That statement should be such an unquestionable fundamental truth for all of us. Indeed to live otherwise seems objectively absurd.

The relative blips in time when I wasn't happy or was outright deeply sad were the times that my ignorantly blissful consciousness and my subconsciousness were at battle. Neuroplasticity provides the ability to have them sync.

Abuse messes with your mind though and it takes a lot of reflection and self awareness to find your healing path. Abuse often results in feelings of extremely low self worth, which can make it difficult to stop the cycle of abuse. Indeed, your feelings of self worth can be so low that you ***cannot even recognize*** less "blatant" forms ***as abuse.*** If you don't deem yourself worthy of anything better, you won't be motivated to do the work. It is painful to say but I had to realize that I didn't deserve the abusive treatment before I could stop it.

Abuse can be extremely ***self-perpetuating*** based on the beliefs it instills in you. I was always responsible for living my life the way I wanted to and for not letting anyone take advantage of me. The power to stop the abuse was always within me. I am eternally thankful for all the "earth angels" who helped me discover that innate power and those who helped keep me moving forward before I realized I always had the ability to do so.

I needed to change my belief in order to change my behavior. It was relatively easy once I discovered how. I'm still a work in progress - maybe will be forever. That's ok, I'm progressing and moving in the right direction - truly forward - for the first time in my life. I finally managed to stop the cycle of abuse - primarily by changing my underlying negative core belief of being a means to an end. *I am now in control* of my beliefs, my behaviors and my *limitless* life.

What troubled me most about my abuses was that they had, at times, temporarily left me feeling *lethargic, apathetic, impassioned*. I desperately missed my energetic, happy, passionate self. I was more or less just biding time. I fervently wanted more for the rest of my life - for me and my relationships. I realize now that in those times of relative unhappiness, I was stuck either in "freeze" mode (particularly after the attempted murder and after Yanni abandoned me) or "flight" mode (particularly when I flirted with the ultimate escape of suicide). It took me a lifetime to realize that *I needed to heal* to *live* - truly live - an authentic, fulfilled happy life.

Acknowledging that I allowed myself to be used as a puppet *all my life* and affirming things as fundamental as that *I am loveable simply for being me* is both the low point and high point of my life. The low point given the undeniable, starkly-articulated recognition of the prior reality and the high point given my absolute resolve that that reality stops *now*.

This. This is why I am writing this book. Now I am full on sobbing with distinct physiological excitement rushing throughout my body because I don't want anyone else to continue living their lives dictated by utterly false, despicable core limiting beliefs. I want to help provide insight into *why* it's crucial to heal and *how* to heal. I want to inspire others who may be plodding through a half-lived life like I was to *live a beautiful, authentic, fulfilled life*.

I am no longer blissfully ignorant; I'm blissfully free. I am *free* to channel my energetic, resilient and adaptable nature in pursuit of *my health, happiness and harmony*. This is my individual "Declaration of Independence" from limiting beliefs and the shackling constraints of subjugation they created. I am replacing my "T3" self diagnosis of trauma brain, body and bonds with an optimistic prognosis of "H3" in the form of authentic health, happiness and harmony.

As I was "unraveling" my "unraveling" so to speak, as I wrote this book, I appreciated that my healing required distinct steps and that it made sense to chronicle them separately. This book is focused on coming to grips with *why* I needed to heal my unresolved traumas to **stop a pattern of abuse** and how I was finally able to do that. That part of my healing was extraordinarily transformative, paving the way for loving and respectful relationships, including with myself. The relationships that weren't healthy ended while the good ones became priceless to me. Good stuff, right? I am now ***primed for peace***.

Notwithstanding that progress, however, I was very cognizant that my nervous system had suffered substantially from the cycle of traumatic abuses. Simply putting an end to the abusive patterns was woefully insufficient. I could not truly be at peace without undoing the significant damage that those abuses had cumulatively caused over a lifetime. My nerves were taut and frayed and I was frazzled. This is a book about putting an end to the ***destruction*** and being ***primed for peace***. The sequel, "***Soar: Pretty in Peace: Rewire Your Magical Mind to Live Happily Ever Now***" is focused on ***reconstruction*** of my messed up mind and nervous system so that I am wired for ***a limitless life***. Life is good, my friends, and it's only going to get better....

After I pass, I want my epithet to be "***She lived. She loved.***" I don't personally know anyone who has experienced more than I, had more relationships than I, lived more than I, or loved more than I. Living with an open heart and soul has risks, risks I am more than willing to take again and again as the price of a life lived well, fully, multidimensionally. I reject ordinary; I want the extraordinary. Mediocrity scares me more than the occasional mis-step or heartache even. My heart is huge with unlimited, infinite capacity to love. It may break from time to time but I never will...

This is not the "story of my life" or a "memoir". As I stated, I don't personally know anyone who has lived more than I. I have been beyond blessed to have been all over the world and have incredible memories - with countless more to come. You have only seen glimpses of that in this book. I write about my adventures, my passions, my travels and endless extraordinary experiences in other books. This is a book of healing so of course focuses on the abuses I have endured. Those abuses, however, are mere transient excerpts from the innumerable "chapters" of my life.

I noted in the ***Foreword***, that this was not a book about abuse. This book is my ***book of healing***. When I started, I had no idea how incredibly healing writing this book would be. It truly is my gift of love. The realizations and revelations that came to me via writing this book have been profoundly healing and equipped me to truly live the ***rest of my life as the best of my life***. My new insights acquired from the process of writing have equipped me to ***be all I want to be***. I am extraordinarily grateful to be blessed with the unexpected benefit that writing this book will have on my relationships going forward. My relationships with myself, romantic partners, family, friends and humanity in general have been elevated.

Throughout my life, I have been blessed with my own strength, courage, adaptability and tenacity. I have also been equally blessed to have my life beautifully saturated by the love of true friends and by random acts of kindness from virtual strangers, all "earth angels". My healing is a testament to the beauty of true love and the wondrous magic it can work - my love for myself and my life and the compassionate love of so many I am blessed to call friends. Their love sustained me even when my own could not.

My friends, my chosen family, have believed in me when I didn't even care to believe in myself, buoyed me when I was drowning in apathy, gave me the motivation to move forward when I didn't have the will or strength and guided me with loving and sage advice. My life may have been tempered periodically with "clouds of darkness" but I'm the lucky one. The sun *always* reappeared...

It's Over
Time to Soar...

THE "BEGINNING".... and then she lived happily ever now...

About the Author

Sophia M. Elan, aka, "***Mediterranean Me***" *i*s a University of Chicago Law School alum and retired corporate lawyer. She traded her professional career to feed her soul. Sophia is an insatiable foodie and an avid health, fitness and travel enthusiast with a masters degree in natural health and certifications in fitness and nutrition. She happily travels the world with her fourth passport and an unquenchable zest for life in quest of simple pleasures. These passions provide endless inspiration for her literary career. She is currently enjoying the stunning Turkish Riviera while working on her sequel, "***Soar: Pretty in Peace: Rewire your Magical Mind to Live Happily Ever Now.***" Wherever she is, you can find Sophia with her trademark smile and her heart overflowing with gratitude and love. Sophia warmly invites you to follow her life and adventures and feel free to get in touch.

Read more at https://linktr.ee/mediterraneanme.

About the Publisher

In the pursuit of **health, happiness and harmony**, my *mission* is to live the *rest of my life* as *the best of my life*. My *wish* is for you to as well. My *hope* is that you internalize this as a fundamental promise to yourself and use it as a guide to optimize your life. My *belief* is that this is achievable via simple, natural, enjoyable, holistic lifestyle factors, collectively dubbed, the "K.I.S.S. Plan", as in "keep it simple, sweetheart". Holistically, the body, the mind and the spirit have the beautiful innate power and wisdom for you to achieve that. My purpose in life has now become sharing intuitive, easily accessible ways to optimize your health and life, a la the Mediterranean lifestyle I am blessed to live. I fervently believe everyone can live to *"be all you want to be"*.

I sincerely hope you enjoy my debut book and find some inspiration and insights from my experiences and revelations. I would greatly appreciate it if you could leave a review on the site you purchased this book on and/or at www.goodreads.com. Please follow my literary career and escapades at www.mediterraneanme.com. As an independent writer, I am very grateful for your support! xo, *Sophia*